UNDER
COVER

JOHN BEVERE

THOMAS NELSON
Since 1798

NASHVILLE DALLAS MEXICO CITY RIO DE JANEIRO BEIJING

Published in Nashville, Tennessee, by Thomas Nelson, Inc.

Unless otherwise noted, Scripture quotations are from THE NEW KING JAMES VERSION. Copyright © 1979, 1980, 1982, Thomas Nelson, Inc., Publishers.

Scripture quotations noted NIV are from the HOLY BIBLE: NEW INTERNA-TIONAL VERSION®. Copyright © 1973, 1978, 1984 by International Bible Society. Used by permission of Zondervan Publishing House. All rights reserved.

Scripture quotations noted NLT are from the *Holy Bible,* New Living Translation, copyright © 1996. Used by permission of Tyndale House Publishers, Inc., Wheaton, Illinois 60189. All rights reserved.

Scripture quotations noted NCV are from the New Century Version.

Scripture quotations noted KJV are from the *King James Version.*

Scripture quotations noted TLB are from *The Living Bible,* copyright © 1971. Used by permission of Tyndale House Publishers, Inc., Wheaton, Illinois 60189. All rights reserved.

Scripture quotations noted CEV are from THE CONTEMPORY ENGLISH VERSION. © 1991 by the American Bible Society. Used by permission.

Scripture quotations noted The Message are from *The Message: The New Testament in Contemporary English.* Copyright © 1993 by Eugene H. Peterson.

Scripture quotations noted AMPLIFIED are from THE AMPLIFIED BIBLE: Old Testament. Copyright © 1962, 1964 by Zondervan Publishing House (used by permission); and from THE AMPLIFIED NEW TESTAMENT. Copyright © 1958 by the Lockman Foundation (used by permission.)

Scripture quotations noted NASB are from the NEW AMERICAN STANDARD BIBLE (R), © Copyright the Lockman Foundation 1960, 1962, 1963, 1968, 1971, 1972, 1973, 1975, 1977. Used by permission.

ISBN 0-7852-6991-6

I dedicate this book to my first born son,
Addison David Bevere.

"A wise son makes a glad father."
PROVERBS 10:1

Your name means "Beloved who is worthy of trust."
You have certainly lived up to this name, and walked in the
precepts of this book. May you inherit God's richest blessings
and promises and may His face continue to shine upon you.
May you live long and prosper in life.

Your mother and I love you and are blessed
to have you as our son.

CONTENTS

Acknowledgments   vii

SECTION 1:
Introducing Under Cover

1. Introducing Under Cover   3
2. It's Hard to Kick Against the Goads   9

SECTION 2:
God's Direct Covering

3. Sin Defined   23
4. The Secret Power of Lawlessness   34
5. The Consequences of Disobedience I   48
6. The Consequences of Disobedience II   57
7. Bewitched   71

SECTION 3:
God's Appointed Covering

8. Does God Know Who Is in Charge?   87
9. Honor the King   100
10. Double Honor   113
11. Obedience and Submission   130
12. What If Authority Tells Me . . . ?   142
13. Unfair Treatment   160
14. Self-Inflicted Judgment   178
15. Odds and Ends   194
16. Great Faith   210
17. Conclusion   225

About the Author   228

ACKNOWLEDGMENTS

My deepest appreciation to . . .

My wife, Lisa. For the hours you spent editing this work. But most of all thanks for being my dearest friend, most faithful supporter, wife, and mother of our children.

To our four sons, Addison, Austin, Alexander, and Arden. Each of you have brought tremendous joy to my life and are special treasures. Thank you for sharing in the call of God, and encouraging me to travel and write.

To my parents, John and Kay Bevere. Thank you for the godly lifestyle you have continuously lived before me. You both have loved me not only in word but most of all in your actions.

To Pastor Al Brice, Loran Johnson, Rob Birkbeck, Dr. Tony Stone, and Steve Watson, thank you for serving on the advisory board of our United States and European ministry offices. The love, kindness, and wisdom you have selflessly given has touched and strengthened our hearts.

To the staff of John Bevere Ministries. Thank you for your unwavering support and faithfulness. Lisa and I love each of you.

To David and Pam Graham, thank you for your sincere and faithful support in overseeing the operations of our European office.

To Michael Hyatt and Victor Oliver, thanks for your encouragement and belief in the message God has burned in our hearts.

To Cindy Blades, thank you for your editing skills in this project as well as your encouragement.

To all the staff of Thomas Nelson Publishers. Thanks for the support of this message and for your professional and kind help. You are a great group to work with.

Most important, my sincere gratitude to Jesus, my Lord. How can words adequately acknowledge all You have done for me and for Your people. I love You more than I am able to express.

INTRODUCING UNDER COVER

CHAPTER 1

INTRODUCING UNDER COVER

*Often the painful words, not the smooth ones,
ultimately bring the greatest freedom and protection.*

Under cover—this phrase can apply to a vast number of situations. In its simplest form it could describe a small child nestled under the warmth and protection of a blanket, or behind the protective frame of a parent in danger. A civilian description may include a city under police or military protection. It could describe an animal hidden away in a thicket, cave, or subterranean refuge. Or it could describe a family enjoying the shelter and safety of their home while a storm rages just outside.

As a child I remember living in an area where we experienced frequent storms. We would watch the dark clouds roll in from our picture windows to the accompanying beat of distant thunders. In a matter of minutes the storm was on top of us in full force. Lightning flashes were followed by immediate explosive thunders. The rain sounded like thousands of tiny hammers pounding away at our roof. The storm actually made our house feel that much more safe and secure. Everything outside the windows was wet, cold, and in danger of fatal lightning strikes. Yet inside we were safe and dry shielded by our roof from the tyranny of the storm. We were under cover.

Taking this point further, we can pull these two words together and come up with another term—*undercover*. This term describes the safety found in hidden identities. An agent who is undercover can move freely about without being apprehended by his enemy. His government has put him under the cover of an alias, and he is a free agent in a hostile area. In short, no matter how we use this word or phrase in it's vast applications, they all seems to include *protection* and *freedom*.

But how does this term *Under Cover* apply to Christians? David writes, "He who dwells in the secret place of the Most High shall abide *under* the shadow of the Almighty. I will say of the LORD, 'He is my refuge and my fortress; my God, in Him I will trust'" (Ps. 91:1–2). Again we see protection for those under His cover. However, from the initial words of his statement, "He who . . .", we discover the all important question, Who is under His cover? The book you hold in your hand is a quest for this most important answer. To put it briefly, the one who is under cover is the one who is under God's authority.

Adam and Eve enjoyed freedom and protection in the garden under God's cover. However, the moment they disobeyed they found themselves in great need of the very thing they had voluntarily slipped out from under . . . it was the need, "to cover themselves" (Gen 3:7 NLT). Their disobedience to God's authority robbed mankind of the sweet freedom and protection they'd once known.

Let's face it. *Authority* is not a popular word. Yet by rejecting or fearing it, we lose sight of the great protection and benefits authority provides. We shudder because we don't see it from God's perspective. Too often our attitude toward authority reminds me of a situation that occurred with my third son.

When Alexander entered first grade, he had a bad experience with his teacher. She was constantly on edge with the class—grumpy and out of control, yelling and screaming at the students frequently. Too often Alexander found himself the focus of her outbursts because he is a creative and energetic young man who would rather talk than be still. To him school was a wonderful social gathering. Needless to say, his approach to school clashed with the teacher's personality and impatience.

Many times my wife and I ended up in her room after school for consultation sessions. We worked with the teacher, encouraging Alec to submit to her rules and to cooperate, but the whole stressful process hindered his love for structured academic learning.

Then we moved to a new state, and Alec moved into the second grade. He had a very different teacher. She was almost overly nice and extremely sensitive to the happiness of her students. She thought Alec was adorable, and with his disposition, he probably fell in love with her, but got away with about everything and learned very little. Alec seemed to be slipping through the cracks of academia, so we moved him to a wonderful charter school that stressed academics.

He felt lost and frustrated there. He was in the midst of children who had excelled in learning for their first two years. Alec was now under the tutelage of a good and kind, but firm, teacher. It was soon discovered that he was behind the other students. Again, there were frequent, but this time beneficial, meetings with his teacher. Lisa and I got more involved with his work.

Going to school all day and having parents breathing down your neck at night can become overwhelming. Many times Alec would just shut down. Tears frequently flowed as he felt like he was drowning, even though he was actually making progress.

One day the bottom fell out for him emotionally. His brothers were going to a school roller skating party, but he had to stay home to do some unfinished schoolwork he had hidden in his desk. He was missing out on the fun due to his stack of work from the teacher! He could do nothing but weep. It was time for another daddy-son talk. After a few words, I could easily see the problem. In his eyes the whole thing was utterly hopeless. The tears of frustration continually flowed, and he just wasn't hearing what Dad was saying. There was a time of silence with both of us out of words. He just hung his head and sobbed.

I'll never forget what happened next. He straightened up, gained his composure somewhat, and wiped his face dry, then looked at me with those big chocolate brown and now confident eyes. An idea had obviously dawned on him, one that would solve his problems and dry his tears. He straightened up and crossed his arms. With a grave voice he said, "Daddy, I want to tell you something. Did you know Jessica in my class . . . she doesn't believe in doctors?" He hesitated, then added, "Well, Daddy, I don't believe in teachers."

It was hard for me to refrain from smirking or laughing. He had successfully surprised me with this one. He continued, "If Jessica in my class can not believe in doctors, well I just won't believe in teachers." I couldn't contain my laughter any longer. If he had spoken this out of frustration, it wouldn't have been so humorous. But it was his tone. He really thought he was letting me in on a new revelation that could solve all his problems. He was as serious as someone testifying in a courtroom.

Of course, I took the opportunity to explain to him where he might be if he did not have teachers. I shared with him what it was like when I went to Angola, Africa, the previous year to work at feeding stations for starving young children. How those children would have given almost anything to trade opportunities with Alexander! They would have jumped on the chance to learn because they understood its importance in one day providing for their families. After my lengthy explanation, he reluctantly released his newfound philosophy and returned to the kitchen table to conquer his stack of work.

For the next several weeks I kept thinking about this encounter with my son and couldn't help drawing the parallel between it and the way that some people look at authority. Too often there is a history of unpleasant experiences with authority; some, because the leaders they were under were unnecessarily harsh; others, like Alexander, out of sheer frustration have come to view authorities hindrances to their enjoyment or to what they believe best for themselves when, in reality, they have fine leaders and authorities over them. But out of these distasteful experiences has developed a subtle attitude: *I just don't believe in authority*, or to put it in more adult terms, *I'm just not going to submit to authority unless I first agree with it.*

But what is God's position on all this? Are we to submit to authorities even if they are unfair? What if they are corrupt? What if they tell us to do what we perceive as wrong? What if they tell us to sin? Where can the line be drawn? Besides, why should we have to submit? Are there any benefits? Couldn't we all just be led by the Spirit of God?

The Word of God holds specific answers to all these questions. I believe this is one of the most important books the Lord has commissioned me to write because it deals with the root cause of many difficulties people currently experience in the church. What caused Lucifer to fall? Rebellion. What caused Adam to fall? Rebellion. What causes many to drift in their walk with God? Rebellion. What is really sobering is that most rebellion is not blatant, but subtle.

In this book I have shared examples of my own failures. I am not a power-hungry leader who desires to beat his sheep, staff, or family into submission. I have a wonderful staff and family. And I am not a pastor. So I write as a man who has made many mistakes or, more accurately put, sins. I served under two international ministries in the 1980s, and from these experiences I draw most of my errant examples. What is most sobering about each incident is that I believed with all my heart I was right in each one when, in reality, I was wrong. I am so grateful to our Lord that His Word exposed my motives.

My heartfelt desire is to see you learn from my hardships and avoid the same mistakes. I pray you'll draw instruction and godly insight from my foolishness, and reap the benefits. For what I later learned as a result of my experiences and the truths revealed in the process was both beneficial and wonderful. Through repentance came safety and provision.

I believe the same can occur with you as this book unfolds. As you read the biblical and personal examples, light will be shed on your heart as well. Some points may strengthen what you already know, while others will set you free. In either case, I pray you will receive His word with meekness, for that is truly my heart in bringing it.

Confronted with truth, we can respond two ways. We can become angry and defensive, like Cain, Adam's son, and forsake the very revelation we need (Gen. 4). Or we can be humble and broken, like David when challenged by Nathan, and let the pain and repentance raise us to another level of godly character (2 Sam. 12). Let's have the heart of David in this matter and reject the pride endeavoring to keep us from God's plan of provision and protection.

As you embark on this path, remember that often the painful

words, not the smooth ones, ultimately bring the greatest freedom and protection. As a child, right before I received my second grade immunization shot, a friend told me how much it hurt. After hearing that I was determined to avoid the needle at all costs. I fought with two nurses until they finally gave up. Then my parents sat me down and explained to me what could happen if I didn't get the tuberculosis vaccine. I had already watched my sister die of cancer, so I knew they wanted only my protection. I knew the shot would be somewhat painful, but it would keep me from experiencing much greater pain from contracting a dreadful and possibly deadly disease. Once I understood, I willingly went back for the shot.

Remember this example when you encounter any uncomfortable, or even painful, immunizing truths from the Word of God. Know your heavenly Father's ways are perfect, and what may at times look presently detrimental or hurtful will actually be His positioning for protection, blessing, or another's salvation. Never forget His love for us is pure, complete, and everlasting!

Before we begin our journey, let's pray:

Heavenly Father, I desire truth in my inward parts more than I desire comfort or pleasure. So I place my heart and soul in Your hands, knowing that Your ways are perfect. You love me enough to send what was most important to You, Your Son, Jesus, to die for me that I might have eternal life. If You love me that much, You surely desire to complete the work in my life, that You have begun. As I read this book, I ask that You would speak to me by Your Spirit and show me Your desired ways for my life. Open my eyes to see and my ears to hear Your Word. Reveal Jesus to me greater than I have ever seen Him before. Thank You in advance for what You will do in me through Your word in this book. In Jesus' name I pray. Amen.

CHAPTER 2

IT'S HARD TO KICK
AGAINST THE GOADS

---

*It is hard to understand kingdom principles with a
democratic mind-set.*

A challenge now looms before me, one perhaps impossible without the grace of God. Mine is to attempt to teach authority in the midst of a world that increases daily in lawlessness. Therefore, a lot of what I outline in this book will go against or resist the very reasoning processes of this world. In so many ways we have been programmed to think differently from the foundational truths we are about to encounter. Yet this is the exact tactic of Satan, the enemy of our souls— he loves to make what brings us into bondage appear desirable and even good while portraying what is liberating as bondage.

That is how it all started in the first place. Remember the Garden; his method worked so well, he hasn't changed it since then. That is why we are urgently warned, "Do not be deceived, my beloved brethren" (James 1:16), and "Do not be conformed to this world, but be transformed by the renewing of your mind, that you may prove what is that good and acceptable and perfect will of God" (Rom. 12:2).

My experience has been that Westerners (dwellers of democratic nations of America and Europe) are some of the most resistant people to truly hearing the word of God. The reason is fundamental. It is hard to understand kingdom principles with a democratic mind-set. Democracy is fine for the nations of the world, but we must remember the kingdom of God is just that—a kingdom. It is ruled by a King, and there are rank, order, and authority. The laws of His kingdom are not superseded by, or subject to, popular opinion, voting, or polls. The laws are not swayed by what we believe to be good for us, as Eve was so cleverly deceived into thinking. Therefore, just as Samuel "explained to the people the behavior of royalty, and wrote it in a book" (1 Sam. 10:25), we must be instructed in kingdom principles today since our society does not foster in us kingdom ways.

If we attempt to live as believers with a cultural mind-set towards authority, we will be at best ineffective and at worst positioned for danger. Our provision as well as protection could be blocked or even cut off as we disconnect ourselves from the Source of true life. It could be likened to playing baseball in life while God is directing a football championship. We could compare it to attempting the use of an electric appliance without plugging it into the power source.

Too often today, if we don't agree with authority, we can challenge it through complaint or protest. After all, government should be "of the people, by the people, for the people," right? This and other democratic mind-sets have trickled into our Christianity and marched many down the deceptive path of self-rule. As this path continues they go beyond challenging authority to blatantly resisting it. Then there are those who have developed a greater degree of contempt for authority, which they display by totally ignoring its existence. Thus, they betray a complete loss of the fear of God.

But none of these approaches will bring the very freedom we seek. For the Scripture says,

> If they obey and serve him,
>> they will spend the rest of their days in prosperity
>> and their years in contentment.
> But if they do not listen,

> they will perish by the sword
> and die without knowledge. (Job 36:11–12 NIV)

"Him" is none other than God. Notice the promise: provision and protection in exchange for our submission to His authority. Also note the impending danger that accompanies our ignoring His government. The freedom we seek when resisting authority we lose in our insubordination to it. My wife has a saying, "There is freedom in submission and bondage in rebellion." It sums up what we read in these verses from Job.

Some may say, "I submit to God, but not to man, unless I agree with him." This is where our upbringing and incorrect church thinking can hinder us. We cannot separate our submission to God's inherent authority from our submission to His delegated authority. All authority originates from Him! Hear what the Scripture admonishes:

> Let every soul be subject to the governing authorities. *For there is no authority except from God*, and the authorities that exist are appointed by God. Therefore whoever resists the authority resists the ordinance of God, and those who resist will bring judgment on themselves. (Rom. 13:1–2)

There is so much to think about in this passage, and we will dig through it later, but now I want to just comment on only a few points. First, God appoints all existing rulers. The truth is, no one can get into a place of legitimate authority without God's knowledge. We must settle this idea in our hearts. Second, to rebel against those authorities is to rebel against the ordinance of the Lord, or God Himself, and those who do bring judgment on themselves. We must remember, our Father—not a power-hungry leader—is the One who authored these words, for, "all Scripture is given by inspiration of God" (2 Tim. 3:16). Just because it has been twisted by man doesn't mean it was not authored by God.

Although they may not be quick to admit it, too many see themselves accountable only to God, and not to authorities. Those who think this way are on a collision course with the very One they call

Lord. Recall Jesus' words to Saul (who would become Paul), "It is hard for you to kick against the goads" (Acts 9:5). Farmers in biblical days used goads. A common goad was an eight-foot-long straight branch of oak or other strong wood from which the bark had been stripped. At the front end a pointed spike was used to prod the oxen while plowing. An ox would certainly not resist such a sharp instrument capable of administering a good deal of pain and harm. Hence in Paul's day this proverbial expression was used to describe the futility of resistance to superior authority or power.

Those who resist the authority of God, whether directly, as Paul did, or indirectly to His delegated authority, will find themselves kicking against the goad in God's hands. More often than not this can be a painful experience and lesson too many of us end up learning the hard way, as I did.

MY OWN EYE-OPENING EXPERIENCE

Speaking of pain, I remember when my eyes were painfully opened to the fact that resistance to delegated authority was resistance to God's authority. For me it is stamped forever as a monument to the foolishness of kicking against the goads.

In the mid-1980s I was offered the position of youth pastor at a large international church. After prayer and an amazing confirmation, I accepted this position as the will of God.

I felt overwhelmed because I had no previous youth ministry experience, but found myself part of the staff of one of the fastest-growing and most influential churches in America. I started devouring youth ministry books and manuals. One book was by the senior youth pastor of a church in Louisiana that had an outstanding youth program. I had my secretary call and ask if I could fly in for two days and spend time with the group. The leaders graciously welcomed me, and we selected the dates.

Upon arriving, I was whisked immediately to a Wednesday night youth meeting. I was amazed. They had their own youth auditorium, which seated 1,500, and it was almost full! They were not playing games or preaching easy, compromising messages; the messages were of purity and power. To top it off, the young people were actually excited to be there. I was thrilled and felt certain I had picked the right group to glean from.

The next day I met at the church with the leaders. Again I could hardly believe what I found. They had their own youth administration building, two full-time youth secretaries, and four full-time youth pastors. I spent the next two days in and out of meetings with all four youth pastors. The statistics were mind-boggling. At that time they had 1,250 young adults in their high school ministry and it was growing at an astounding rate.

Each of the four pastors told me the exact same thing. The success of the ministry was due to the "parties" they had every Friday night at more than one hundred locations around the city. The parties were actually home cell groups with the objective of getting young people saved.

The concept was simple enough, but profound. It is hard to get unsaved teenagers to a church, but easy to get them to a party. During the week each member of the youth group was encouraged to target one person in school and invite him or her to the party Friday night. Once there, they enjoyed food, socializing, and contemporary Christian music; then the appointed leader, a high-school or college student, started an organized Bible-based group discussion that eventually steered the conversation to the topic of salvation. Next he presented an opportunity for those there to give their lives to Jesus. As a result, many first-time visitors were saved. They were taken aside and instructed in the importance of fellowship and church, names and phone numbers were exchanged, and they were invited to the Wednesday night youth services.

I attended one of the parties and was inspired when several unsaved students gave their lives to Jesus. I returned to my church and shared what I had learned with my assistant. After prayer, we felt led to do the same thing with our group. I also excitedly shared the vision with the senior pastor in the parking lot one Sunday after the service. He encouraged me, "Great, brother. Go for it!"

EIGHT MONTHS OF PLANNING AND WORKING

While in prayer, God gave me a plan. I would immediately begin a school of leadership to prepare my leaders. I announced it Tuesday night to the entire youth group, and to my delight, seventy of them showed up for the leadership class the following Sunday morning. I would teach them weekly for the next six months on principles of leadership, such as faithfulness, integrity, commitment, serving, and vision.

After five months, the Lord spoke to my heart in prayer again and said, *Choose twenty-four of the young people in your leadership class, and start a discipleship class for them. You will select from them your first leaders of the parties.* I began immediately to train those leaders for the first round of home cells.

For the next two months I prepared those leaders for the home group parties, and I preached the vision of the parties to the Tuesday night main youth group. My assistant pastor and I worked on the leader's curriculum and many details, such as the parties' locations, the division of the city by school districts and zip codes, as well as how the groups would expand and how follow-up would be handled. We poured ourselves into this effort with the purpose of reaching lost souls propelling us.

Everyone was excited. The vision had trickled down from the leaders to the regular attendees of the youth services. The young people were already talking about the individuals they wanted to invite first to their parties. We were praying that God would touch hearts to respond, that they would see their need for Jesus and be saved. My assistant and I could envision the entire sanctuary filled with 2,500 young people on Tuesday nights. To say the least, we were charged with vision and passion.

A MEETING I'LL NEVER FORGET

Three weeks before the launch of the first parties, I walked into the weekly pastors' meeting, totally unprepared for what I was about to hear. In the meeting the senior pastor shared with all eleven of us associate pastors the following devastating words, "Gentlemen, the Holy

Spirit has shown me that the direction of this church is not to have home cell groups. So I want you all to cancel any small group meetings you are having in members' homes."

I couldn't believe what I was hearing. There had to be some kind of mistake or misunderstanding. My assistant's shocked eyes met mine as we struggled with our confusion. I tried to comfort myself with the thought, *He doesn't mean the youth . . . he is just talking about the other pastors.* The singles' pastor, the seniors' pastor, the couples' pastor, and others had home groups, but they were not doing very well and were really not the focus of their ministries. Besides, I had talked to my senior pastor about my idea a few months back in the parking lot, and he said, "Go for it," so I concluded the youth department must be exempt from this moratorium.

I couldn't wait any longer. "Excuse me, Pastor. You mean except the youth ministry, correct?"

He looked back at me and said, "John, the Holy Spirit spoke to me and told me the direction of this church is not to have cell groups."

I spoke again, "Pastor, remember I flew several months ago to that youth group in Louisiana? They have 1,250 high school students in their youth group. All four pastors said it was due to their home cell groups."

The senior pastor looked at me and said, "John, the Holy Spirit spoke to me and told me the direction of this church is not to have home cell groups."

I spoke again, my intensity rising, all the while thinking, *He doesn't understand.* I reasoned, "Pastor, it is hard to get unsaved young people into our church, but we can get almost any high school student into a party, which as I explained to you a few months back would actually be a home group focused on getting the lost saved."

He repeated, "John, the Holy Spirit told me the direction of this church is not to have home cell groups."

Becoming quite impassioned, I argued, "But, Pastor, we can fill our auditorium with 2,500 students. We could see all the youth of Orlando, Florida, saved!"

He repeated the same words.

I argued with him for approximately fifteen minutes. Everyone in the room could feel the tension mounting. Fortunately for me, the only words that kept coming out the pastor's mouth were ones he believed God told him to say.

Finally I was quiet, but I was steaming inside. I heard nothing else for the rest of the meeting. All I could think was, *We have worked on this for eight months. He knew we were doing this; I told him months ago. How can he shut down the vehicle that would bring hundreds or even thousands into the kingdom? He is stopping a move of God! What am I going to tell the youth? What will my leaders think? I flew to Louisiana. What a waste of money, of time! I can't believe this is really happening!* My thoughts were almost endless, and in all of them, I was right and on God's side, but the pastor was missing it!

When the meeting was over, I did a beeline out of the conference room. An older, wiser associate pastor tried to stop me to speak wisdom, restraint, and comfort to me, but I looked at him and said, "Fred, I don't want to talk!" He saw he would get nowhere and backed off.

I pulled into my driveway, opened my front door, and received a greeting from my wife. I did not greet her, but said in a very frustrated voice, "You're not going to believe what he did!"

Upon hearing the tone of my voice, she responded with concern, "Who, and what did he do?"

"Pastor! He canceled the home group parties! What we've worked on for eight months. He canceled them! Can you believe it?"

She looked at me and said with the most straight forward and serious voice, "Well, it looks like God is trying to teach you something." Then she walked out of the foyer and into our bedroom.

Now I was mad at her. I stormed into the kitchen, put my foot up on a chair, looked out our front window, and continued my thoughts of how wrong my pastor was. Only added to those thoughts were thoughts of how insensitive and undiscerning my wife was.

AN ENCOUNTER WITH THE MASTER

As I stared out the window, the Holy Spirit spoke to my heart. He said, *John, whose ministry are you building? Mine or yours?*

I blurted out, "Yours, Lord!"

He quickly responded, *No, you're not! You're building your own.*

I said, "Lord, we can't get most unsaved students to our church, but we can get them into parties . . ." I started going through the whole reasoning process and plan with Him—as if He didn't know. How easily we can be deceived!

The Lord allowed me to vent it all out, then said, *John, when I brought you to this church to serve this man, I made you an extension of the ministry I entrusted to him. I called you to be his arms and legs; I put only one man in charge of a ministry.*

He brought to my mind Moses. The Bible says, "Moses certainly was faithful in the administration of all God's house" (Heb. 3:5 AMPLIFIED). He was the leader God put over the congregation.

Then He brought to my mind James in the New Testament. James was the leader of the church in Jerusalem. He reminded me of the incident where circumcision was in question among the believers (Acts 15). Paul, Barnabas, Peter, John, and all the rest of the apostles and elders of the church of Jerusalem came together to talk it out.

Some of the believing Pharisees who were also leaders spoke first. Then Peter spoke. After him, Paul and Barnabas shared what God was doing among the Gentiles. Once they had finished, James stood up, summarized what had been spoken, and then made this ruling, "Therefore I judge . . ." As the head, he gave his decision, and all of them, including Peter, Paul, and John, submitted to his decision.

I saw this dynamic illustrated in the Scriptures when the angel released Peter from prison. Peter said to the believers at the house of Mary, "Go, tell these things to James and to the brethren" (Acts 12:17). The same was true for Luke and Paul. When they came to Jerusalem, Luke recorded, "The brethren received us gladly. On the following day Paul went in with us to James, and all the elders were present" (Acts 21:17–18). Why would Peter and Paul identify James in those two accounts? It is clear he was the lead man by the way he is separately mentioned by name.

Once the Holy Spirit clarified this point, He continued, *John, when you stand before Me in judgment for the time period that I have had you serve this pastor, you will not first give an account of how many youth you led to salvation in Orlando, Florida. You will first be judged on how faithful you were to the pastor I've put you under.*

Then He made the statement that shocked me: *In fact, you could win all the youth in Orlando and stand before Me and be judged for not submitting to and being faithful to the pastor I put you under.* With those words came a renewed sense of the fear of God! With all my defenses down, I was putty in the Master's hand.

He went on, *John, if you continue in this direction, the youth will go one way while the church goes another direction. You will bring a* division *to the church.* The prefix *di-* means "two." Putting it together, *division* means "two visions"! Why are so many churches and homes dividing today? There is more than one vision, which means one is not submitted to God's ordained authority. God ordains set men or leaders because any two-headed organization is doomed for division!

THE RESPONSE AND FOLLOW-THROUGH OF REPENTANCE

I immediately repented of my rebellious attitude. After praying, I knew what I had to do. I picked up the phone and called the senior pastor. When he answered, I said, "Pastor, this is John Bevere. I'm calling to ask your forgiveness. God has shown me I have been in rebellion to your authority, and I have sinned greatly. Please forgive me. I will cancel the home groups immediately."

He was very gracious, and he forgave me. As soon as I hung up, I heard the Holy Spirit pose this question: *Now, how will you tell your twenty-four leaders this weekend?*

I saw a vision or image of me walking into the room with the leaders and in a sad monotone voice reporting, "Guys, you're not going to believe what has happened."

They would all look at me with concern, asking, "What?"

I would continue in my heavy monotone voice, "You know we have worked on this for months, but Pastor has canceled the home cell groups. We will not have our parties on Friday night."

I saw all of them moan and groan in disgust over the decision. It was easy to perceive they were upset with the senior pastor. We were all his victims, and of course, I looked good at his expense.

After mulling this scene in my mind, I heard the Holy Spirit question, *Is that what you are going to do?*

I answered, "No, Sir!"

At the next meeting I walked into the roomful of leaders with confidence and a smile on my face and excitement in my voice. With enthusiasm I announced, "Guys, I've got great news."

They looked up with eager anticipation. "What?"

I continued, "God has spared us from birthing and building something that is not from Him. Our senior pastor told us in a staff meeting this week that the direction of the Holy Spirit for this church is not to have home groups. So effective immediately the parties are canceled!"

They all seemed to reflect my excitement and in one accord shouted, "Yeah . . . all right!" I never had one problem with them! I wasn't the only one who grew out of this experience; we all did. At a later date I was able to share with them what had transpired. Many of those young twenty-four are in full-time ministry today and doing well.

A Broken and Contrite Heart

As I look back, I am convinced that was a pivotal point in my life and ministry. Had I not broken, but persisted in my own reasoning and continued in my stubbornness, I would be at a very different place today. Oh, I may have canceled the parties because I had no other choice, but my heart would have remained resistant, proud, and hard. Never forget: it is not just outward obedience that God desires, but a broken and contrite heart, one that thirsts and hungers for the will of God. For this reason David said,

> For You do not desire sacrifice, or else I would give it . . .
> The sacrifices of God are a broken spirit,
> A broken and a contrite heart—
> These, O God, You will not despise. (Ps. 51:16–17)

We can make great sacrifices in our lives, serve long hours, labor without pay, give up sleep, seek ways to reach more people, and do all sorts of things because in ministry the list can be endless. Caught up in all this sacrifice, we could easily imagine ourselves and our efforts as pleasing to God. However, in all this activity our core motive could still be deceptively fueled by self-will.

Hear these words: God is pleased with submission that leads to true obedience. The purpose of this book is not only to reveal the importance of submission to God's authority, but also to create a love and passion for obedience to it.

I realize there may be many unanswered questions in your mind about the testimony given here. One may be, "Didn't God tell you in prayer to do those home groups?" Another may be, "What if the pastor was wrong about the direction of the church? What if you were supposed to have cell groups, and he was wrong and you were right? What if he had been influenced wrongly?" As we move forward in this study, we will answer these questions and many more.

However, before further discussion of delegated authority, we must first establish the importance of submitting to God's direct authority. Watchman Nee writes,

> Before a man can subject himself to God's delegated authority he must first meet God's inherent authority. Our entire relationship with God is regulated by whether or not we have met authority. If we have, then we shall encounter authority everywhere, and being thus restrained by God we can begin to be used by Him. (*Spiritual Authority* [New York: Christian Fellowship Publishers, 1972])

A firm scriptural foundation of the importance of submission to God Himself must be laid first. Only after this is accomplished can we move on to the importance of submission to delegated authority. It will be the cornerstone for everything we will build upon.

GOD'S DIRECT COVERING

CHAPTER 3

SIN DEFINED

The church often veers away from the core definition of sin.
We do not connect with its true meaning.

F or a moment, let's play a game. For the lack of a better title, let's call it the psychologist and patient game. You're the patient reclining on the couch, and I'm the psychologist sitting on the chair beside you. I'll say a word, and you tell me the first thing that comes to your mind. Ready? Here's the word: sin. What came to mind first?

After speaking with numerous believers and leaders the world over, I can guess what came to mind. You may have thought of adultery, fornication, perversion, or some other form of sexual misconduct. I hear this tragic statement quite often, "He fell into sin." This usually refers to the fall of a leader in the sexual realm. The one informing me doesn't have to explain further; I know immediately what he is alluding to. In church circles this thought seems to be in the forefront as far as association with the word *sin*.

Or perhaps an image of drunkenness or drug abuse flashed through your mind. Believers certainly view them as major sins. Maybe gambling, murder, theft, or witchcraft came to mind. It is possible, but not as likely, that you may have entertained hatred, strife, jealousy, or unforgiveness in your sin category. I think we can safely assume the list looms quite large.

NOT CONNECTING WITH THE CORE DEFINITION

After thinking this through, allow me to say this: Adam did not jump in bed with a strange woman in the Garden, nor did he smoke a joint! Yet his sin was so serious it brought all creation into captivity and bondage. We need to consider Adam's situation when we define sin, for the nature of his transgression spread throughout the veins of the human race. What did he do that brought so much destruction on mankind? Simply put, he was not obedient to what God told him.

Ponder this for a moment. I am not saying the list I've just cited is void of sin, but I am stressing a point that the church often veers away from the core definition of sin. We do not connect with its true meaning. Without this important link, we can easily be led into deception, as we are about to learn in this chapter.

Let me give another example. Let's say your total awareness or core understanding of sickness is anyone with a body temperature exceeding 98.6 degrees, accompanied by general discomfort in the body and coughing, sneezing, or throwing up. In my seven-year-old mind, that was my complete understanding of sickness when my beloved fourteen-year-old sister was diagnosed with cancer. She made frequent trips to the doctors and was hospitalized for a couple of weeks. My mother explained to me, "Johnny, your sister is very sick." Yet she did not have a fever and wasn't coughing or sneezing. I couldn't figure out why my parents and older sister were so worried. I reasoned she was just tired. I didn't comprehend the severity of her illness because I processed it through what I knew and had experienced.

It never really sunk in until I was called out of my first grade classroom one day, was taken home, and found a priest sitting in our living room beside my mother and father. Then I was told my sister was dead. Then and only then did I realize she had been *very* sick. During all those months, I never connected with what was actually going on because my definition of sickness was limited to just one aspect of it. I asked questions and probed further. I learned a sick person to be one who is afflicted with ill health or disease. No longer would I measure sickness in the same way; I became aware of what the true definition of sickness encompassed.

24

THE TRUE DEFINITION OF SIN

The same is true of many people in the church. Too often we lack the core understanding of what sin really is. To move forward, we must look at how Scripture defines it. The Bible declares, "Sin is lawlessness" (1 John 3:4). The Greek word for "lawlessness" is *anomia*. Thayer's Greek dictionary defines this word: "the condition of [being] without law, because of ignorance of it or because of violating it." Simply put, lawlessness means not to submit to the law or authority of God. Vine's dictionary states that this verse gives "the real meaning of the word [sin]." Vine goes on to say, "This definition of sin sets forth its essential character as the rejection of the law, or will, of God and the substitution of the will of self."

To confirm this definition, let's look at a parable of Jesus. He was eating with some people, and one of them said, "Blessed is he who shall eat bread in the kingdom of God!" (Luke 14:15).

The Lord took advantage of the man's comment to tell who would eat at the table of the marriage supper of the Lamb. He started by saying, "A certain man gave a great supper and invited many, and sent his servant at supper time to say to those who were invited, 'Come, for all things are now ready'" (Luke 14:16–17).

The man giving the supper represents the Father, and the servant is Jesus Himself. The use of the singular "servant" reinforces this interpretation. Scripture specifically states, "God, who at various times and in various ways spoke in time past to the fathers by the prophets, has in these last days spoken to us by His Son" (Heb. 1:1–2). Jesus is our Spokesman. Those who preach, teach, or write in these New Testament times are commanded to speak as the Lord's oracles. We must hear what He is saying to us and accurately communicate it.

In this parable the Father's will is spoken: "Come, for all things are now ready." This announcement is directed toward those already invited, that is, those in the church, not unbelievers who have never heard the gospel.

However, these people begin to make excuses for not heeding the call: "Come." The first one says, "I have a fifth of vodka and a kicking party to go to this weekend, and I really want to be there; please have me excused."

The second one says, "I won an all-expense-paid trip to Las Vegas. And on top of that I have five thousand dollars that was given to me to spend at the casinos. I really want to go, so please excuse me for not coming."

The third one says, "I have fallen in love with my secretary, and we are going to take a trip together this week and check into a Hawaiian resort to fill our week with love. Please don't say anything to my wife; she thinks I'm going on a business trip. So I can't come."

Is that what they say? If you read your Bible, you will find their responses are very different. Let's examine each one.

"The first said to [the servant], 'I have bought a piece of ground.'" Now I have a question before we go any farther: is buying a piece of ground a sin? If it is, a lot of us are in trouble. The answer is no. We all know that. Let's look again at what he said: "I have bought a piece of ground, and I must go and see it. I ask you to have me excused" (v. 18). As I stated, buying land is not sin, but when interest in possessions becomes more important than immediate submission to the word of God, it falls under the core definition of sin. It is lawlessness; it does not submit to God's authority.

The next fellow wasn't embarking on a gambling trip. He said, "I have bought five yoke of oxen, and I am going to test them. I ask you to have me excused" (v. 19). Is buying oxen or any necessary equipment for our livelihood a sin? Of course not, but when industry or business becomes more important than instantly obeying the word or will of God, it is sin! Remember, Adam did not gamble in the Garden of Eden. He simply did not submit to what God said.

The last one said, "I have married a wife, and therefore I cannot come" (v. 20). Is taking a wife a sin? Of course not. If it was, most of us would be in big trouble. However, when the desire to please a mate becomes more important than submitting to the will of God it is sin. Again, recall the Garden. Eve was deceived (2 Cor. 11:3), but it was a different story for Adam: "Adam was not deceived" (1 Tim. 2:14). Referring to the nature of Adam's sin, the Scripture says, "For just as through the *disobedience* of the one man the many were made sinners" (Rom. 5:19 NIV, emphasis added). Adam disobeyed because his wife had already eaten, and she wanted him to do the same. He chose her over submitting to the authority of God. This is sin. As a result of Adam's disobedience, "many were made sinners," or we can say it like this: "Many were made lawless or disobedient to the authority of God." This is true sin. In the case of this parable, Jesus showed how the man chose his wife at the expense of not obeying the word of God.

Now hear what Jesus said about those men who made very polite excuses but did not submit themselves to the calling voice and authority of God: "For I say to you that none of those men who were invited shall taste my supper" (Luke 14:24). How sobering! Those men would not be permitted to dine at the wedding supper to which they had previously held honorary invitations. They were barred from the marriage supper of the Lamb, not because of sexual misconduct, or drug or alcohol abuse, but because of simple disobedience to the word of God. Why should this surprise us? If we think it through, was it not Adam's disobedience that brought the greatest consequence of judgment on mankind?

Isn't it interesting there is no mention in this parable of drug addicts, prostitutes, pimps, alcoholics, murderers, or thieves, right?

Wrong!

If you read on, you will notice the servant reported to the master and relayed all the excuses. The master of the house instructed the servant, "Go out into the highways and hedges, and compel them to come in, that my house many be filled" (Luke 14:23). The people of the highways and hedges in Scripture represent the prostitutes, pimps, thieves, gang members, murderers, alcoholics, and so on! Wow, they are in the parable, but in a good sense!

The Lord knows that in these last days, many of these people will realize their lives are empty and have brought them nothing but sorrow, and they will tire of kicking against the goads. When they hear the call of the Master, they will respond with instant obedience. In contrast, those who were invited, who attend church and consider themselves godly, but obey God only when it is convenient or doesn't interfere with their schedules, agendas, blessings, or pleasure, will find themselves with Adam, shut out from God's glorious presence.

"I Will, Sir"

Sin reveals its true definition in the parable of the wedding supper as disobedience to God's authority. Jesus made it clear in yet another parable, in which He opened with the question, "What do you think?" With those opening words He attempted to get His outwardly righteous listeners to look deeper and glimpse the truth within their answer.

Jesus spoke of a man with two sons. The father went to his first son and told him, "Son, go and work today in the vineyard."

The son replied, "I will not." However, later he changed his mind and left what he was doing and worked in the vineyard.

Then the father approached the second son and asked the same thing of him. The son answered his father, "I will, sir." Sounded like a great son, and he certainly spoke with respect to his father. Yet Jesus said, "He did not go."

Then Jesus asked the all-important, but easy-to-answer question, "Which of the two did what his father wanted?"

The group He was addressing answered correctly: "The first."

Then Jesus went right to the heart of the matter and said, "I tell you the truth, the tax collectors and the prostitutes are entering the kingdom of God ahead of you" (Matt. 21:28–31 NIV). Now, it is obvious any parent would prefer his son to say, "Yes, sir, I will go," and actually go with joy, not only obeying the command, but having a willing attitude as well. Yet this parable showed these leaders that the core meaning of sin is ultimately disobedience to the authority of God. It is not confined to adultery, murder, theft, and so forth.

The leaders were proud and confident in themselves because they weren't ensnared in what they considered "gross sins." However, with their limited definition of sin, they were easily deceived into committing what they professed to avoid so diligently—sin, or disobedience to divine authority.

What About the "Big Ones"?

We can walk throughout the Bible and find this same message repeatedly. You might be thinking, *What about lying, getting drunk, committing adultery, stealing, committing murder? Aren't these sins?* Absolutely! They go against His authority as well. God is the same One who tells us to put away lying, and "let each one of you speak truth with his neighbor" (Eph. 4:24–25). As far as getting drunk, He commands, "Do not be drunk with wine" (Eph. 5:18). Regarding adultery, He warns, "Flee sexual immorality" (1 Cor. 6:18). What about stealing? We are instructed, "If you are a thief, stop stealing" (Eph. 4:28 NLT). In regard to murder, we are told, "Whoever hates his brother is a murderer, and you know that no murderer has eternal life abiding in him" (1 John 3:15). The New Testament emphasizes that people who practice these things will not inherit the kingdom of God (1 Cor. 6:9–11; Gal. 5:19–21; Rev. 21:8). Yet let's not lose sight of the fact that all manner of sin destroys, not just the ones we have labeled "the big ones."

Let's return to our game of psychologist and patient. The patient on the couch with a good understanding of sin could readily answer, "Not submitting to divine authority." He understands that connection between sin and lawlessness.

The Days of Lawlessness

The disciples of Jesus asked Him about the end of the age. He responded by telling them events that would take place and by describing conditions that would be prevalent in the days preceding His second coming. One of the conditions is this: "Because lawlessness will abound, the love of many will grow cold. But he who endures to the end shall be saved" (Matt. 24:12–13).

Whenever I ask congregations whether this applies to our present society, I am greeted with raised hands and nodding heads; most view our society as sinful. Very few, if any, question whether this is an accurate assessment. Yet Jesus was not describing society in that statement.

He was describing the church! You may be wondering how I could reach this conclusion. Well, two distinct phrases in the two verses show He was talking about the church, not society in general.

The first is the key phrase "the *love* of many will grow cold." The Greek word for "love" is *agape*. W. E. Vine, who is an expert in Greek words, writes that *agape* is used "by the Spirit of revelation . . . to express ideas previously unknown." Remember, Jesus said, "A new commandment I give to you, that you love [*agapao*, the verb form of the noun *agape*] one another; as I have loved you" (John 13:34). This love had not been previously known to mankind; He was the very One who introduced it. He defined it with the phrase "as I have loved you." Vines goes on to say, "This love expresses the deep and constant 'love' and interest of a perfect Being towards entirely unworthy objects." In essence it speaks of the unconditional love of God, the love poured out in our hearts by the Holy Spirit, whom Jesus said, "The world cannot receive" (Rom. 5:5; John 14:17). In essence this love can be found only in those who have received Jesus Christ as their Savior.

There are other Greek words translated "love" in the New Testament. However, each of them can be applied just as easily to non-believers as to believers. One such word is *phileo*. This word, according to W. E. Vine, "is to be distinguished from *agapao* in this, that *phileo* more nearly represents 'tender affection' . . . *Phileo* is never used in a command for men to 'love' God." This word is not used uniquely to believers as *agape* is.

In Jesus' statement, "Because lawlessness will abound, the love of many will grow cold," the Greek word used for "love" is not *phileo* but *agape*! Jesus was not directing His statement toward society; rather, he was speaking to the church. He was saying that lawlessness is going to abound in the church in the last days.

We cannot overlook other corresponding statements He made. One such statement is found in the gospel of Matthew: "Not everyone who says to Me, 'Lord, Lord,' shall enter the kingdom of heaven, but he who does the will of My Father in heaven" (Matt. 7:21).

This statement abolishes our general concept and definition of who is saved. We have taught and believed that all you have to do is confess a "sinner's prayer," and you are ensured a secure place in heaven. We have neglected or placed no emphasis on keeping His commands. This counterfeit grace leads many astray, causing them to make light of obedience. Jesus said those who will be in heaven are those who *confess* and *do* the will of God, thus keeping the commands of God.

True grace has been given to empower us to obey what He demands of us. The writer of Hebrews said it best: "Let us have grace, by which we may serve God acceptably" (Heb. 12:28). Grace empowers us to serve God in an acceptable manner, which is in accordance with His will.

Jesus went on to say, "Many will say to Me in that day, 'Lord, Lord, have we not prophesied in Your name, cast out demons in Your name, and done many wonders in Your name?'" (Matt. 7:22).

Not a few, but *many* are referenced in this scripture. Remember the word *many* in His previous statement? "The love of many will grow cold." These multitudes will say to Jesus, "Lord, have we not prophesied, cast out demons, and done miracles in Your name?" An unbeliever cannot cast out a demon in Jesus' name (Acts 19:13–17). So again He was addressing those in the church.

He then will say to these professing Christians: "Depart from Me, you who practice lawlessness!" (Matt. 7:23). Notice what they practice—*lawlessness*. In other words, they have a lifestyle similar to those in the parable of the wedding. They have developed a pattern of placing their agenda, pleasure, or plans before the commands of the Master. Today this seems normal or natural behavior. Simply put, they do not live out their confession of submission to His lordship. They obey what fits in with their plans. They are unaware of their present lawlessness. This, I am sad to say, is the state of too many professing Christians today!

The second reason we know Jesus was addressing the church is found in His next phrase, "But he who endures to the end shall be saved." To endure a race, you must have begun it. Unbelievers have yet to begin the Christian race.

THE SHOCK AND AGONY OF DECEPTION

When Jesus and the apostles speak to the people of the last days, we find repeated warning against what best describes the atmosphere of their time, *deception*. One reason for widespread deception is the misapprehension of the core meaning of sin. It is not too different from my frame of reference with my sister. I was shocked when I came home and found she had died because I never accepted the fact she was really sick. This relates to an experience I had in the late 1980s.

While in prayer I received a sobering spiritual vision that changed the course of my life and ministry. I saw a multitude of people, too great to number, the magnitude of which I had never seen before. They were amassed before the gates of heaven, awaiting entrance, expecting to hear the Master say, "Come, you blessed of My Father, inherit the kingdom prepared for you from the foundation of the world" (Matt. 25:34). But instead they heard the Master say, "Depart from Me, you who practice lawlessness." I saw the look of terrible shock, agony, and terror on their faces. They really believed they were destined for heaven because they professed the lordship of Jesus and their Christianity. Yet they did not understand the true or core meaning of sin. Though they desired heaven, they lacked the passion to obediently do the will of the Father.

God is looking for children whose hearts yearn to walk in obedience. No matter what area of life it may touch, we as believers should delight in doing His will. At the close of a life filled with success from obedience and hardship from disobedience, Solomon breathed wisdom to stand for all time, "Let us hear the conclusion of the whole matter: Fear God and keep His commandments, for this is man's all" (Eccl. 12:13).

The entire verse of Matthew 7:23 states, "And then I will declare to them, 'I never knew you; depart from Me, you who practice lawlessness!'" Some may question that this could not apply to believers because Jesus said, "I never knew you." Remember, unbelievers cannot cast out demons in Jesus' name. When Jesus said, "I never knew you . . . ," it is important to understand the Greek word translated "knew" is *ginosko*. It is used to describe intercourse between a man and a woman in the New Testament (Matt. 1:25). It represents intimacy. Jesus was actually saying, "I never intimately knew you." We read in 1 Corinthians 8:3: "But if anyone loves God, this one is known by Him." The word translated "known" is the same Greek *ginosko*. God intimately knows those who love Him. Those who love Him are those who submit to His authority by obeying His words. Jesus said, "He who does not love Me does not keep My words" (John 14:24).

CHAPTER 4

The Secret Power of Lawlessness

Revealed, not communicated,
knowledge is our greatest guard against deception.

The phrase "the last days" is frequently mentioned in the Scriptures. It is quite possible these days will prove to be the most exciting as well as frightening time in the history of mankind. Exciting because we stand to witness the greatest revelation of God's glory any generation has yet to experience, which will be accompanied by an unimaginable harvest of souls. It will be a time of glory and joy, judgment, and fear.

Fearful because the apostle Paul explicitly told us, "There will be terrible times in the last days" (2 Tim. 3:1 NIV). Prior to this statement he said, *"But mark this."* In other words make careful note of what I am about to write; highlight and underline it in your mind! He then expounded on this trouble in detail in the third chapter. The reason for the terrible times would not be persecution from government or atheists. The reason for the perilous times would stem from widespread *deception* within the church. This warning is repeatedly sounded throughout the New Testament.

Deception is a scary thing. Why? Because it is deceptive! A person who is deceived believes with all his heart that he is right when, in reality, he is wrong. Jesus repeatedly warned against deception in the Gospels. In Matthew 24 alone, He warned four times to beware of it.

In fact, when His disciples asked about His return, the first words out of His mouth when describing our day was, "Take heed that no one deceives you" (Matt. 24:4). It is easy to sense the urgency in His warning. There is a serious and solemn tone. He wanted the words imprinted on their souls and ever before them. His words have stood for thousands of years, and we would be wise not to neglect His counsel.

Two Important Questions

We must ask two important questions. First, what is the root cause of this deception? Second, why is this deception able to run its course unchecked? To answer the first, the root cause of deception is none other than what we discussed in the previous chapter: disobedience to divine authority, or lawlessness. We are admonished,

> "But be doers of the word, and not hearers only, deceiving yourselves" (James 1:22).

Sobering! Scripture tells us when a person *hears* the Word of God yet does not *obey*, deception enters his heart and mind. This person now lives under the conviction that he is on target when he is actually in error. Where there is not true submission to God's authority, which includes the authority of His Word, the door is opened to subtle but great deception.

Why will deception run rampant in the last days? Paul told us many will be deceived "because they did not receive the love of the truth" (2 Thess. 2:10). To love the truth is not just to enjoy hearing it, but to love obeying it. God said to one prophet,

> As for you, son of man, the children of your people are talking about you beside the walls and in the doors of the houses; and they speak to one another, everyone saying to his brother, "Please come and hear what the word is that comes from the LORD." So they come to you as people do, they sit before you as My people, and they hear your words, *but they do not do them*; for with their mouth they show much love, but their hearts pursue their own gain. (Ezek. 33:30–31, emphasis added)

Many people in our churches love good preaching and teaching, but when it comes down to reality, they still love their own lives more than they love God's will (2. Tim 3:1–4). We must love truth more than anyone or anything else. We must passionately desire His will more than our comfort or lives. Then we will delight in putting our personal desires aside for His wishes. We will take up our crosses and deny our rights and privileges for the sake of fulfilling His will. Why? Because He is God, our Creator, our Redeemer, and His love toward us is perfect. This alone keeps us from deception.

But is this the type of devotion we see in the church? Reality is much different. It is amazing how these writers of Scripture foresaw our day with greater accuracy than we see it.

The Secret Power of Lawlessness

There is another factor to consider in understanding why lawlessness is so rampant in our day. We are warned, "For the secret power of lawlessness is already at work" (2 Thess. 2:7 NIV). This word translated "lawlessness" is the same Greek word *anomia,* we studied in the previous chapter. Notice there's a secret force or power behind it. The New King James Version refers to it as the "mystery of lawlessness." The mystery is hidden in its secret power. With believers, lawlessness would not be effective if blatant, only if subtle and deceptive. That is its mystery. Because God does not want us ignorant of this mystery or secret power, He warns us (2 Cor. 2:11).

Satan is the master of deception. Think of it: he led a third of the angels in an uprising against God (Rev. 12:3–4). That took place in a perfect environment, in the very presence of our glorious Lord! Jesus warned that Satan was not only a deceiver but the very father of it (John 8:44). Jesus also warned us that Satan's delusions and deceptions would become so strong in the latter days that if it were possible even the elect would fall prey to them (Matt. 24:24).

Why should we be surprised? If he could mislead millions of angels in heaven, why would it be difficult to mislead multitudes in this earthly environment, of which he is called the "prince of the power of the air" (Eph. 2:2)? We now live in the very days Jesus spoke of, so examine carefully Paul's passionate plea to the Corinthian church:

"But I fear, lest somehow, as the serpent deceived Eve by his crafti-ness, so your minds may be corrupted" (2 Cor. 11:3).

Paul compared the vulnerability of believers to the deception of Eve. Without a doubt one of the devil's most spectacular feats was the deception of Eve. She lived in a perfect environment, free from demonic rule and influence. She walked in the very presence of God, unhindered by her flesh. Causing her to rebel must have been one of Satan's most crafty schemes. He resorted to subtle and cunning tactics to corrupt the purity of her mind. By understanding his tactics with Eve, we expose his best weapon; we gain an understanding of how he tries to deceive us as well as why so many fall into disobedience today.

Recall that Eve was beguiled into disobedience, but Adam knew exactly what he was doing. I have watched people in the church trans-gress God's commands with their eyes wide open, fully aware of what they do. They are not deceived. They are treading on dangerous territory and advancing toward spiritual death (Rom. 8:13). These are the hard of heart and difficult to reach. Then there are others—these constitute the majority of the disobedient in the church—*the deceived*. As with Eve, ignorance has opened them to deception, the secret power of lawlessness.

Ignorance is a breeding ground for deception. God said, "There-fore my people have gone into captivity, because they have no knowl-edge" (Isa. 5:13). The revealed knowledge of God's ways and His spiritual laws guard us from the enemy's deceptions. The light of His truth exposes and protects us from any lie.

REVELATION VERSUS COMMUNICATED KNOWLEDGE

God placed man in the Garden and said, "Of every tree of the garden you may freely eat; but of the tree of the knowledge of good and evil you shall not eat, for in the day that you eat of it you shall surely die" (Gen. 2:16–17).

After that, the Lord removed the woman from the man. We can assume this took place a while later, for the man had named and viewed every animal and bird of the air before the woman left his side.

Unlike Adam, the woman did not hear the command directly from the mouth of God. Adam probably conveyed it to her as they enjoyed God's garden. We can surmise this situation by her response to the serpent. Read carefully the following verses:

> Now the serpent was more cunning than any beast of the field which the LORD God had made. And he said to the woman, "Has God indeed said, 'You shall not eat of every tree of the garden'?" And the woman said to the serpent, "We may eat the fruit of the trees of the garden; but of the fruit of the tree which is in the midst of the garden, God has said, 'You shall not eat it, nor shall you touch it, lest you die.'" (Gen. 3:1–3)

First, notice when the serpent questioned God's command, the woman responded, "We may . . .," rather than a reply such as, "God has said . . ." This is a classic response of one who has heard orders or rules secondhand. It is not the response of a person who has the heartbeat and motive of the One who originated the command.

Second, notice her response differs from God's original commandment. She added, "God has said, 'You shall not eat it, nor shall you touch it, lest you die.'" God never said anything about touching it. Here we have another example of what happens when you have heard from another what God said rather than having it revealed directly by the Lord.

When God reveals His word by His Spirit, it then becomes a part of us. This can happen as we read a book, as we listen to another teach, or as we are alone reading the Bible, or in communion with the Spirit of God. To Adam, God's command was as real as everything else around him; it was part of him. Conversely, when we hear God's command, but it is not revealed to us by His Spirit, it is not a part of us. It's just a law to us, and "the strength of sin [disobedience] is the law" (1 Cor. 15:56).

As I stated, I believe Adam repeated God's command to Eve. More than likely Eve did not seek God personally about it. She just accepted Adam's information as "this is the way it is." For her it was not revealed knowledge, but communicated knowledge. Hearing it secondhand would make her more vulnerable to deception. For that reason the serpent targeted her rather than Adam.

Revealed, not communicated, knowledge is our greatest guard against deception. Many are bound by legalism because they've heard only the knowledge, instruction, or confines of Scriptures. Whether it comes from parents, preachers, tapes, or books they have yet to seek to know God's very heart in the matter, which would give them the understanding that would guard them from deception. They have the letter without the heartbeat. They can even accurately repeat chapter or verse, but they have lost the breath of life behind the Scriptures.

They may even have enthusiasm as they share a new teaching they just heard at a seminar or conference. However, they appear unable to live out what they so excitedly share. It is not a part of them. They carry the words, yet they remain barren and incapable of producing the life of God. When this happens, they are easily tempted to add to or take away from what God has said. They can be easily deceived because they lack an understanding of God's way.

Here is an example I've heard numerous times: "Well, you know, brother, money is the root of all evil!" That is not what God said. He said, "The *love* of money is a root of all kinds of evil" (1 Tim. 6:10, emphasis added).

If money was the root of all evil, then Jesus was out of order because He had a treasurer and a money bag! At one point a woman broke a bottle of perfume that was worth an entire year's salary and poured it on Him. Judas, who loved money, was upset at the act, yet the Lord rebuked him and commended her (John 12:3–7).

No, it's not money itself, but the love of it, that is a root of all evil. It is an unhealthy desire for and dependency on money. This legalistic view causes people to have an unhealthy attitude toward money that God never intended. God warns us of an unhealthy desire for, and dependency on, money. Therefore, they can never operate in the area of finances in a truly godly manner. This ignorance confirms God's

Word has not been revealed in their hearts. They have only a communicated knowledge of His Word, and they are candidates for deception.

So how do we receive revelation knowledge? By walking humbly before God with the fear and love of God burning in our hearts. God said,

> But on this one will I look:
> On him who is poor and of a contrite spirit,
> And who trembles at My word. (Isa. 66:2)

The one who trembles at His Word will instantly obey Him, whether he sees the advantage or not. He is the one who truly fears God. And Scripture clearly declares, "The secret of the LORD is with those who fear Him, and He will show them His covenant" (Ps. 25:14).

Now we better understand Solomon's statement at the end of his life: "Fear God and keep His commandments, for this is man's all" (Eccl. 12:13). God reveals His secrets or ways to those who fear Him, and John said to this group of people,

> These things I have written to you concerning those who try to *deceive* you. But the anointing which you have received from Him abides in you, and you do not need that anyone teach you; but as the same anointing teaches you concerning all things, and is true, and is not a lie [deception], and just as it has taught you, you will abide in Him. (1 John 2:26–27, emphasis added)

This shows us how the revealed Word of God keeps us from deception. Eve was deceived into disobedience because she lacked God's revealed knowledge. Therefore, she did not detect the trickery and perversion in the words of the serpent.

HOW DID THE SERPENT DO IT?

Let's move on and answer the question: How did the serpent deceive the woman? What was his subtle scheme of attack? Knowing the answer is vital. Think about it: How did he maneuver her into deception? Eve lived in an entirely perfect environment. She had never been abused by anyone in authority. She had no bad experience with a father, boss, or minister. She lived in a flourishing garden, free from demonic oppression. All she had known was God's goodness and provision. She had walked and talked in His presence. So how did the serpent go about deceiving her?

Recall God's command: "Of every tree of the garden you may freely eat; but of the tree of the knowledge of good and evil you shall not eat, for in the day that you eat of it you shall surely die" (Gen. 2:16–17).

God's goodness granted, "You may freely eat . . . ," while His authority restricted, ". . . but of the tree of the knowledge of good and evil." God emphasized their liberty to eat of every tree with the exception of one.

It is God's very essence to love and give. He desired companions in His garden who would love and obey Him. He did not want robots who lacked the freedom of choice. He longed for children, made in His image, with a free will. When He restricted their access to the tree, He gave them a choice that protected them from death. It involved their will. Would they trust and obey? Without the command there would be no choice.

Examine closely the serpent's words: "Now the serpent was more cunning than any beast of the field which the LORD God had made. And he said to the woman, 'Has God indeed said, "You shall not eat of every tree of the garden"?'" (Gen. 3:1). To put his question in more contemporary terms, the serpent said, "I hear that God said you can't eat from every tree. Is that right?"

The serpent began his strategy by first distorting the emphasis of God's command. By twisting its meaning, he brought into question God's motive. He wanted to lead Eve down a path of reasoning where she would eventually question God's goodness and integrity. Once he accomplished that, it would be all too easy to turn her against His authority.

The serpent ignored God's generosity and pointed to His exception. He implied something good for them was being withheld. With a single question the serpent distorted the only command, given to protect, into an unjust denial of good. Can you hear the sneer in his voice as he questioned, "So, God said you can't eat from every tree?" Despite their access to an entire garden to eat from, the serpent called Eve's attention to the one tree denied them. He made God look like a "taker" rather than the "giver" He is.

By causing the Lord to appear unjust, the serpent could attack God's dominion. Satan is no fool; he went after the very foundation of the Lord's authority: "Righteousness and justice are the foundation of His throne" (Ps. 97:2). His throne represents His authority. If Satan can pervert His righteous character through deception and distortion, then the very foundation of His authority is under question in the eyes of His creation.

In response to the serpent's question the woman corrected him: "We may eat the fruit of the trees of the garden; but of the fruit of the tree which is in the midst of the garden, God has said, 'You shall not eat it, nor shall you touch it, lest you die'" (Gen. 3:2–3).

It is quite possible, even as she answered, she wondered about the reason behind the command. She was questioning the goodness of God. Can you hear her thoughts? *It looks good . . . I don't know why we can't eat from that tree. What could be the harm in it? What's in it that is so bad for us?* With newly raised doubts of His motives, she was open to the questioning of God's authority.

The serpent seized the opportunity to undermine God's authority, truthfulness, and integrity by boldly countering His word: "You will not surely die. For God knows that in the day you eat of it your eyes will be opened, and you will be like God, knowing good and evil" (Gen. 3:4–5).

The master of deception sought to destroy the very foundation of her loyalty by blatantly contradicting God and assuring her she would not die. He quickly followed his reasoning up with, "Instead of dying, you'll become more like God. You'll be able to choose for yourself between good and evil because you will be wise. You won't have to hear everything secondhand or be subject to unfair commands anymore."

SIN CONCEIVED—SLAVERY FOLLOWS

Eve was shocked and confused. She wondered, *Why would God keep this fruit from me?* She looked at the tree again to survey its fruit, although through different eyes. She judged the fruit to be good and pleasant, not bad and injurious. She thought, *Surely it looks great for eating, and best of all it will make us wise.*

That reasoning blinded her to all else around her. She forgot the abundant goodness provided as she focused on the single tree. She thought, *This tree bears something good for us, and God has kept it from us. Its fruit could have been ours all along. Why has He done this to us? If He is withholding something we need in this tree, what else has He withheld from us?*

With God's character, integrity, and goodness in question, and the assurance of no harm, there no longer remained any reason for submission to His authority in the matter. Her self-will overrode the Father's will. Eve reached for the fruit and turned it in her hand—nothing happened. The serpent must have been right. She then ate and gave some to her husband.

After they ate it their eyes were suddenly opened, and they felt a wave of shame and fear as they realized their nakedness. With their disobedience came spiritual death. Flesh had now become the strong taskmaster that would dominate them. By questioning God's word and taking the path of reasoning to deception, they opened their lives to the master of disobedience. He became their dark lord. As Scriptures confirm, "Do you not know that to whom you present yourselves slaves to obey, you are that one's slaves whom you obey, whether of sin [disobedience to God's authority] leading to death, or of obedience leading to righteousness?" (Rom. 6:16). The lord of death was granted not only access to their lives but also legal entrance to the world. Paul explained it this way: "Therefore, just as through one man sin entered the world, and death through sin, and thus death spread to all men" (Rom. 5:12).

Before their disobedience, there was no hatred, anger, unforgiveness, strife, gossip, corruption, fraud, bitterness, or extortion. There was no sexual perversion, drug abuse, drunkenness, murder, or theft.

There was no wife or child abuse. Sickness, disease, and poverty were nonexistent. Natural disasters, pestilence, and plagues were implicitly unknown to mankind. The animal kingdom lived in complete harmony. The earth's atmosphere was tranquil with the will of God presiding over all creation.

Disobedience brought forth these horrid behavioral problems that plague mankind, and the list multiplies and grows fouler with each passing generation. Their one act of insubordination marked the beginning of the secret power of lawlessness. Out of its deception man lost his divine provision and protection. Rebellion patterned after Satan's own had opened wide the door to his dominion and destruction. He took full advantage of his opportunity to be like God but not subject to Him. By enslaving God's creation, he enthroned himself (Isa. 14:12–14).

THE SCHEME IS NO DIFFERENT TODAY

Satan's mode of operation differs little today. He still desires to pervert God's character to turn us against His authority. The book of James makes this absolutely clear: "Do not be deceived, my beloved brethren. Every good gift and every perfect gift is from above, and comes down from the Father of lights, with whom there is no variation or shadow of turning" (1:16–17).

The writer wanted to make sure we believers would not fall to the same secret power of lawlessness that Eve did. He gave us warning to protect us, as did Paul. We must carefully heed his words and settle them in our hearts; there is nothing good outside the realm of God's will. It may appear good, but if it doesn't line up with God's will, make no mistake, there is nothing good in it for us.

James reiterated that if you believe there is good outside God's provision, then you can be deceived, just as Eve was. Carefully consider what we've discussed. No matter how good it looks, tastes, or feels; no matter how rich, abundant, wise, or successful it may make you, if it is not from God, it will eventually lead you down a path of intense sorrow, regret, and, in the end, death. Divine provision and protection will be compromised by way of deception. Every perfect and good gift is from

God; He is the Source. Embrace this truth, and settle it in your heart, then looks won't deceive you! If Eve had done this, she wouldn't have been swayed. She looked outside God's provision to fulfill her desires.

How many marry the wrong person for the wrong reasons? God may have warned them through parents or pastors, or spoken directly to their hearts, but they allowed reasoning to drown out these voices. Perhaps they were lonely and desired companionship. Perhaps the person was pleasant to the eyes and appeared helpful in making decisions. They inevitably chose their will over God's, and all too often suffered greatly.

Of course, God can redeem our misjudgments. David's sin of taking Bathsheba was redeemed later in the birth of Solomon. However, he reaped much sorrow for his disobedience, as the sword never left his home. He lost three sons in early age or in their primes to death. How much better when we choose obedience.

Too often people leave the very places—jobs, churches, cities—where God has planted them because they disagree with authorities set over them. Or perhaps they see their lives stagnating, or they believe there is no future for them where they are. Soon an opportunity comes along, and even though there is no witness from the Holy Spirit to depart, they leave. Not only that, but often the departure compromises the purity to which God called them. They reason, *I've been on this shelf too long; I have to do something.* Then they end up going against the will of God in the pursuit of what they believe is good for them. They may end up financially well off, yet their hearts have long drifted from an intimate and passionate relationship with the Lord.

In more general terms, how many disobey the will of God? They are enticed by the good and pleasant. Perhaps they find a means of prosperity or success outside the counsel of God's Word. They pursue it and find fun, happiness, or excitement—for a season. They find "good" in what God said "no" to. They fear God withholds the attractive or fun stuff from them! They think He doesn't understand their needs or He ignores the importance of their desires. They believe God is unfaithful if their prayers are not answered within their predetermined time frame. They reason, "Why wait? I'll take the good and pleasant now!"

CONSIDER JESUS

Consider Jesus. He was in the desert for forty days and nights without water, food, or comfort. Hunger pains pierced His belly as starvation began its harsh work. If He didn't have food and water soon, He would die. But what came first: the provision or the temptation?

At that point Satan came to question Him, "If You are the Son of God, command that these stones become bread" (Matt. 4:3). The enemy was again questioning what God had just clearly stated. The Father openly declared Jesus was His Son at the banks of the Jordan. Satan was again attempting to distort God's character: "If you are God's Son, why has He led You out here to starve? Why doesn't He provide for You? Perhaps it is time You provided for Yourself. If You don't get nutrition soon, You'll die, or if You get it too late, You'll end up with severe physical problems. Use Your authority to serve Yourself. Turn these stones to bread."

Jesus resisted and waited for God's provision. He would not allow the enemy to pervert the character of God in His mind. He knew His Father provided for His needs. He remained submitted to God's authority, no matter how unpleasant it was at the moment.

After He resisted Satan's temptation to take matters into His own hands, "the devil left Him, and behold, angels came and ministered to Him" (Matt. 4:11). Why? The writer of Hebrews described Jesus this way: "Who, in the days of His flesh, when He had offered up prayers and supplications, with vehement cries and tears to Him who was able to save Him from death, and was heard because of His godly fear, though He was a Son, yet He learned obedience by the things which He suffered" (Heb. 5:7–8). God heard Him because of His godly fear. He did not doubt the Father's goodness. Even in the face of great temptation and intense suffering, more than any had undergone, He chose obedience, though it meant severe hardship.

Unlike the response of Adam and Eve, this type of obedience and submission blocked all inroads of the enemy to His life. He testified, "The ruler of this world is coming, and he has nothing in Me. But that the world may know that I love the Father, and as the Father gave Me commandment, so I do" (John 14:30–31).

Unlike Adam, Jesus, the last Adam, walked in perfect obedience to His Father and could testify that Satan found nothing in Him. For this very reason, we are admonished, "The one who says he abides in Him [Jesus] ought himself to walk in the same manner as He walked" (1 John 2:6 NASB). He is our example and forerunner. He is the One who paid the price and lit the path for us to walk on. We are no longer destined for the way of the first Adam and his lawlessness, but are called and empowered to walk in the ways of obedience of the last Adam.

The Message passionately proclaims,

> Strip down, start running—and never quit [in obedience to God]! No extra spiritual fat, no parasitic sins. Keep your eyes on *Jesus,* who both began and finished this race we're in. Study how he did it. Because he never lost sight of where he was headed—that exhilarating finish in and with God—he could put up with anything along the way: cross, shame, whatever. And now he's *there,* in the place of honor, right alongside God. When you find yourselves flagging in your faith [obedience], go over that story again, item by item, that long litany of hostility he plowed through. *That* will shoot adrenaline into your souls! (Heb. 12:1–3)

That sums it up. Learn from the First Adam's fall, and follow hard after the last Adam's obedience.

In the next chapter we will examine the consequences of disobedience. They are not always seen immediately, but they will surely follow. Once disobedience is clearly revealed, you should never contemplate tolerating it again.

CHAPTER 5

THE CONSEQUENCES OF DISOBEDIENCE I

Faith and obedience are inseparable because obedience is evidence of true faith.

Various consequences result from disobedience. The aftereffects are not always immediately recognizable or obvious, but just as seeds sown produce a harvest, these, too, are certain. The enemy of the soul longs to keep this knowledge from us in hopes we will esteem obedience lightly and easily fall prey to his deceptive tactics.

Some people subconsciously reason that any consequence of their disobedience will be outweighed by what they perceive as the immediate gain of their decision. I am amazed by how prevalent this deceptive and deadly thought process is. This is the mystery or secret power of lawlessness. It is my earnest hope and prayer that these next three chapters will secure in your heart the commitment to never entertain disobedience.

THE SONS OF ADAM

We'll begin by learning from Cain, the firstborn of Adam. Cain was a farmer by occupation. His brother, Abel, Adam's second born, was a shepherd. Scripture tells us in the course of time Cain brought an offering of the fruit of the ground before the Lord, and Abel brought an offering of the firstborn of his flock. We learn, "The LORD accepted Abel and his offering, but he did not accept Cain and his offering" (Gen. 4:4–5 NLT).

As a side note, this refutes a common saying we often hear in our churches today, "God will accept you just the way you are." That is just not true. God does accept us *if we repent!* Try this statement out on Ananias and Sapphira. It just doesn't fit; they're dead (Acts 5:1–11).

God didn't accept Cain's offering; furthermore, He didn't accept Cain! That He didn't accept Cain doesn't mean Cain's destiny was permanent rejection, but our modern-day theology of God's unconditional acceptance is inaccurate. In fact, it is dangerous because it removes the fear of the Lord from our hearts. The fear of the Lord guards us and causes us to depart from sin (Ex. 20:20). After the deaths of Ananias and Sapphira, the Bible tells us, "So great fear came upon all the church" (Acts 5:11). No longer was disobedience a casual matter!

I would like to slightly modernize the story of Adam's two sons in order to bring it forward. His sons were raised in a home that called on the name of the Lord. Both brought an offering to the Lord, which represented their lives. The Bible says we are to offer our bodies as living sacrifices (Rom. 12:1). Whenever a sacrifice is brought before God, it represents our service to Him. So we are not talking about Abel, who served God, and brother Cain, who did not. Cain wasn't hanging out at the sports arenas, strip joints, or bars and avoiding any possible church attendance. Don't mistake Cain with a man who doesn't want anything to do with God. Both would presently be considered believers who had communication with God.

Both men were diligent in their work to bring an offering to the Lord. In fact, we could safely say Cain worked harder than Abel. I know very little about farming and shepherding, but I know enough to know shepherding is work, but farming is harder. With shepherding, you have responsibilities in the morning and afternoon, but usually in the heat of the day, you can rest under a shade tree and sip on a cool drink.

Farming is more labor intensive. Cain's offering came by the sweat of his brow, brought forth by toiling against the very ground God had cursed (Gen. 3:17–19). Cain cleared the ground of rocks, stumps, and other debris. Then he plowed and cultivated the soil. He planted, watered, fertilized, and protected his crops. He expended a lot of effort to supply an offering.

WHY DIDN'T GOD ACCEPT CAIN?

So we must ask, Why didn't God accept Cain's offering when He knew he worked harder? The answer is found with his parents. In the Garden everything God created had a covering. Animals have fur, fish have scales, and birds have feathers. You never see a polar bear wearing jeans; it doesn't need additional covering.

Adam and Eve were no exception. They did not have physical covering or clothing; rather, they were "crowned" with glory (Ps. 8:5). The word *crowned* means "to circle or surround." They were covered by it. The very glory that God placed on them was so overwhelming that, in their eyes, it concealed their physical nakedness. For this reason Scripture says, "They were both naked, the man and his wife, and were not ashamed" (Gen. 2:25). They were not ruled by self-consciousness; rather their lives were before God. The thought of wanting clothing didn't cross their minds because it wasn't necessary.

That changed the moment they disobeyed. Prior to their disobedience, their spirits completely dominated, whereas afterward their flesh would dominate. The first words recorded in Scripture after they ate were, "Then the eyes of both of them were opened, and they knew that they were naked" (Gen. 3:7). The key words are *they knew.* They had knowledge they did not have before.

The principle of the knowledge of good and evil is to live life according to what is right and wrong. Before the Fall, their actions were governed not by the knowledge of good and evil, or by right and wrong, but by the knowledge of God. They were motivated by a sense of obedience birthed out of trust and love. Right and wrong were not in their minds, but in God's hand. We are told,

His work is perfect;
For all His ways are justice,
A God of truth and without injustice;
Righteous and upright is He. (Deut. 32:4)

Adam and Eve lived before God, completely God conscious. By taking of the fruit of the Tree of the Knowledge of Good and Evil, they found a source of the knowledge of what was good and evil outside God. We can identify this as the principle of reasoning. They no longer needed God to govern them; they had a sense of right and wrong within themselves. That was why the first question God asked them after their fall was, "Who told you?" (Gen. 3:11).

Whenever God asks a question, He is not looking for information. He is drawing you into what He is communicating. God already knew they had eaten from the tree and were speaking from their own wisdom. They had replaced obedience with reasoning. He was actually saying, "So you have now found a source of the sense of right and wrong outside Me. You have obviously eaten from the Tree of the Knowledge of Good and Evil."

Immediately after their disobedience, they covered their nakedness with fig leaves, or the *fruit of the ground*. Even with the covering they still felt naked and hid. God then questioned, "Who told you that you were naked?" (Gen. 3:11). Out of their newly found sense of right and wrong, they attempted to do right in their eyes, and yet still felt naked. That covering was not God's way. He demonstrated His acceptable covering, or offering for nakedness, by slaying an innocent animal and covering Adam and Eve with its skin. That was God's prescribed way, not the fruit of the ground.

At that point Adam and Eve were ignorant of what God was looking for, but Cain and Abel were not. Their parents had taught them the acceptable offering to God. So when Cain brought an offering of the fruit of the ground, it was again an unacceptable offering. He was serving God his own way! He gravitated toward the curse that operates by way of reason and draws on the logic of right and wrong, rather than from the purity of childlike obedience as his brother, Abel, had done.

You Should Rule over It

The Scriptures tell us, "By faith Abel offered to God a more excellent sacrifice than Cain, through which he obtained witness that he was righteous, God testifying of his gifts; and through it he being dead still speaks" (Heb. 11:4). The New Testament writer equated the obedience of Abel with faith. We will learn in a future chapter that true faith is equated with, as well as founded on, obedience. True faith operates out of obedience rather than a sense of right and wrong.

Once Cain realized his efforts and offering were unacceptable to God, "Cain was very angry, and his countenance fell" (Gen. 4:5). This is the classic response of a religious person when he is confronted with truth. He gets angry. You will find this to be true throughout the Scriptures. This anger is fueled by pride, and pride rejects God's will or ways in order to cling to its own.

God in His mercy attempted to open Cain's eyes by way of questioning, "Why are you angry? And why has your countenance fallen? If you do well, will you not be accepted?" (Gen. 4:6–7). To do well with God is to obey. He desires obedience over sacrifice. Numerous times He told His people to get rid of their songs and instruments, and quit bringing the sacrifices. Why? "Because, when I called, no one answered, when I spoke they did not hear" (Isa. 66:4). They sacrificed, but did not listen to or obey what He said. The highest form of worship is obedience.

Knowing this, we could insert the words *obey Me* for *do well* in the verse from Genesis without changing the meaning. It would read, "Cain, why are you angry? You don't need to be. Learn from this. If you obey Me as your brother did, I will accept you and your sacrifice as I did Abel and his."

The Lord warned, "And if you do not do well [if you do not obey and you persist in your reasoning], sin lies at the door. And its desire is for you, but you should rule over it" (Gen. 4:7). Note two things here. First, sin (disobedience) has desire. The lord of lawlessness, Satan, is the force behind disobedience. Once this force was granted entrance by Adam, it had one objective: to control or rule everyone and everything.

It is similar to a wicked scientist who released an uncontainable amount of radioactive gases into our atmosphere. The gases would permeate everywhere, even though the actual presence of the scientist would not. He set in motion a deadly and powerful force. The only ones protected from these deadly gases would be those wearing protective gear. The Scriptures are very clear: "We know that we are children of God and that the world around us is under the power and control of the evil one" (1 John 5:19 NLT).

Another way to view this would be to compare the desire of sin to the law of gravity. It is a constant force that is always in place and affects all matter. If you step off the top of a building, you will find its law in effect and fall to the lowest point, in fact, very hard. You may not want to fall or have an awareness of or belief in the law of gravity; nevertheless, you will encounter it.

One day scientists discovered yet another law—the law of lift. They learned that the law of lift supersedes the law of gravity if conditions were right. Innovative men designed the airplane based on the law of lift. When you fly in a plane, you are on a level free from the law of gravity and do not fall to gravity's lowest point. Scripture tells us, "For the law of the Spirit of life in Christ Jesus has made me free from the law of sin and death" (Rom. 8:2). What wonderful news!

I fly frequently. Last year alone I flew approximately two hundred thousand miles to preach the gospel globally. When I get on these jets, I'm delighted that the law of lift sets me free from the law of gravity. However, if the pilot decided to turn off the engines, and the wings fell off, the plane would feel the full effect of the law of gravity, and the plane would come down hard. We would no longer enjoy a mastery of the law of gravity, but would find ourselves mastered by what we previously enjoyed power over.

Scripture further declares in this same chapter, "Therefore, brethren, we are debtors—not to the flesh, to live according to the flesh. For if you live according to the flesh you will die" (Rom. 8:12–13). Although the law of the Spirit of life makes us free from the law of sin, the law of sin remains intact. Our protection or mastery of it comes from true faith or obedience.

The "law of the Spirit of life" is also called "the law of faith" (Rom. 3:27). We know the law of faith supersedes the law of sin. True faith is described as having corresponding works of obedience (James 2:19–23). Faith and obedience are inseparable because obedience is evidence of true faith.

Abel mastered the law of sin and death by faith, or obedience to God. In speaking to Cain, God warned: sin's desire is for you (not unlike gravity's desire or influence on any solid matter); if you obey Me, you will master it (just as lift overrides gravity). Sin is mastered through obedience.

OPEN ACCESS

The second point God made to Cain was that "if you do not do well [do not obey Me], sin is crouching at the door" (Gen. 4:7 NASB). Notice He used the word *door*. There is a figurative door in the life of every person; whether you are aware or unaware, it is there. This door represents entrance into your life. In this case it is an access for sin and demonic power. God tells us right from the start what opens it to sin and demonic influence and what shuts it. Disobedience opens it, whereas obedience slams it shut.

What happened with Cain? He persisted in his wisdom and reasoning. Envy entered his heart, closely followed by offense. Then came hatred. Murder was premeditated, and it wasn't long before Cain killed his brother in a rage. He was belligerent, and he lost his fear of God. He exemplified his attitude in his defiant response to God's questioning about where his brother was: "I do not know. Am I my brother's keeper?" (Gen. 4:9). He was lying to God, for he knew exactly where his brother was.

Anyone in his right mind would realize God knew where Abel was, but this is what happens when someone turns to reasoning and allows disobedience in his life. He loses touch with the reality of spiritual things. He attempts to lower the image of God to his level and limitations, and imagines himself as wise as God—or sometimes even wiser. He is not in his right mind. Lucifer is a prime example; reasoning birthed from iniquity led him to believe he could overthrow God. How foolish! Yet he has led many in his way (Isa. 14:12–17).

If you were friends with Cain and Abel and didn't know the inside story, you might be baffled by the whole situation. How could a man who started out diligently serving God end up an irreverent murderer? How could this be? He had opened the door of his soul to the law of sin by persisting in disobedience. Do you know the saying, "Give them an inch and they'll take a mile"? It perfectly describes the law of disobedience. If you open your life to it just a little, it is like a crack in a dam. The force of the water eventually breaks through like a flood.

I have had the honor of ministering full time for almost eighteen years. During that time, I have witnessed this law in countless incidents. I have seen those who start out on fire for the things of God. They are active in their churches and constantly telling others about Jesus. They are like Cain, who started out diligently. But in the course of time situations arise that expose areas of self-will still within them. It could be, as with Cain, by way of God's direct authority or by way of delegated authority. Either way, it always seems to deal with authority.

I have watched as they refused to submit their will and persisted in their own way. It is only a matter of time before lawlessness floods their lives. It may not manifest itself in murder, but one thing is certain: it manifests in some form. Perhaps a flood of greed, hatred, anger, unforgiveness, strife, gossip, sexual sin, or countless other forms of bondage grip their flesh. Often in this deceived and offended state, they imagine they are right with God, and all other authorities are extreme, legalistic, or out of touch.

In cases like Cain's, if they rebel against God's direct authority, they reduce the image, authority, and power of God to a more manageable level and thus become increasingly irreverent. They profess His lordship, but in reality serve a Jesus fashioned after their own image. Without a consciousness of it, in their hearts they have elevated their reasoning above the throne and authority of God. Either way, they are blinded to their true condition by the deception in their hearts.

If you had told Cain when he was a young man, still tender of heart and serving God, "One day, you will murder your own brother," he would have been shocked and quickly responded, "That is impossible. I'd never do that!" Yet later he opened himself up to lawlessness and committed what was previously unthinkable to him.

People both in and out of churches will one day stand before God and be judged for their lawlessness. Yet if you could have followed the course of their lives, you could never have imagined they would end at such a destination. Even now they would never dream themselves lawless, but on the Day of Judgment when truth is revealed, they will wonder, *How did I drift so far from obedience to the ways of God?* The sad answer will be, they did not love and embrace the truth of being under His cover.

There is only one hope for people in deception: that God's mercy will open their eyes; that the light of His truth will dispel the dark shroud of deception. The cry of my heart—and the purpose of this book—is to safeguard people from the mastery of the deceptive power of lawlessness and to expose the light of truth to those already ensnared in its grip and thus set them free. I have preached this message all over the world, and when I ask how many have fallen into areas of disobedience, the response is always overwhelming, usually well over 50 percent. Most confess, "I didn't know the rebellion was there until the truth exposed it in my heart."

I also confess, I do not write this book as one who has never been deceived by this secret power of lawlessness. No, I have found myself under its terrible grip, and God in His mercy exposed the error of my heart and ways. I share with you what I know and have been delivered from. I am so grateful to our precious Lord for His tender mercy!

God graciously attempts to open our eyes to areas of disobedience, but as with Cain, we will not see truth until we first humble ourselves. In the next chapter, we will see the overwhelming importance humility plays in our deliverance and, at the same time, see the deadly consequences of pride.

CHAPTER 6

THE CONSEQUENCES OF DISOBEDIENCE II

Partial obedience is not obedience at all in the eyes of God.

The life of Saul, the first king of Israel, lends us a vivid picture of what transpires when a person flirts with disobedience. His is a tragic story that holds many relevant lessons to us as believers. There are keys of understanding hidden within the corrective word of the Lord spoken to him. A look at his life grants us an even clearer understanding of the spiritual consequences of not fully obeying divine authority. If we permit it, this understanding will strengthen us, and his failure will become our warning. We are told, "For whatever things were written before were written for our learning" (Rom. 15:4); and "These things happened to them as examples and were written down as warnings for us, on whom the fulfillment of the ages has come" (1 Cor. 10:11 NIV).

PARTIAL OBEDIENCE

Let's begin where the senior prophet of Israel, Samuel, went to Saul with a command from the mouth of God. He warned Saul to carefully heed the instructions: "Now go and attack Amalek, and utterly destroy all that they have, and do not spare them. But kill both man and woman, infant and nursing child, ox and sheep, camel and donkey" (1 Sam. 15:3). The command was direct and very specific. Nothing Amalek possessed—whether human or beast—was to be left alive. Everything with breath was to be destroyed.

Watch Saul's response. He did not say, "I won't do it . . . this is too harsh!" Too often we limit the understanding of rebellion to merely the obvious—blatant disobedience. Yet we'll soon discover this is far from accurate. Nor did Saul agree, then later change his mind. Most of us understand this form of disobedience as well. Nor did Saul neglect to make it a priority and eventually disobey out of forgetfulness. Most will admit that behavior would not be obedient, but would excuse it because of its good intentions. More than likely, all would agree these scenarios represent disobedient behavior patterns, but let's turn our attention again to Saul.

He immediately gathered his army and made ready to attack Amalek. Everything looked great. He attacked and killed every man, woman, infant, and nursing child. Tens of thousands were put to the edge of the sword by Saul and his great army.

However, Saul spared the king of Amalek. Why? Possibly he was conforming to the culture of that time. If you conquered a nation and took alive its leader, you brought back to your palace a slave, a sort of living trophy.

Saul also slaughtered thousands of animals. Yet he spared the best of the sheep, oxen, fatlings, lambs, and all that was good, and gave it to his people so they could sacrifice to God and do the "scriptural" thing. Imagine how the people must have viewed his actions. While they sacrificed the doomed animals to Jehovah, they thought, *What a godly king we have, always putting the Lord first.*

But God had a very different take on it. He lamented to Samuel, "I greatly regret that I have set up Saul as king, for he has turned back from following Me, and has not performed My commandments" (1 Sam. 15:11). Saul killed tens of thousands and spared but one. He did 99.9 percent of what was commanded of him. Most of us would see obedience in his campaign, yet God saw disobedience. In fact, through the prophet a few verses later He called it rebellion. Thus, we learn that partial obedience is not obedience at all in the eyes of God. In fact, almost complete obedience, even 99 percent, is not considered obedience; rather, it is rebellion.

How often we hear this comment: "Why don't you look at all I have done? You're just focusing on the little I didn't!" Saul could have said that for sure. Though this is in line with human reasoning, it is not in line with the divine!

Samuel left to meet Saul, and when Samuel reached him, Saul enthusiastically greeted him, "The LORD bless you! I have carried out the LORD's instructions" (1 Sam. 15:13 NIV). You can hear the joy and confidence in his voice. I fully believe Saul was sincere. He really believed he did what was commanded, yet God said he rebelled.

How do we account for the vast difference of opinion between what God said the night before and what Saul believed in his heart? The answer is found in these words: "But be doers of the word, and not hearers only, deceiving yourselves" (James 1:22). The moment a person disobeys the Word of God clearly revealed to him, a veil goes over his heart, and that veil distorts and obstructs his view. It is deception. Saul was deceived in his reasoning and confident he did right when, in reality, he was wrong. His belief conflicted with God's reality, even though it might agree with human reasoning.

That was not the first time Saul had failed to fully obey the word of the Lord. Samuel previously rebuked him for disobedience (1 Sam. 13:1–13). There could have been other incidents as well that were not recorded. Saul had a pattern of disobedience. Once this pattern forms, it becomes increasingly difficult to discern truth from error.

THE VEIL OF DECEPTION

Do you remember the first time you sinned after salvation? I do. I felt as though a knife had passed through my heart. As children of God, we are all acquainted with this feeling. It is the conviction of the Holy Spirit and our hearts smiting us. But what happens when we justify what we did, thereby turning our backs on true repentance? Two things. First, we are positioned to repeat the same act of disobedience. Second, the veil of deception covers our hearts, thereby lessening the sense of conviction and replacing it with reasoning.

At the next infraction, we don't feel the knife so keenly because a veil shrouds it; rather, there is only a pinch of discomfort. Again we justify ourselves, and another veil blankets our hearts, muffling further the call of truth. The next time we transgress we sense a mere tingle of conviction. If again we justify, another death shroud veils our hearts. If we sin again, the veil is so thick, there is no conviction at all—only justification. Deception has hidden the truth from us, and the conscience is seared.

At this point a person may fall away from any semblance of godliness, or more frequently he may continue with a form of godliness, but live religiously under the curse of the knowledge of good and evil.

His sense of right and wrong is now drawn from a source other than the living Word of God, breathed by the Holy Spirit, into his heart. He lives by the deceived dictates of his heart. It could be the letter of the Scripture, which kills (2 Cor. 3:6), or what society deems right or wrong. Either way, he is out of touch with the living God. Now the only way he can be reached is through a prophetic messenger sent to him by God.

THE THREE-STEP PROCESS

The Lord will take a person through a progressive process in order to reach him in his disobedience. First, He always attempts to reach a person through conviction. But if he has repeatedly disobeyed, he is in a place where he has lost touch with the heart and directives of God due to the veil of deception, God then sends a prophetic messenger, just as He sent Samuel to Saul. The true ministry of a prophet opens eyes to see the ways of God. God can send any person on a prophetic mission. It doesn't necessarily have to be an actual prophet; the message could come through a pastor, parent, boss, child, or friend. James explained, "My dear brothers and sisters, if anyone among you wanders away from the truth and is brought back again, you can be sure that the one who brings that person back will save that sinner from death and bring about the forgiveness of many sins" (5:19–20 NLT). Notice the message was directed toward believers who were in sin. Also note the phrase "many sins." The wandering resulted from repeated disobedience.

Once the prophetic messenger is (or messengers are) sent, if we still don't listen, God attempts to reach us through judgment. Paul wrote, "For if we would *judge* ourselves, we would not be *judged*" (1 Cor. 11:31, emphasis added). The root word *judge* appears twice in this scripture. However, each is a different Greek word. The first, "For if we would *judge* ourselves," is the Greek word *diakrino*, which means "to separate extensively." (This occurs when we examine ourselves thoroughly to remove the vile from the precious.) We accomplish this through confession and repentance of our disobedience. The second occurrence, "we would not be *judged*," is the Greek word *krino*, which means "to punish or condemn." Paul continued, "But when we are judged [*krino*, punished], we are chastened by the Lord, that we may not be condemned with the world" (v. 32). God longs to separate us from our disobedience so we will not be punished with the world (Matt. 7:20–23; Luke 12:45–48).

So the question becomes: How does God judge or punish His people when they ignore or refuse prophetic warning? The answer usually comes in the form of hardship, sickness, or some other type of affliction. The psalmist declared,

> Before I was afflicted I went astray,
> But now I keep Your word . . .
> I know, O LORD, that Your judgments are right,
> And that in faithfulness You have afflicted me. (Ps. 119:67, 75)

If we look at what Paul said through a different translation, it becomes quite clear: "That is why many of you are weak and sick and some have even died. But if we examine ourselves, we will not be examined by God and judged in this way" (1 Cor. 11:30–31 NLT).

A VIVID EXAMPLE

I have witnessed many cases of people who received judgment by not responding to the first two methods of God's corrective process. One vivid illustration occurred in the early 1990s when I was preaching at a youth camp in Texas. The beginning of the week was very confrontational because many young people had lost their tenderness toward the Lord through sin. Several young men and women came forward at each service and repented of their sins, most of which were sexually related, and were gloriously cleansed by the blood of Jesus. I was excitedly expecting a blowout final night in God because of the repentance that had been sown all week.

When I walked into that final service, I realized it would not start out the way I had anticipated. Again, I sensed the need to bring correction and call for repentance. When the time came for me to speak, I took the microphone and began to pray. The Holy Spirit showed me: *There is still a person in this auditorium who is in rebellion. Give this person another opportunity to come forward.* (I had already preached on rebellion in a previous service.) I gave the call, a few young people came forward, but I knew in my heart none was the one the Holy Spirit was targeting. These were sensitive young men and women probably wanting to deal with other issues.

The Holy Spirit spoke again to my heart: *Tell this person if he or she does not respond tonight, judgment will come on his or her life.* I spoke exactly what He spoke to my heart, and more young men and women came forward, but again I felt the person the Spirit of God was targeting was missing.

The Holy Spirit spoke again to my heart: *Tell this person what the judgment will be if he or she fails to respond.* He impressed it within me, then I heard His voice again: *Tell the person he or she will be in a head-on car collision in three weeks if he or she does not respond tonight.*

With fear and trembling I firmly repeated the words He'd spoken to my heart. More young men and women came forward, yet again, I knew none of them was the one the Lord was targeting. The Lord released me to minister and pray with those who had come forward. I did, and after that, we had the powerful service I anticipated. Many young people received impartations from the Lord; others received the call to ministry. Some were healed and received direction for their lives. It was a night none of us would soon—and possibly ever—forget.

A few months passed, and the youth pastor and I talked by phone. He was giving me follow-up reports from the youth camp. He shared, "John, there is a young high school girl in our youth group who had given us more problems than anyone else. She was always disobeying us and causing trouble. I knew in my heart she was the one the Holy Spirit was speaking to that last night. I was so disappointed when she didn't respond." (I had no idea of who this girl was.)

He continued, "Three weeks after camp she was in a head-on car collision accident, just as you warned. The car was totaled."

I was trembling; I wanted to know what happened to her. I knew I had spoken by the Spirit of God, but I hoped this person would hear His call before tragedy befell her.

He continued, "God spared her life! She was in serious condition, but has since recovered. She is now one of the most on-fire girls in our church. She's a totally different person. Her life has been completely transformed!" I was relieved and excited for her. Hear David's words again, "Before I was afflicted I went astray, but now I keep your word."

Now let me make a very clear point. It is not God who brings these things on us. Rather, He lifts His hand of protection and allows the enemy to bring on us what obedience would have protected us from. The psalmist declared,

> You let men ride over our heads;
>   we went through fire and water,
>   but you brought us to a place of abundance. (Ps. 66:12 NIV)

Another translation puts it this way: "You brought us out to rich fulfillment" (NKJV). This young woman's attention was arrested in the accident. She repented in the hospital and came out into a place of rich fulfillment. It wasn't God's first choice of correction, but when the other failed, it was effective.

I wish I could say all similar incidents end this way, but they haven't. Another comes to mind. A young man, also in rebellion, was warned by a minister I know. He did not heed and was shortly there-after in a head-on automobile wreck and died instantly. I could give countless other testimonies—many who repented and were blessed, and others who ended up similar to the outcome of King Saul.

OBEDIENCE VERSUS SACRIFICE

Let's return to Saul's story. Samuel saw Saul's deception and immedi-ately went to the heart of the issue like a true prophetic messenger. Samuel questioned, "What then is this bleating of the sheep in my ears, and the lowing of the oxen which I hear?"

Saul quickly answered, "They have brought them from the Amalekites; for the people spared the best of the sheep and the oxen, to sacrifice to the LORD your God; and the rest we have utterly destroyed" (1 Sam 15:14–15).

He diverted the blame from himself to the people when confronted by the truth. "I wanted to obey," he implied, "but the people com-pelled me." A man with an unrepentant heart diverts blame to others when caught in disobedience, thus failing to take responsibility for his own actions.

Adam blamed God and Eve. Eve blamed the serpent. Adam was right; God had given him the woman, and the woman had given him the fruit. But no one forced him to eat. He ate of his own free will. Yes, Eve was deceived, but she still made the choice to disobey.

Saul led the people; they did not lead him. He was accountable not only for his disobedience but for theirs as well. He was the one in authority to lead and instruct. Leaders, listen carefully: you will give account for the disobedience you allow in the lives of those entrusted to your care.

Eli, Israel's leader and Samuel's mentor, knew his sons despised the ordinances of God, yet he did nothing. He gave them a token slap-on-the-hand rebuke, but he did not exercise his authority and remove or restrain them. Therefore, God decreed, "I have told him that I will judge his house forever for the iniquity which he knows, because his sons made themselves vile, and he did not restrain them" (1 Sam. 3:13). It was not just his sons who were judged, but Eli was judged as well.

Next, Saul justified his disobedience because the sheep and oxen were spared as offerings to the Lord. You know he was deceived if he thought by disobedience he could render an acceptable sacrifice or service to God. It was a subtle and deceptive form of rebellion.

Jesus made this statement: "If anyone desires to come after Me, let him deny himself, and take up his cross, and follow Me" (Matt. 16:24). Some take the cross and concentrate on its image of suffering as representing a life of sacrifice. However, in these words of Jesus the cross is not the only or complete focus. You can live a life of self-denial and sacrifice and not fulfill God's purpose or will! In fact, you could choose self-denial and sacrifice and still be in rebellion to God!

The focus of what Jesus was saying is *obedience*. The only way we can obey is to take up the cross. For without death to our own agendas and desires we will eventually have a face-off between the will of God and the desire of man. If we do not lay down our lives, we will find a way of fulfilling those desires contrary to His and even use Scriptures to back it, just as Saul did. We must ask ourselves, "Does service to God include disobedience?" If so, Satan would receive glory from our "scriptural" religious practices or sacrifices since he is the originator and lord of rebellion.

At that point Samuel silenced Saul's reasoning:

> "Be quiet! And I will tell you what the LORD said to me last night." And he [Saul] said to him, "Speak on." So Samuel said, "When you were little in your own eyes, were you not head of the tribes of Israel? And did not the LORD anoint you king over Israel? Now the LORD sent you on a mission, and said, 'Go, and utterly destroy the sinners, the Amalekites, and fight against them until they are consumed.' Why then did you not obey the voice of the LORD? Why did you swoop down on the spoil, and do evil in the sight of the LORD?" (1 Sam. 15:16–19)

Samuel said, "When you were small in your own eyes, were you not made the leader of the tribes of Israel?" In other words, Saul, when you were first king, you were unassuming, humble, and meek. We saw that years earlier when Samuel first told Saul he would be king. Saul responded in disbelief, "Am I not a Benjamite, of the smallest of the tribes of Israel, and my family the least of all the families of the tribe of Benjamin? Why then do you speak like this to me?" (1 Sam. 9:21). Saul did not see himself as king. He was perplexed about why God would choose an insignificant man like him.

Later, when the Lord chose to reveal him before all Israel, each tribe was brought to cast lots. Out of them, the tribe of Benjamin, was chosen. Out of it, Saul's family was picked. Then Saul himself. "But when they sought him, he could not be found. Therefore they inquired of the LORD further, 'Has the man [Saul] come here yet?' And the LORD answered, 'There he is, hidden among the equipment'" (1 Sam. 10:21–22).

Saul was overwhelmed by the thought of ruling God's people. He was small in his own eyes. Samuel brought that to his remembrance, then proceeded, "Now the Lord sent you on a mission and said, 'Go, and utterly destroy' . . . Why now do you think you know more than the Lord? When did your wisdom supersede God's? Have you now taken His place? Why do you seek right and wrong from a source outside God? What happened to the humble, unassuming man?"

Do any of us know more than God? Of course, we don't! But when we disobey, that is the message we communicate to God and those around us. How foolish to think ourselves wiser than He who sits on the throne of glory. The very One who not only created the universe but also contains the universe. The Creator who put the stars in the heavens with His fingers. Yet we exalt the wisdom of mere men above His when we ignore His counsel!

REBELLION AND WITCHCRAFT

Samuel fixed his gaze on Saul and, with the boldness of his prophetic office, declared,

Behold, to obey is better than sacrifice,
And to heed than the fat of rams.
For rebellion *is as* the sin of witchcraft,
And stubbornness *is as* iniquity and idolatry. (1 Sam. 15:22–23)

Samuel directly linked rebellion with witchcraft: "For rebellion *is as* the sin of witchcraft." Notice the words *is as* in this verse are in italic type. This is common in both the King James and the New King James Versions when words are used that did not appear in the original text. They were added later by the translators to lend clarity. A more accurate translation would have used only the word *is* (*Interlinear Bible*, vol. 2, p. 750).

This text should read, "For rebellion is witchcraft." This clarifies the context of this scripture. It is one thing to liken rebellion to witchcraft, but an entirely different issue to say it is actually witchcraft. Obviously a true Christian would never knowingly practice witchcraft. But how many are under its influence unknowingly because of the deception of rebellion?

The word *witchcraft* conjures up images of women wearing black, reciting incantations, traveling by broom, or scanning the future in crystal balls while a cauldron simmers on the open fire. Or perhaps the more modern version is one who casts spells and curses upon others for influence. Let's leave behind both concepts and discover the very heart of witchcraft, no matter what form it takes.

The Hebrew word used here for "witchcraft" is *qesem*. Its English counterparts are *divination, witchcraft,* and *sorcery.* However, experts tell us the exact meaning of these words in reference to occultism is unknown, which accounts for the variety in translations of this word (*Theological Wordbook of the Old Testament*, vol. 3, p. 805). The importance lies not in the form or method but in the result or goal of witchcraft.

Witchcraft directly opens one to the demonic realm. Its goal is to *control* circumstances, situations, or people through various avenues, often without the participant's understanding of what is happening in the spirit realm. There is a range from total ignorance of what one is doing to complete understanding and awareness of the powers of darkness involved. In essence witchcraft can be practiced either with total unawareness or with complete knowledge. Its goal is control, but inevitably the controller becomes the controlled due to the involvement with the demonic realm.

SLAVERY THROUGH DISOBEDIENCE

As a former youth pastor, I had the opportunity to come in contact with the occult. The area high schools were populated with young people who dabbled in spiritualism to various degrees. My youth group leaders regularly reported encounters with classmates involved in witchcraft or satanism.

One of the most interesting principles I learned about occultic practices was this: when initiating an individual into a coven (a group of individuals practicing witchcraft), the leaders encouraged him to take drugs, drink, engage in illicit sex, steal, and carry out various other acts that defied the laws of God or our land. I was uncertain why until God opened this truth to me: "Rebellion is witchcraft."

They are taught, the more you rebel, the more power you obtain, and they seek power. This is true because rebellion is witchcraft. The more they rebel, the more they give legal access to demonic powers to influence, control, and empower their lives. By rebelling against the order and laws of God and His delegated authority, they knowingly grant legal access to the controlling demonic realm.

This idea is reflected in what sorcerers call their satanic bible. A few years ago, while changing channels in a hotel room after a service, my wife and I came across a network special on satanism and witchcraft. I was about to flip the channel, which ordinarily is wise to do, because I believe all we need to know about spiritual warfare should come from the Spirit of God. However, I felt impressed to watch it a moment. The show discussed the satanic bible. The journalist reported the number one commandment: "Do what thou wilt."

That got my attention. Scriptures started coming to mind immediately. The psalmist proclaimed,

> Behold, I come;
> In the scroll of the book it is written of me.
> I delight to do Your will, O my God,
> And Your law is within my heart. (Ps. 40:7–8)

Jesus said of Himself, "I do not seek My own will but the will of the Father who sent Me" (John 5:30). I knew from years of study, the Lord is drawn to those who live obediently toward Him. It hit me that the opposite is true as well: spirits of darkness are drawn to those who live in rebellion. This command of "Do what thou wilt," is a direct perversion of the Word of God, and it lines up exactly with what God said concerning rebellion.

Those who willfully commit themselves to the service of Satan understand this principle, yet others are deceived. The ignorant ones mistake lawlessness for liberty. But there is no freedom in rebellion. The New Testament reveals a clear picture of what actually takes place. They become slaves to depravity. Peter exposed their error this way: "They [those leaders who encourage insubordination] promise freedom, but they themselves are slaves to sin and corruption. For you are a slave to whatever controls you" (2 Peter 2:19 NLT).

The truth is evident. There is no freedom; there are instead bondage and control, which open the soul to demonic oppression and control. Paul reemphasized this point: "Don't you realize that you can choose your own master? You can choose sin (with death) or else obedience (with acquittal). The one to whom you offer yourself—he will take you and be your master and you will be his slave" (Rom. 6:16 TLB).

Jesus stressed this principle: "Most assuredly, I say to you, whoever commits sin is a slave of sin" (John 8:34). Remember Cain's disobedience in his choice of offerings to the Lord? Afterward God made it clear to him his choices would determine his destiny. He could honor God's will and close the door to sin's control (witchcraft), or he could rebel and face without divine protection or strength the crouching form of sin that sought to master or control him.

Samuel warned Saul, just as God Himself warned Cain. Rebellion opened his soul to the influence of a controlling spirit that caused him to behave in a manner he never would have if he was in his right mind. Saul did not truly repent, and the Bible indicates in 1 Samuel 16:14 that not long after his rebellion, an evil, tormenting spirit came upon his life and troubled him. The evil spirit had legal access in his life from that point on. There was no rest for Saul because there was no true repentance. Saul became a very different man from the one we first met.

He had gone from an unassuming young man who obeyed authorities, such as his father and the prophet Samuel, and who respected the things of God to one who violated all he held dear. If you had approached him in his early years and foretold him, "Saul, the day will come when you will kill eighty-five innocent priests, their wives, and their children in a fit of rage," he would have dismissed you as crazy. "Impossible! I could never do that!" he would have reasoned. The sad truth is, he did (1 Sam. 22)!

The evil spirit manipulated him into a life of jealousy, anger, hatred, strife, murder, and deception. It controlled him by way of his unrepentant disobedience. He chased and tried to kill David, one of God's and his own most faithful servants. He believed David a traitor, when in reality he was a man after the heart of God. As a result of the demonic control, Saul saw only fleeting glimpses of truth through a thick cloud of deception. Truth became a lie, and the lies became truth.

Oh, how many times I have seen this happen! Not only with others but with myself. I look back to seasons of my life when I dabbled with disobedience, and I want to weep at the deception I walked in. In those times, I viewed godly authorities as legalistic or in error, and godly friends often as my adversaries. I drew near to other rebels, only to have fuel poured on my already raging fire of disobedience. We saw ourselves as closer to the Lord and were convinced we were the "new breed" of ministers God was raising up. Oh, the Lord has been merciful to me! May your eyes be opened wide to this trick, so you are not deceived as I was.

CHAPTER 7:

BEWITCHED

The light of God's Word exposes deception and discerns the thoughts and intentions of the hearts of men.

Rebellion is witchcraft. The effects of this hidden principle of law-lessness are obvious in our society, and no less apparent in our churches, even though it is more subtle in its entrance. This chapter provides an in-depth vantage of witchcraft's influence over a believer in rebellion. We'll draw from the Old Testament, the New Testament, and present-day accounts to study the control that occurs from disobedience.

A CURSE DENIED

First, let's look at Israel. During their wilderness journey, the descen-dants of Abraham camped on the plains of Moab. They had just attacked and defeated Bashan and had already destroyed the Amorites when they were refused passage through the territory.

As the Israelites camped in the plains of Moab, Balak and the people he led, the Moabites and the Midianites, were worried. The people trem-bled with fear. The Lord had promised the Israelites, "I will send My fear before you, I will cause confusion among all the people to whom you come" (Ex. 23:27). They knew the Isrealites had conquered each nation that opposed them and had utterly destroyed the most powerful nation, Egypt.

King Balak sent ambassadors to the prophet Balaam requesting his help. He was well known for his spiritual accuracy and insight. The king knew that Balaam's prophecies happened. If he blessed, they were blessed; if he cursed, they were cursed. After receiving two sets of ambassadors from Balak, Balaam consented to travel with the princes to the king with the intent to curse the children of Israel. The king's offer of money and honor swayed him.

The next day they climbed the high places of Baal, and Balaam observed the nation of Israel. He instructed the king to erect seven altars and prepare a sacrifice for each. Then Balaam opened his mouth to curse Israel, but instead he pronounced a blessing over them.

Needless to say, the king was upset! "What have you done to me? I took you to curse my enemies, and look, you have blessed them bountifully!" (Num. 23:11).

So Balaam suggested they move to a higher level, hoping to give Balak what he wanted. Maybe there would be more energy to curse from a higher site. Again seven altars were erected and additional sacrifices offered. But as Balaam opened his mouth again to bring a witchcraft curse, again he blessed Israel instead.

The process continued. Each time Balaam attempted to curse, he was compelled to bless. In Balaam's second oracle we find this profound statement: "For there is no sorcery against Jacob, nor any divination against Israel" (Num. 23:23).

Balaam declared there was no sorcery or divination effective against the people of God! What an exciting and powerful statement! To bring this truth forward into today's time frame, we would say, "There is no witchcraft that works against God's people, nor any divination against His church!" (Num. 23:23, author's paraphrase).

This promise should encourage us. The witches and warlocks can rant, rave, and burn their candles. They can recite their hexes, spells, and curses, but they cannot harm a child of God. They will not prevail against the church of the living God. Proverbs 26:2 reinforces this truth: "Like a fluttering sparrow or a darting swallow, an undeserved curse does not come to rest" (NIV).

THE CURSE REVERSED

Again, back to my youth pastor days. A girl who was one of the lead witches in her high school came to Jesus. Her mother dedicated her to Satan when she was yet in her mother's womb. After her conversion, she discussed with my assistant her former life. She made a statement that caught his attention. She said, "We cannot put witchcraft curses on Christians."

My assistant questioned, "Why not?"

She said, "Because if we placed a curse on them, it would come back on us." He was thrilled.

As you can see, her words line up with what Balaam spoke. In his first oracle he posed this question: "How shall I curse whom God has not cursed?" (Num. 23:8). Even if Balaam *had* pronounced a curse over the children of Israel, it would have returned upon his head. David said it this way:

> Hide me from the secret plots of the wicked,
> From the *rebellion* of the workers of iniquity,
> Who sharpen their tongue like a sword,
> And bend their bows to shoot their arrows—bitter words,
> That they may shoot in secret at the blameless. (Ps. 64:2–4, emphasis added)

Curses will be released by the rebellious (those involved in witchcraft), but they will not rest upon the righteous. Watch what happens to those who release curses:

> But God shall shoot at them with an arrow;
> Suddenly they shall be wounded.
> So He will make them stumble over their own tongue. (Ps. 64:7–8)

They will stumble over their own tongues. The very words they release to hurt others will circle back to them. David used this vivid word picture to describe it: "They have dug a pit before me; into the midst of it they themselves have fallen" (Ps. 57:6).

SEDUCED TO DISOBEY

Balaam knew it was impossible to curse the Israelites the way they were. There was no way he could make a curse stick, even though he wanted to. Moses recounted the situation: "They hired against you Balaam the son of Beor from Pethor of Mesopotamia, to curse you. Nevertheless the LORD your God would not listen to Balaam, but the LORD your God turned the curse into a blessing for you, because the LORD your God loves you" (Deut. 23:4–5). This is true for us as well.

The furious King Balak shouted, "I called you to curse my enemies! Instead, you have blessed them three times. Now get out of here! Go back home! I had planned to reward you richly, but the LORD has kept you from your reward" (Num. 24:10–11 NLT).

The king had planned to give Balaam a large monetary reward and social honor for successfully cursing his fatal enemy. But in essence the king said, "You can forget your reward. It is obvious your God doesn't want you to have it. Get out of my sight!"

Balaam had a problem: he really wanted that reward. It was the whole reason he was there, and he was about to lose it all. To avoid the loss, he shared another plan of attack with King Balak. Though he knew he couldn't curse the Israelites, he did understand how to get them to bring themselves under a curse.

With his understanding of the spiritual relationship between rebellion and witchcraft, Balaam advised the king to send Moabite women to infiltrate Israel's camp. He had them take their idols along and lure the men of Israel into sexual sin and rebellion against God's statutes. He knew the rebellion would bring them under a witchcraft curse.

We know this transpired because both Moses and Jesus referenced his counsel to the king. Moses confirmed it: "Look, these women caused the children of Israel, through *the counsel of Balaam*, to trespass against the LORD in the incident of Peor, and there was a plague among the congregation of the LORD" (Num. 31:16, emphasis added). Years later Jesus said Balaam had "*taught Balak* to put a stumbling block before the children of Israel, to eat things sacrificed to idols, and to commit sexual immorality" (Rev. 2:14, emphasis added).

This is laid out in Scripture. Immediately following Balaam's prophecies, we read, "Now Israel remained in Acacia Grove, and the people began to commit harlotry with the women of Moab [and Midian]. They invited the people to the sacrifices of their gods, and the people ate and bowed down to their gods. So Israel was joined to Baal of Peor, and the anger of the LORD was aroused against Israel" (Num. 25:1–3). As a result, a severe plague broke out and ravaged the people of Israel.

Disobedience caused this nation, which could not be cursed, to come under a curse of the plague: "And those who died in the plague were twenty-four thousand" (Num. 25:9). Twenty-four thousand! Do you realize the tragedy of this statement? Today if there is an airplane crash or a hurricane that takes hundreds of lives, it makes world news. We are not talking about hundreds, but twenty-four thousand people! That was the greatest single loss of life Israel experienced in the wilderness, and it all resulted from the people's rebellion.

Radical disobedience opened the door to a radical plague. Their rebellion was flagrant. In fact, one shameless Israelite man openly flaunted his Midianite woman in the sight of Moses and the entire congregation of Israel as they cried to God (Num. 25:6).

What stopped the plague? You probably guessed it—radical obedience!

> Now when Phinehas the son of Eleazar, the son of Aaron the priest, saw it [the man showing off his Midianite girlfriend], he rose from among the congregation and took a javelin in his hand; and he went after the man of Israel into the tent and thrust both of them through, the man of Israel, and the woman through her body. So the plague was stopped among the children of Israel. (Num. 25:7–8)

Again allow me to point this out: God is not the Author of plagues and diseases. The children of Israel blatantly rebelled and violated His authority. Therefore, the Lord's covering of protection was lifted, and the enemy had legal access by the permission of God. Once again this affirms rebellion as witchcraft and grants legal entrance to demonic powers of control. Israel escaped the curse of a soothsayer, only to be decimated by disobedience.

WHO HAS BROUGHT YOU UNDER A CURSE?

We've seen an Old Testament example that rebellion is witchcraft, and there are plenty more. Now let's examine the New Testament. The apostle Paul wrote a stern letter to the churches in Galatia. It was not a letter to the general populace of Galatia, but specifically directed to the churches. Carefully read Paul's statement: "O foolish Galatians! Who has bewitched you?" (Gal. 3:1).

Wait a minute! Paul was telling the churches they were under a witchcraft curse! You may question, "I thought there was no divination or witchcraft against God's people?" That is correct. No curse can be released against the obedient. But remember, rebellion or disobedience places a person under witchcraft.

Recall my assistant's meeting with the former witch, delivered from sorcery. When she saw his excitement upon learning that curses couldn't be placed on Christians, she quickly added, "But, Pastor, we could affect lukewarm people in the church [the disobedient]." In confirmation, hear what Paul said, "Who has bewitched you that you should not obey the truth?" (Gal. 3:1).

The bewitchment involved disobeying God's word, not any curses that sorcerers had conjured up. Why? Because rebellion is witchcraft! In essence the church in Galatia came under a witchcraft curse because of disobedience.

Before going any farther I must clarify this point. We come under bewitchment when we disobey what God has made clear to us, not when we disobey what has not been revealed to us. This becomes clear as Paul continued, "Who has bewitched you that you should not obey the truth, before whose eyes Jesus was clearly portrayed among you as crucified?" (Gal. 3:1).

This specific incident yields a universal truth. God had revealed His salvation by grace to those churches through Paul's preaching. But it wasn't long before they embraced the reasoning and traditions of another and disobeyed what was once made so very clear to them by the Holy Spirit. They began to teach and live under the belief that salvation came by keeping the works of the law. However, the universal premise we want to focus on is this: *whenever we disobey what God has clearly revealed to us, we bring ourselves under the influence of a witchcraft curse.* Why? Because rebellion is witchcraft.

I have seen this with entire congregations, families, and individuals. I have met many churchgoers who for some reason or another live in an almost constant state of disobedience. Most are unaware of its severity because they have been numbed by a lopsided teaching of grace that downplays the importance of obedience. One crisis follows another in their lives. There is always some problem or sin over which they just can't seem to gain victory. They escape one snare to find themselves entrapped in another. Each scenario seems progressively worse. These problems consume their time, energy, and livelihood. Somewhere an access has been legally given to demonic oppression or influence. Their disobedience has made them vulnerable.

I have watched their marriages suffer or, even worse, end in the broken state of divorce. Others are passed over for promotions or, worse, lose their jobs. Some fall prey to theft, financial crisis, and tragedy. Frustrated, they frantically look for someone to blame. Many times they blame the treatment they received from parents, pastor, boss, spouse, children, government, or anyone else available who doesn't agree with their reasoning.

Two culprits at work actually feed off each other. The first is deception. Darkness has clouded their hearts because they failed to obey God's Word. The second culprit is a tangled snare of controlling spirits who attack at will because of disobedience. Paul instructed those dealing with professing believers in rebellion, "The Lord's servant must gently teach those who disagree. Then maybe God will let them change their minds so they can accept the truth. And they may wake up and escape from the trap of the devil, who catches them to do what he wants" (2 Tim. 2:25–26 NCV). The problem: deceived captives blame others in order to hide from their own disobedience, and doing this blinds them to exactly what they need to be free.

Thank God for His Word. Its light exposes deception and discerns the thoughts and intentions of the hearts of men. Unfortunately when afflicted due to disobedience, most people refuse to learn. They continue in the wilderness of disobedience, blaming everyone else rather than learning from the error of their ways.

"YOU HAVE NO COMPASSION"

I recall an incident where someone did learn. I had the honor of ministering regularly at an international ministry that consisted of a church and Bible school. I loved and respected this ministry, that had impacted my life. One day a leader of the ministry called and told me, "John, I am calling all the close friends of this ministry to tell them what is about to happen so they don't hear it from some other source. I need to tell you I am divorcing my spouse. We've been married for eighteen years and seem to be going separate directions in our thinking and outlook in life. We don't do things together as a couple, and what we like is just so different. We have tried for years to improve, and it has only gotten worse."

I couldn't believe what I was hearing. I kept thinking, *No, please, don't do this.* I loved this couple and their ministry. I was so shocked, I was speechless.

In my silence this person continued, "Now, John, you know I love Jesus very much, and if I'm doing the wrong thing, He will show me." This minister talked with me about the situation a few more minutes, then ended the phone call. I had said very little because I was still taking it all in.

All day long I couldn't shake what I'd heard. I rehearsed the words again and again. I thought, *This seems like a bad dream.* In the midst of my troubled thoughts I sensed the Holy Spirit telling me to call this person back and speak the truth.

The next morning I made the call. I had slept on it, so it wouldn't appear reactionary, but as a Spirit-led response. Upon recognizing my voice, the minister asked, "Hi, John, what's up?"

I began, "I want to talk with you some more about the divorce. Has there been any immorality on the part of your spouse?"

The response was, "Absolutely not!"

I then said, "What you are doing is wrong. Jesus makes it clear that the only reason to consider a divorce is sexual unfaithfulness (Matt. 5:32), and the book of Malachi tells us that God hates divorce because it covers our garment with violence (2:16). You said to me yesterday that you loved Jesus, and if you were doing the wrong thing, He would show you. But why should He show you when He has already made it clear through His Word what His will is? How can you willfully go against what God has declared? If you do this, how can you stand before your congregation or Bible school and tell them to walk in holiness by resisting sin or devils? You are opening yourself and ministry to trouble and deception."

The minister interrupted me and said sternly, "John Bevere, you've not walked in my steps, and you have no compassion!"

The next thing I heard was the receiver of the phone slammed down. The minister had hung up on me. Thirty minutes later I received word from my office that I'd been canceled. (I was scheduled to go there in three months.) I told my wife, "I knew they'd do this, but not so soon." All communication was completely cut off, and later another minister who had passed through there told me my name was "mud." I kept thinking, *All I was trying to do was to be a true friend.*

AWAKENED BY JUDGMENT

To my surprise, seven months later I received a call from this minister: "John, I need to have a heart-to-heart talk with you. Do you know what happened after I hung up the phone and canceled you? Well, one month later my kidneys failed, and I was given a 50 percent chance of survival. After the second dialysis, I awoke and said to myself, 'What am I doing getting a divorce?' I realized I was very wrong. My kidney failure was a wake-up call. I called my spouse and repented. I went before our church and Bible school and repented. I told the Bible school, 'I canceled John Bevere because he told me I was wrong to divorce. I am going to call him and see if he'll come back.' So, John, would you please come back?"

"Of course," I responded. I was so excited for this person, and my respect for this minister grew immensely. In addition to all this, the recovery was much faster than expected, and a perfect kidney match was found and donated a year later. This minister didn't miss one service. This person's progress astounded the doctors. Also, with this repentance a greater spiritual authority and strength came on this minister's life. Now, years later, this person leads more effectively than ever before and is a sought-after speaker with a very happy family. Every time I am with the couple, it is easy to see their love for each other. You would never know a few years previously they were a few steps away from divorce.

SICK FOR THREE AND A HALF MONTHS

It was easy for me not to judge this minister, for I had gone through a similar experience a few years earlier. It wasn't with my marriage, but with an area of disobedience in the ministry. When we first founded John Bevere Ministries, the Lord gave us a clear directive not to accept an opportunity for the ministry just because it looked good until we first knew His will.

Well, a few years passed, and what appeared to be a great opportunity arose for our ministry to expand. Yet in prayer, God was clearly saying "no" to my wife and me separately; we were not to accept the offer. However, the offer was made persistently, and I was flattered, so I listened. It wasn't long before I began to reason away the word that God had impressed in my heart. I became confused, and my mind became clouded with all the words. My wife tried to counsel me against it, but quickly realized I would not be convinced otherwise. I ended up accepting the proposal.

Since I've been saved, I've been blessed with virtually no sickness or health problems (to God be the glory). I rarely catch anything, and if I do, it's gone in twenty-four to thirty-six hours. I believe Jesus provided divine health as well as forgiveness of sins when He died on the cross (Isa. 53:4–5 AMPLIFIED; Ps. 103:2–3). But on the day I moved forward with this opportunity, I became sick and couldn't shake it.

It started out as the flu. I threw up for the second time since I was nineteen. After several days of battling the flu, I caught a virus. My wife and I had gone out of town to celebrate our anniversary, and for days my temperature hovered over 100 degrees and ruined our vacation. At the close of the week I preached while suffering from a fever and chills. The fever dragged on into the next week during meetings in Canada. I preached with a high fever, only to return to my room and shiver in bed until the next service. I had very little strength.

The fever continued to hold for the third week. We couldn't understand what was happening. I'd never fought sickness like that. I prayed and fought, using the Word of God, but I couldn't shake it. I went to the doctor. He prescribed a strong antibiotic, and soon I was back to normal.

But a week after finishing the antibiotic, I caught a severe head cold, the kind that drains all your strength. I was miserable. Sore throat, stuffed head, and all the other annoying conditions. It dragged on for weeks as I continued to minister.

After recovering from my head cold, I injured my knee climbing a wall overseas. It was so severe I was in a wheelchair in my travels and limped with a brace for several weeks after that. At the tail end of this, I was hit with another virus. My temperature rose to 101 to 102 degrees, and again I couldn't shake it. Again I had to get a prescription to get over it. It seemed I couldn't go more than a week without some kind of infirmity. The cycle lasted three and a half months.

Through all my ills, my wife did not become sick, not even one day. Besides the physical problems, numerous other problems arose. I was in a struggle with an opponent who seemed not to budge because he was more powerful than I was. My willful disobedience brought me under a curse!

INSTANT RELIEF FROM TRUE REPENTANCE

Four months passed, and I admitted my sin. However, I still had to deal with my commitment, and if there wasn't a miraculous intervention, I saw no way out. Lisa and I joined hands; I repented and asked for God's mercy. He got us out of the long-term commitment I'd ensnared us in.

A few months later, my wife and I discussed all that had transpired, and we linked all my sickness to my disobedience. We realized as soon as I repented, my previous good health was restored. The other problems that loomed over us were resolved and disappeared.

In that time period the words of James became clear to me. I had frequently quoted his words, "Resist the devil and he will flee from you" (James 4:7). In the past if I sensed an attack, I passionately resisted the darkness with the Word of God and always saw results. Yet that time I got nowhere. When I came through it, I realized I was quoting only half of what James was saying: "Therefore submit to God. Resist the devil and he will flee from you" (4:7).

We resist the devil by obediently submitting to God's authority. We can quote scriptures until we are blue in the face, but if we are in disobedience, we will not see results.

AN IMPORTANT CLARIFICATION

Please understand this point: every time a person faces difficulty, sickness, problems, or hardships, disobedience is not necessarily the cause. Many suffer while living obedient lives. David was such a man. He was not in any sort of rebellion. He did nothing wrong to bring upon himself his leader's wrath. Yet he was driven out to live in caves, deserts, and wildernesses. He was a man without a home or country. For years he lived as a vagabond in a state of hardship. Some judged him and felt he suffered because of disobedience, but the discerning could perceive God's hand forging a new type of king and could sense God's favor on his life. It was evident by his wisdom.

There are numerous examples of obedient people who suffered:

Jesus, Joseph, Hannah, Daniel, Jeremiah, and Job, among others. The difference between the hardship of the obedient and those under witchcraft is that there is spiritual progress for the obedient. They are not banging their heads against a wall; they are not circling a mountain getting nowhere.

Cain was a different story. His disobedience caused great suffering. Offended, he refused to repent, which resulted in a curse on his life. He lived his years as a fugitive and a vagabond. His aimless and hopeless wanderings are an example and warning to future generations.

I will conclude with this statement: don't take the truths of the last two chapters and use them to judge others. Their hardships may be trials from which God will receive glory. The purpose of this chapter is to help you realize the severity of disobedience to the authority of God. If you are in disobedience, may you use these truths to judge yourself and get back on the path of life.

GOD'S APPOINTED COVERING

CHAPTER 8

DOES GOD KNOW WHO IS IN CHARGE?

*If we learn how to obey God, we will have no trouble recognizing
God's authority on another.*

We have established the importance of submission to God's direct authority. Let's now discuss the equal importance of submission to His delegated authorities. To set the stage, we'll begin with the scripture highlighted in the second chapter:

> "Let every soul be subject to the governing authorities. For there is no authority except from God, and the authorities that exist are appointed by God. Therefore whoever resists the authority resists the ordinance of God, and those who resist will bring judgment on themselves" (Rom. 13:1–2).

THE GOVERNING AUTHORITIES

First, who are these "governing authorities"? In this specific text Paul referred to civil or governmental authorities. However, these words of exhortation apply not only to governmental leaders but also encompass other areas of delegated authority. What we glean from this text should be applied to all areas of delegated authority.

The New Testament speaks of four divisions of delegated authority:

civil, church, family, and social. In social I include employers, teachers, and bosses. The New Testament gives specific guidelines for each area; however, in most cases, the counsel spans the borders and extends to all areas of delegated authority.

Notice the opening line, "Let every soul." No one is exempt, so implant this in your mind. It is a command, not a suggestion. The Lord does not give hints or recommendations.

He continued, "Let every soul be *subject* to the governing authorities." The Greek word for "subject" is *hupotasso*. It is a Greek military term meaning "to arrange (troop divisions) in a military fashion under the command of a leader." In nonmilitary usage, it was "a voluntary attitude of giving in, cooperating, assuming responsibility, and carrying a burden" (Thayer's Greek dictionary). Simply put, this word as used in this verse exhorts us to voluntarily place ourselves under submission to authorities with the full intent of obeying them.

Every soul is to be subject to authorities because God has appointed all governing authorities in our lives. The origin of all authority goes back to God. There is no exception. In fact, the English word *appointed* in this verse is the Greek word *tasso,* which means "to assign, ordain, or set." In no way does this word have "by chance" implications. It is direct appointment. Since God has appointed all authorities, we refuse the authority behind them if we dishonor or refuse to submit to them. Whether we know it or not, we resist the ordinance or rule of God. When we oppose God's delegated authority, we oppose God Himself!

When we as Christians have contact with authorities, we must see beyond personality and honor position. We obey men in authority because God's authority is upon them. Whether we are drawn to the personality or not, or we think they should have the position or not, we honor them. Too often believers profess submission to God, but neglect submission to delegated authority. They are deceived!

If we learn how to obey God, we will have no trouble recognizing God's authority on another. Are there times when we must choose between God's direct authority and His delegated authority? Yes! But not as often as most believers think. There is only one exception, which we will cover at length in a later chapter. However, the issue here is that most Christians think obedience is the exception and personal free choice is the rule. Following this type of reasoning can lead us into a course of destruction. The consequences, as we saw in earlier chapters, are severe. Not only does it place us under the judgment of God, but it grants legal access to demonic powers. If we want to remain obedient to God and blessed, we have but one choice when it comes to delegated authority—submission and obedience.

ARE EVIL AUTHORITIES APPOINTED BY GOD?

So, we are instructed that all authority is appointed by God, and we are to respond by respecting and submitting to the position. Often at this point walls go up in people's minds. The common rebuttal is, "I know leaders who are harsh and downright evil. How can you tell me they were appointed by God?" To answer, let's take a worst-case scenario, someone in the Hitler or Stalin category. Those two distinguished themselves as possibly the top two most evil leaders of the past century. We'd all agree someone from this category is about as cruel and evil as you can get. Correct?

Let's talk about Pharaoh, ruler of Egypt. He definitely falls under the same category. Under his lead, the nation of Israel was brutally treated. He enslaved and impoverished the people, physically and mentally abused them, and if all that wasn't enough, he murdered thousands of them in cold blood. He was defiant and arrogant with no regard for human life or the Lord. Where did his authority come from? How did God's people end up under him? Was it an accident?

According to Scripture, God told Pharaoh through Moses, "I have raised you up" (Ex. 9:16). Paul confirmed this in his epistle to the Romans (9:17). From both references we know this to be accurate and not misconstrued; a thing is established by the testimony of two witnesses (John 8:17). There is no doubt that God, not the devil, raised up and set Pharaoh in his position of authority. In other words, God granted Pharaoh authority over Abraham's descendants. This correlates perfectly with "the authorities that exist are appointed by God."

Let's discuss how they got under this wicked leader's authority. God appeared to Abraham when he was seventy-five and told him he would make a great nation out of him if he obeyed. Abraham did, and his obedience pleased God so much that he is called the "father of faith" (Rom. 4:11–12). In response to Abraham's obedience, God cut covenant with him. In cutting the covenant, the Lord said, "Know for certain that your descendants will be strangers in a country not their own, and they will be *enslaved* and *mistreated* four hundred years" (Gen. 15:13 NIV).

In another translation (NKJV) the word *afflicted* is used instead of *mistreated*. What a hard pill to swallow! As a father of four sons, I would not be particularly excited to hear this heritage for my children, grandchildren, or great-grandchildren. I wouldn't call this an edifying or comforting prophecy. Think of it. We live in the first century of a new millennium. This treatment would affect my generations well into the century of A.D. 2400! I could be easily tempted to think, *is this my promise and blessing for obeying God?* Even of more interest, this was foretold before Isaac was conceived.

Was It Their Bad Behavior?

Some may reason, "The Lord told Abraham this in advance because his descendants would be disobedient and would therefore be placed under Pharaoh as punishment for bad behavior, yet God would never actually plan this for them!" Let's explore and find out whether this reasoning is accurate.

To answer, we must first know how they came under Pharaoh's leadership. Abraham's son Isaac was a God-fearing man who lived a life of obedience and holiness. He and his wife, Rebekah, had two sons: Esau, the elder, and Jacob, the younger. They were very different men in many ways. God revealed His thoughts before their birth by saying, "Jacob I have loved, but Esau I have hated" (Rom. 9:13).

Though Jacob started out a bit deviant, he ended up having a radical encounter with God at Peniel (Gen. 32). The encounter established God's covenant of blessing in his life, and his name was changed from Jacob to Israel, which means "Prince with God." After that, we see strong devotion in his lifestyle. He commanded his family to flee idolatry and remain pure before God. As a result, the terror of God fell on the unbelievers as his family journeyed (Gen. 35).

Israel was the father of twelve sons. The eleventh, Joseph, was despised by the elder brothers because their father favored him. God gave Joseph two separate dreams that prophetically showed him he would be a great leader and his brothers would serve him. The dreams so upset the brothers, they plotted a way to get rid of him and carried it out when they sold Joseph as a slave to Egypt.

Even through times of extreme loneliness and disappointment, Joseph remained faithful to the Lord while in Egypt. After ten years of service to one of Pharaoh's officers, he was falsely accused of raping his master's wife. He found himself in a dungeon for more than two years, but remained steadfast and loyal. Then the Lord used him to interpret the dreams of two of Pharaoh's servants, who had also been put in prison. One was executed; the other was restored, but for a season the restored one did not remember Joseph as he had asked. Nevertheless, Joseph was faithful.

Later when Pharaoh was troubled by a dream, the restored servant told him of Joseph. Joseph was called out of the dungeon to interpret Pharaoh's dream. The interpretation warned of a severe famine that would follow seven years of plenty. God gave Joseph wisdom to instruct Pharaoh to store up reserves in the years of abundance. Pharaoh was so in awe of his wisdom, he immediately elevated Joseph to number two man in Egypt, under only Pharaoh.

Back home was Joseph's godly father, Israel, who knew nothing of what was to happen. God didn't reveal it to him. This would be the vehicle that would transport all Abraham's descendants to Egypt. Two years into the famine Israel sent his sons to Egypt to buy grain. Without it they would perish. Egypt was the only place to go, for only Egypt was prepared for famine and equipped with the Lord's wisdom. God made the nation rich as a result of what He revealed through Joseph. He was grooming Egypt to become the most powerful and influential of all nations. That, too, was for a purpose.

When the sons of Israel arrived in Egypt, they were brought before Joseph, but they did not recognize him. It is no wonder. Who would have expected a slave on the throne? Joseph, on the other hand, recognized them—and might even have been expecting them—but he kept his identity secret. He blessed them with free grain, but devised a scheme to retain one brother in order to cause all to return. When their supplies ran out, they returned with all the sons of Israel. When all of them gathered, Joseph revealed himself.

Upon learning his identity, his brothers were terrified. Joseph was in a position to take revenge for their betrayal. But instead he comforted them:

> I am Joseph your brother, whom you sold into Egypt. But now, do not therefore be grieved or angry with yourselves because you sold me here; for *God sent me* before you to preserve life. For these two years the famine has been in the land, and there are still five years in which there will be neither plowing nor harvesting. And God sent me before you to preserve a posterity for you in the earth, and to save your lives by a great deliverance. *So now it was not you who sent me here, but God.* (Gen. 45:4–8, emphasis added)

After his response, you may wonder whether he spent so much time in Egypt that it warped his views. Maybe he forgot the years of pain, betrayal, and loneliness. After all, how could a loving God put him through so much suffering? How could He allow the most faithful and obedient son of Israel to endure the hardship of slavery and a lonely dungeon for more than twelve years when he was blameless? Did Joseph actually believe God not only allowed it, but also planned it?

Remember, out of the mouths of two witnesses every word is established. Hear what the psalmist wrote years later:

> Moreover He [God] called for a famine in the land;
> He destroyed all the provision of bread.
> He sent a man before them—Joseph—who was sold as a slave.
> They hurt his feet with fetters,
> He was laid in irons.
> Until the time that his word came to pass,
> The word of the LORD tested him. (Ps 105:16–19)

Wow, Joseph wasn't delusional in his assessment! Let's look closer at this passage. First, God, not the devil or circumstances, planned the famine. Second, as Joseph said, God sent him ahead of his family. It's not anyone else's doing when the phrase "sent by God" is used. Joseph wasn't in denial; he was speaking by the Spirit of God. Third, all his suffering was a test, or purifying process, for Joseph. Last, he was hurt with fetters and laid in irons. Dungeons then were much, much worse than our prisons today. But Joseph was the most godly son! Does that mean good people can go through harsh treatment by authority, and it is not an accident or the plan of the devil? Do you mean such circumstances can actually be the plan or provision of God?

A GREAT DELIVERANCE?

Let's continue to answer these important questions. Look again at Joseph's words. Remember he was speaking under divine inspiration: "And God sent me before you to preserve a posterity for you in the earth, and to save your lives by a great deliverance. So now it was not you who sent me here, but God" (Gen. 45:7–8).

Great deliverance! Wait a minute. It was not the disobedience of Abraham's descendants that brought them under the rule of Pharaoh, but God's plan. To top it off, God knew beforehand that shortly after Joseph's death, another Pharaoh would rise up and treat Israel with cruelty (Ex. 1:8–14). God had told Abraham years earlier they would be afflicted four hundred years. So that was the Lord's great deliverance? How could that be considered deliverance when they experienced such hardship?

Some may question, "Why didn't God give Abraham's descendants the wisdom that would have given them, not Egypt, food provisions for the seven-year famine? Then Joseph could have avoided all the suffering." The reason is clear: God wanted them under Pharaoh. He planned it. You may say, "But Pharaoh was like an ancient Hitler. He murdered thousands of them and afflicted God's people with great hardship." Yes, it is true, but we must remember God's priority is not for us to have the comforts and enjoyments of this world—His priority is redemption!

Hear the wisdom of God as He spoke to Pharaoh: "But indeed for this purpose I have raised you up, that I may show My power in you, and that My name may be declared in all the earth" (Ex. 9:16).

Before then, the only ones who knew the Lord God were Abraham, Isaac, Jacob, and their descendants. The rest of the world did not know the God of Abraham, Isaac, and Jacob. That was why when Moses approached Pharaoh and commanded him in the name of the Lord to let Israel go, Pharaoh responded, "Who is the LORD, that I should obey His voice to let Israel go? I do not know the LORD, nor will I let Israel go" (Ex. 5:2). Pharaoh and all Egypt did not know God. However, when God performed His signs to deliver His people, that changed.

After a few plagues, some Egyptians hearkened to the word of God. Before the hail came, we read, "He who feared the word of the LORD among the servants of Pharaoh made his servants and his livestock flee to the houses" (Ex. 9:20). Soon they were pleading with Pharaoh, "Let the men go, that they may serve the LORD" (Ex. 10:7). Even the magicians of Egypt said to their king, "This is the finger of God" (Ex. 8:19).

Their newly found knowledge of Jehovah became quite evident as we read, "Moses was very great in the land of Egypt, in the sight of Pharaoh's servants and in the sight of the people" (Ex. 11:3). They deeply respected the man of God, for they then knew who was Lord. And we read that the descendants of Abraham were given what they requested from the people of Egypt, such as articles of silver, gold and clothing (Ex. 12:35–36). Even Pharaoh eventually said, "The LORD is righteous, and my people and I are wicked" (Ex. 9:27). Finally all Egypt knew who the living God was.

THE WHOLE EARTH CAME TO KNOW

Not only Egypt, but the whole earth came to know of Jehovah as the true and living God. That knowledge was a direct result of His humbling the most powerful nation on the earth. God gave the nation wisdom through Joseph, which positioned it to be the greatest—only to later be defeated by Israelite slaves. The defeat had a much more profound impact on the watching world than if slaves had defeated a poor and weak or even an average nation. God made such an impression on the whole earth that after years of Israel's wandering in the desert, the nations still feared Him and trembled before Israel.

The effects were evident an entire generation later. Joshua, Moses' successor, sent two spies to the mighty nation of Jericho. The men were met by Rahab the harlot, who told them,

> I know that the LORD has given you the land, that the terror of you has fallen on us, and that *all the inhabitants* of the land are fainthearted because of you. For we have heard how the LORD dried up the water of the Red Sea for you when you came out of Egypt . . . And as soon as we heard these things, our hearts melted; neither did there remain any more courage in anyone because of you, *for the LORD your God, He is God in heaven above and on earth beneath.* (Josh. 2:9–11, emphasis added)

She declared the Lord is God, and "all the inhabitants" of the land were fainthearted. The Lord's name was known throughout the earth!

The knowledge was not only for His glory, but for redemption as well. The first fruits were manifested when the foreign prostitute and all her household were saved. Even more significant, she was the great-grandmother of King David and in the lineage of Jesus Christ. That would not have happened if God had not declared throughout the whole earth His name through humbling Pharaoh.

A few hundred years after the exodus from Egypt there was still evidence of the fear of God among the nations. During the time of Eli, priest and judge over Israel, God's name was remembered again for what He did to Pharaoh. Israel was at battle with the Philistines and suffered a loss the first day. The next day the Israelites brought the ark into the war camp. They rallied, and "all Israel shouted so loudly that the earth shook" (1 Sam. 4:5). The Philistines heard the noise and questioned among themselves what it could mean. Then they understood that the ark of the Lord had come into the Israelite camp. Consider their response:

The Philistines were afraid, for they said, God [Hebrew, *elohiym*] is come into the camp. And they said, Woe unto us! for there hath not been such a thing heretofore. Woe unto us! who shall deliver us out of the hand of these mighty Gods [*elohiym*]? these are the Gods [*elohiym*] that smote the Egyptians with all the plagues. (1 Sam. 4:7–8 KJV)

The Hebrew word used for "Gods" is *elohiym*. This word is used almost two thousand times in the Old Testament to identify the Lord God we serve. It is written thirty-two times in the first chapter of Genesis alone, identifying our God and Creator. Therefore, it could have been accurately translated "God" rather than "Gods." Even Philistines quaked hundreds of years later; though they did not serve Him, they knew who the true and living God was.

THE DEPTH OF THE WISDOM OF GOD

God was not caught off guard when the wicked leader. Pharaoh reigned: "For there is no authority except from God, and the authorities that exist are appointed by God" (Rom. 13:1). Every leader through the years who has had legitimate authority, whether good or harsh, has been appointed by God. He has been ordained for a specific reason, never by accident.

You may now ask, "What good came out of a leader like Stalin or Hitler?" To answer, let me quote the apostle Paul,

Therefore God has mercy on whom he wants to have mercy, and he hardens
whom he wants to harden . . .
Oh, the depth of the riches of the wisdom and knowledge of God!
How unsearchable his judgments,
and his paths beyond tracing out!
Who has known the mind of the Lord?
Or who has been his counselor? (Rom. 9:18; 11:33–34 NIV)

He can do things beyond our tracking. We must accept what He deems inappropriate to presently reveal.

Again Paul described His wisdom, "But who are you, O man, to talk back to God? Shall what is formed say to him who formed it, 'Why did you make me like this?'" (Rom. 9:20 NIV). Hear his words, "Who are you?" In other words, are we in a position to cross-examine Him?

God showed us His reasoning behind the raising up of Pharaoh to give us a pattern as well as insight and understanding so we might trust His wisdom and goodness. However, He doesn't always show us this with every leader. He wants us to trust His wisdom and goodness.

In His wisdom, He never allows suffering without purpose. He can always turn it for His redemptive purposes, even when we are not able to see the purposes at the time. However, eternity reveals them. In His goodness, He never allows harm to us within the scope of eternity. You may argue, "But harm, much harm, has come to people at the hands of corrupt leaders." This is true in the physical sense, yet God judges the spiritual above the physical. Abel's death appeared vain, but it wasn't because his blood still speaks (Heb. 11:4). Thousands of Christians were put to death by corrupt leaders during the Inquisition and persecutions that preceded and followed, yet their blood was not shed in vain. Their blood still speaks.

We have opportunities when we can affect leaders through humility, obedience, and prayers. When God's people humble themselves, pray, and turn from their wicked ways, God will hear from heaven and heal their land. An example is the appointment of godly leadership, illustrated in the book of Judges. The New Testament declares, "Therefore I exhort first of all that supplications, prayers, intercessions, and giving of thanks be made for all men, for kings and all who are in authority, that we may lead a quiet and peaceable life in all godliness and reverence. For this is good and acceptable in the sight of God our Savior" (1 Tim. 2:1–3).

Existing leadership is affected by our prayers. The effects can be as far-reaching as the appointment and selection of leaders. However, even with all this in place there can be exceptions. The apostles and saints of the early church frequently encountered harsh and cruel authorities who persecuted them. They were not suffering because of ungodly lifestyles or prayerlessness; rather, those leaders played a role in the redemptive purposes of God.

HEROD AGRIPPA I

Let's look at one of them, Herod Agrippa I. The name Herod was used to identify several Roman rulers in the Palestine region prior to the birth of Jesus, during His earthly ministry, and after His resurrection. Herod Agrippa I came to power in A.D. 37, after the resurrection of Jesus. He did so through cleverness and tact. With his far-seeing mind he cultivated every means that might lead to his own promotion. A primary political maneuver after the Roman emperor Caligula was murdered was to help Claudius gain the throne. Claudius rewarded his shrewd political move, and he confirmed Agrippa in his present position and added the territories of Judea and Samaria. He became ruler of a kingdom as large as that of his grandfather, Herod the Great.

During his rule, Herod Agrippa I was forced to side in the struggle between Judaism and the Christian sect. Without hesitation he assumed the role of the Christians' bitter persecutor. We read in the book of Acts, "Now about that time Herod [Agrippa I] the king stretched out his hand to harass some from the church. Then he killed James the brother of John with the sword. And because he saw that it pleased the Jews, he proceeded further to seize Peter also" (12:1–3). The ruler was harsh with the believers because it served his political purposes and gained him favor with the Jews. He'd killed James, one of Jesus' three closest apostles, and he intended to kill Peter.

We must ask, "Where did Agrippa's authority come from?" Even though it appeared his maneuvers gained him power, he did not get into his position of authority without God's knowledge and appointment.

Peter, who had suffered at the hands of Agrippa, told believers to "fear God, honor the king" (1 Peter 2:17 NIV). What? Honor the king who had murdered James? Why would God appoint such a harsh leader over the very land in which so many of His children dwelled and then tell them to "honor him"? Part of our answer is found as we continue in Scripture: "Peter was therefore kept in prison, but constant prayer was offered to God for him by the church" (Acts 12:5). As a result, God sent an angel who miraculously delivered Peter from the dungeon to the safety of a home prayer meeting. If the believers had not honored the king, but had rebelled against God's command as it relates to delegated authority, they would not have seen God's hand miraculously move.

Agrippa's plans to execute Peter were thwarted by the prayers and obedience of the church. That event significantly strengthened the believers. Just as He had with Pharaoh, God manifested His power for redemptive purposes. The greatest testimony to that is found in the Scripture itself: "But the word of God grew and multiplied" (Acts 12:24).

The constant prayers of the saints and their obedience to honor authority had a greater impact on the turn of events. As we continue to read, we find that Herod Agrippa I set a day in which he came before the people, sat on his throne in royal apparel, and gave a public address: "And the people kept shouting, 'The voice of a god and not of a man!' Then immediately an angel of the Lord struck him, because he did not give glory to God. And he was eaten by worms and died" (Acts 12:22–23).

Judgment came, but it was by the sword of the Lord, not by God's people. We will soon learn that God is the One who brings judgment on authorities. We are commanded to pray for those in leadership, and to honor and submit to their authority. If there is need of judgment, God says we are to make room for it.

What I have written in this chapter is true, even if it goes against what is taught and perceived in the church. Let's keep an open heart to the wisdom of God. Remember, He is for us, not against us.

CHAPTER 9

HONOR THE KING

We must learn to honor—to revere, respect; to treat with deference and submission, and perform relative duties to—those who are in authority.

A firm exhortation by the apostle Peter, briefly mentioned in the last chapter, needs considerable attention, especially in our day and hour. Before isolating this scripture, let's examine it in the context of preceding statements: "Dear friends, you are foreigners and strangers on this earth. So I beg you not to surrender to those desires that fight against you. Always let others see you behaving properly, even though they may still accuse you of doing wrong" (1 Peter 2:11–12 CEV). We are about to discover that submission to authority is the proper behavior he spoke of. The fight mentioned is the war between a rebellious desire to disobey authority and obedience. However, too frequently we think the opposite; we regard the desire to disobey as our ally and submission as our enemy. This perception couldn't be farther from the truth.

We must not forget what Peter wrote, for even when we do submit and obey, we may still be accused of "doing wrong." I have heard people reason, "What good does it do? I submit, but I still get blamed for things I haven't done wrong." They have lost sight of the fact that their obedience is to the Lord, and their reward comes from Him. *The Message* brings this point out beautifully:

Servants [employees, church members, civilians, etc.], respectfully obey your earthly masters [employers, church leaders, civil authorities, etc.] but always with an eye to obeying the real master, Christ. Don't just do what you have to do to get by, but work heartily, as Christ's servants doing what God wants you to do. And work with a smile on your face, always keeping in mind that no matter who happens to be giving the orders, you're really serving God. Good work will get you good pay from the Master, regardless of whether you are slave or free. (Eph. 6:5–8)

Returning to Peter's exhortation, "For the Lord's sake, yield [submit] to the people who have authority in this world; the king, who is the highest authority, and the leaders who are sent by him" (1 Peter 2:13–14 NCV). The Holy Spirit is exhorting us through Peter, just as He did through Paul, to submit to all governing authorities. Keep in mind, the king he referred to was very harsh, and believers suffered bitter persecution under his rule. Like Paul, Peter exhorted us to recognize the authority of God vested in the man rather than the man himself. He could never submit to the person Herod Agrippa I unless he understood and recognized the authority of God on the king's position. It is difficult to submit to delegated authority if we have yet to encounter the authority of God. The harder we try to obey, the harder it becomes if we fail to see true authority.

Peter warned us because he knew insubordination actually furthers the cause of antichrist or anti-Christian spirits. For this force "opposes and exalts himself above all that is called God" (2 Thess. 2:4), including the ways, methods, operations, and appointments of the true, living God. We believers must ask ourselves, "Are we assisting or restraining the operation of lawlessness?" If we aid it, we operate under the principles of Satan (rebellion), not God.

Peter continued, "Love the brotherhood. Fear God. Honor the king" (1 Peter 2:17). He not only exhorted us to submit but also to honor authorities. The Greek word for "honor" is *timao*, which means "to honor, to have in honor, to revere, to venerate." It is the same word Jesus used when He said, "I honor My Father" (John 8:49).

Webster's Dictionary (1828 version) defines the word *honor* as "to revere, respect; to treat with deference and submission, and perform relative duties to." Let me reiterate: the king Peter referred to was the one persecuting the believers of his day! There is no possible way he referred to the king as an individual; he exhorted us to honor him as an appointed authority of God.

A HEARTBREAKING INTERVIEW

Recently I was interviewed on a live radio talk program of a popular Christian station in a large city in the South. We were discussing one of my books. Ten minutes into the radio interview the announcer took a break. During that time, I heard several commercials and announcements at a lower volume level since I was not actually on air during the break.

All of a sudden, my attention was gripped as I heard a man reporting the national weather. He told the audience of hundreds of thousands how it was so cold in one specific northern state that it froze the lips of the state's governor. He named the governor and reported his lips were so frozen that he couldn't open his mouth and say something stupid, as he normally did.

I was in shock; I couldn't believe what I'd just heard. My thoughts wandered, *Is this a Christian station? Certainly it's not.* Then I thought, *If it is a Christian station, maybe this weather forecast was piped in from an Associated Press source.* I couldn't shake the impact of what I'd heard before the interviewer came back on.

Back on air he asked a vague question to which I responded by saying how important it was to have the heart of God in all we do. My mind was still troubled by what I'd heard, and I said, "A good example would be what I just heard over the intermission." I then asked, "Is this a Christian station?"

He responded, "Yes."

"Well, maybe what I heard was piped in from a secular source because whoever was speaking did not have the heart of God in what was said a few minutes ago."

He asked, "What are you referring to?"

I responded, "The announcement that made reference to freezing the governor's mouth shut."

The interviewer's voice dropped to a disgusted tone, "That person was me."

I said, "The Scripture says we are to fear God and honor the king or those in authority."

He responded in a firmer voice, "Yeah, but there is nothing wrong with a little humor."

I quickly added, "Not at the expense of what God tells us to honor. The apostle Paul said, 'Do not speak evil about the ruler of your people' (Acts 23:5 NIV)."

He closed the live interview before its scheduled conclusion by saying, "Well, John and I don't see eye to eye on everything."

I hung up heartbroken. Was this honoring, revering, or venerating the governor? I can admit, this man he mentioned has not always conducted himself in a way deserving of respect, but he holds the office of governor. As Christians, we are to honor that position of authority. How many believers were affected by the irreverent humor? No wonder we've lost the respect of so many elements of society.

This is a far cry from the behavior of the early persecuted church. They honored authority. When we behave and speak in this manner, we add to the power of lawlessness at work today. Yet the Bible tells us, "For the mystery of lawlessness is already at work; only He who now restrains will do so until He is taken out of the way" (2 Thess. 2:7). This behavior wars against the restraining power of the Holy Spirit. It is the principle of Satan!

THE FEAR OF THE LORD BREEDS HONOR

Let's return to Peter's words, "Fear God. Honor the king." Those who fear God are those who keep before them the Lord of glory's high and lofty position. They have met with and been consumed by His far-reaching authority. They esteem what He esteems and hate what He hates. Firmly implanted within their lives are reverential fear and respect for all in leadership because God has delegated His authority.

A lack of the Spirit of the fear of the Lord is evident when we do not revere authority. Remember Isaiah's description of Jesus:

The Spirit of the LORD shall rest upon Him,
The Spirit of wisdom and understanding,
The Spirit of counsel and might,
The Spirit of knowledge and of *the fear of the* LORD.
His delight is in the fear of the LORD,
And He shall not judge by the sight of His eyes,
Nor decide by the hearing of His ears. (Isa. 11:2–3, emphasis added)

Jesus' delight is in the fear of the Lord. It enabled Him not to judge by natural sight or hearing. That radio host showed by his fruit he was not acquainted with the fear of Lord as it pertained to delegated authorities. Because the governor's behavior had not been honorable, the radio host judged him by the hearing of the ear and the sight of the eye, and by these standards, the radio host could be considered accurate. However, if he had seen through the eyes of the fear of the Lord, he would have perceived the appointed authority upon the governor's life. To slander governmental authority is never an act of godliness.

John the Baptist dealt with the behavior of one in authority named Herod, yet his approach was much different from that of the interviewer. First, John told Herod, "It is not lawful for you to have her [your brother's wife]" (Matt. 14:4). He spoke directly to a sin, not about him disrespectfully. Second, he dealt with Herod from his position of authority as a prophet of God. Last, John wasn't making irreverent jokes about the king.

The only godly person you will find in the Bible making jokes about men who held a position of leadership is Elijah (1 Kings 18:27). He mocked the false prophets of Baal and Asherah, and the gods they represented. Those men, who possessed not true authority, but counterfeit, led many Israelites into darkness. Their positions were not ordained by God. They were not worthy of honor or submission. People who lead occult organizations are not to be submitted to or obeyed. But they are not to be taken lightly, for even "Michael the archangel, in contending with the devil, when he disputed the body of Moses, dared not bring reviling accusation, but said, 'The Lord rebuke you!' But these [the rebellious within the church] speak evil of whatever they do not know" (Jude 9–10). The Spirit of God was upon Elijah to speak in the manner in which he did. For us to flippantly mock any form of leadership, even if it is from darkness, is most unwise.

To return to true appointed authority, it *is* difficult to honor and obey when we do not see authority through eyes enlightened by the fear of the Lord. Yet hear what Scriptures say, "He [God] is especially hard on those who follow their own evil, lustful desires and who despise authority. These people are proud and arrogant, daring even to scoff at the glorious ones without so much as trembling" (2 Peter 2:10 NLT). What is really sobering is that Peter and Jude were talking about those in church settings (Jude 12; 2 Pet. 2:13–15).

I warned as we began this book, it would be hard for some to receive because too often we view God's kingdom through democratic mind-sets. That is why we are commanded to be renewed in the spirit of our minds (Eph. 4:23). If the radio host's mind-set was unique to him, I probably wouldn't have mentioned it, yet this mind-set blankets the church. I made this discovery during the presidency of Bill Clinton.

Two Wrongs Don't Make a Right

When President Clinton was elected in 1992, I was depressed for three days until God dealt with me. He showed me in no uncertain terms that nobody gets into power without His knowledge, and those in authority carry His appointment. Once that was revealed, I began to focus on the authority of the man, not his personal life. When I did, I found a genuine love growing in my heart for this leader and a passionate desire to see him delivered and walking in truth.

I believe the same was true of John the Baptist's heart toward Herod. Though he spoke sternly, he surely had the heart of God for the corrupt leader. That was why Jeremiah wept over the ones he spoke so strongly to. There are those who speak from legalistic, hate-filled hearts, and there are those who speak the corrective word of the Lord from hearts of burning compassion.

What angers the Lord are those who "faultfind" out of self-righteous judgment. I witnessed this in many churches toward President Clinton. Before continuing, let me reiterate I did not vote for President Clinton in either election, and I am heartbroken over what his behavior released into this country.

While traveling in 1992, I was frequently encouraged by believers to watch a certain ultraconservative man on television. He seemed to have a lot to say about our nation's liberal leaders, especially the president and his wife. I heard these comments weekly in different cities. These zealots said, "You've got to hear this guy. He is nailing what is going on in Washington." Out of my trust for them, I thought, *I've got to catch this man and hear what he has to say.* I don't frequently watch television, so it was almost nine months before I finally saw this man.

After returning to my hotel room after a service in California, I flipped on the television, and there he was. He was very funny and had a wild tie on. He then started in on President Clinton. It hit me: *This is the man everyone has been telling me about.* I was excited to finally hear this famous person. I sat down ready to watch and to hear what he had to say.

I listened for twenty minutes as he bashed the president and made him out to be a jerk. The jokes were hilarious, and the words were witty, but the entire time I had a sick feeling in my stomach. I thought, *What's wrong? Everything he is saying is true. He has captured the liberal mindset of our president.* I then questioned, "Lord, why do I have such an uncomfortable feeling in my heart?"

The Holy Spirit immediately answered, *You shall not speak evil of a ruler of your people* (Acts 23:5).

Another Scripture bubbled up in my mind: *I urge, then, first of all, that requests, prayers, intercession and thanksgiving be made for everyone—for kings and all those in authority, that we may live peaceful and quiet lives in all godliness and holiness. This is good, and pleases God our Savior* (1 Tim. 2:1–3 NIV). It hit me like a ton of bricks. God commanded us to honor, pray for, intercede for, and give thanks for those in authority. He also commanded us not to speak against them. He has not told us to bash, criticize, fight with, or make fun of them. Though the television commentator was right about much of what he reported, two wrongs never equal a right!

I was not as upset with this man as I was with the believers who were so excited about his message. As far as this commentator was concerned, I regarded him as someone who didn't know better. What I couldn't comprehend was how believers could proclaim his message. How were they "honoring the king"? God told us what to do as Christians: pray, intercede, and give thanks. Paul not only spoke of the penalty of death, which will occur to those who walk in the various manifestations of lawlessness, "but also approve of those who practice them" (Rom. 1:32).

WHAT LAWS DO WE LIVE BY?

I started preaching what had happened in that hotel room all over the United States. Many saw the light and repented; others became very angry with me. They argued that the commentator stood for right living and the freedom of speech granted by our government. This is true; however, we have commands that supersede this behavior. Do we live by democratic rule or by the laws of the kingdom of God? Just because our land permits the use of alcohol, should we believers drink freely?

We have a higher law. An unbeliever in Rome wrote about the Christians of the first-century church, "They pass their days on earth, but they are citizens of heaven. They obey the prescribed laws, and at the same time, they surpass the laws by their lives" (*Letter to Diognetus*, Chapter 5).

What profit is it to listen to slander? What fruit does it bear? Wouldn't we be more effective to take the time spent watching and spreading that man's message and instead use it to intercede for our national leaders? Didn't God say the outcome of obedient behavior would be "that we may live peaceful and quiet lives in all godliness and holiness"?

I know a minister who met with President Clinton and said, "Any leader who legislates the killing of innocent children will suffer the judgment of God and burn in hell." This minister behaved no differently from John the Baptist with Herod. This messenger of God spoke out of a heart of righteous anger and genuine love for unborn children and the president. While respecting the authority of the president, this minister spoke the truth. This person would never be one to make sport of the president. When men and women listen to television personalities bash authorities, we lose the heart of God. Listening to slander will not produce eternal fruit.

THE HEART TO HONOR AUTHORITY

A heart to honor authority should permeate our behavior, for we honor the Lord's appointment. Paul exhorted us,

> Do you want to be free from fear of the one in authority? Then do what is right and he will commend you. For he is *God's servant* to do you good. But if you do wrong, be afraid, for he does not bear the sword for nothing. He is *God's servant*, an agent of wrath to bring punishment on the wrongdoer. Therefore, it is necessary to submit to the authorities, not only because of possible punishment but also because of conscience. This is also why you pay taxes, for the authorities are God's servants, who give their full time to governing. Give everyone what you owe him: If you owe taxes, pay taxes; if revenue, then revenue; if respect, then respect; if honor, then honor. (Rom. 13:3–7 NIV, emphasis added)

God called those in authority His "servants," and they are worthy to receive due honor and respect. I find this burning in my heart every time I see a policeman, fireman, mayor, councilman, governor, state legislator, judge, congressman, or some other person in a branch of government. I find respect welling up within me when I go to city, state, or federal offices. They are God's ministers to serve His people.

I've received a few speeding tickets, and each time I have told the officer after receiving my ticket, "Sir, I was wrong, and I want to thank you for doing your job and serving our city. Please forgive me for my offense." You should see their faces. One time the officer's demeanor totally changed. He'd started out hard, but softened when he saw my respect for his authority. I thought at one point he was going to take the ticket back, although that was not my intent.

I have a friend who pastors in the state where the governor was dishonored by the "Christian" radio station host. Hear his testimony. He was in prayer for his city, asking God how to really make a difference. At the time his church consisted of a small body of believers. God put it in his heart to honor the civil authorities of his city. After further prayer, he knew what to do. He and his leaders investigated the greatest needs of the city. They found out the fire department needed masks to enable the firefighters to see people through smoke, but the items weren't included in their budget that year. The masks cost $25,000 each. That was a lot of money for a church their size.

The pastor shared the vision with his people, and in one offering they raised every bit of what was needed. He and the leaders of his church presented the check to the city. He shared with me, "John, you would be amazed the way this has ministered to the city officials. They could not believe a church would perform such an act of kindness. They were used to people griping about the needs of government, not giving freely toward them."

Since then the church has exploded in growth. When the congregation dedicated a new building, many city officials attended, and some still attend. Compare this pastor's fruit with that of the radio host.

I've heard numerous believers gripe about the taxes they pay. I've met people in churches who have figured out ways of not paying taxes. They claim it is their constitutional right. To them, I argue, "Your exhortation from God supersedes your supposed constitutional right. God says to 'pay taxes.'" I then say to these people, "Who is paying for the roads you drive on? Who is paying for the policemen, firemen, and lawmakers who protect you?" I have listened as accountants tell me how believers cheat on their taxes by trying to cut corners. It is heartbreaking. I told our accountants, "I don't want any gray areas; I don't want to cut corners." Paying taxes is an opportunity to give back to the government that serves us. We can't be stolen from if we choose to give! When are we believers going to revel in this truth?

If the church would lay hold of this, we would be a greater witness to our nation and the world. We must learn to honor—to revere, respect; to treat with deference and submission, and perform relative duties to—those who are in authority. In doing so we honor our heavenly Father. When we honor the king, we show our fear of the Lord.

SIMILAR TO ALL AREAS OF AUTHORITY

As I wrote in the last chapter, the command to honor the king directly represents civil authority; this counsel also spans other areas of delegated authority. Note the references to honor in the following verses. Concerning the family, God said, "Honor your father and mother" (Eph. 6:2). Again He commanded, "Let the wife see that she respects her husband" (Eph. 5:33). As for social authorities, we read, "Let as many bondservants as are under the yoke count their own masters worthy of all honor, so that the name of God and His doctrine may not be blasphemed" (1 Tim. 6:1). And as for church authority, we are commanded, "Let the elders who rule well be counted worthy of double honor, especially those who labor in the word and doctrine" (1 Tim. 5:17).

As a youth pastor, I too often witnessed young people speaking disrespectfully to their parents. There was no respect in these young people, let alone honor. I corrected them on the spot if their parents didn't. If they only knew they were actually hurting themselves, they wouldn't have dared do it. God says, "'Cursed is the man who dishonors his father or his mother.' Then all the people shall say, 'Amen!'" (Deut. 27:16 NIV). The curse we discussed in early chapters comes on those who dishonor their parents.

On the flip side, God promises great blessings to those who honor their parents: "'Honor your father and mother,' which is the first commandment with promise: 'that it may be well with you and you may live long on the earth'" (Eph. 6:2–3).

God actually promises a child two distinct blessings when he honors his parents. First, it goes well with him. A person who does not honor his parents cannot count on life going well for him. He is under a curse. (I will share my testimony about this in a later chapter.)

The second promise is a long life. What a benefit for honoring your parents! You may think, *Wait a minute. I've known children who honored their parents, yet died young.* I know for sure that the Word of God says this is the first command with a promise. We get in trouble when we allow what we see around us to negate the promises of God. Consider this: our Father promises complete freedom from fear to those who are His. In His words, "In righteousness you shall be established; you shall be far from oppression, for you shall not fear" (Isa. 54:14). Yet precious Christians live in fear. If the promises were automatic, why do so many live under this torment? The answer to this question is: they are received through prayer and won by the good fight of faith.

Abraham's son Isaac is a good example. God made the promise to Abraham concerning Isaac, "I will establish My covenant with him for an everlasting covenant, and with his descendants after him" (Gen. 17:19). God declared the promise, yet after marriage they discovered Rebekah, his only wife, was barren! To complicate matters, he had not chosen her; the Holy Spirit picked her out. You may ask, "Do you mean God handpicked a barren wife?" Yes! The promise was not automatic; it had to be appropriated. Hear what Scripture says, "Now Isaac pleaded with the LORD for his wife, because she was barren; and the LORD granted his plea, and Rebekah his wife conceived" (Gen. 25:21).

Isaac had to fight to obtain the promise by crying out to the Lord. He prayed according to the will of God and was answered. We are encouraged, "Now this is the confidence that we have in Him, that if we ask anything according to His will, He hears us. And if we know that He hears us, whatever we ask, we know that we have the petitions that we have asked of Him" (1 John 5:14–15). God made His will clear in the covenant. If we have His promise, we know we can pray according to His will.

By honoring your parents, you can stand on His two covenant promises through prayer and receive a good, long, and fruitful life. Base your faith on the covenant of God, not the lives of others.

Perhaps you are fretting because you have not honored your parents. This is where repentance comes in. Go to God in prayer and your parents in person, and ask their forgiveness. Begin to honor them, and believe for His covenant promises to be manifested in your life.

The same principle applies for bosses, employers, teachers, et al. If we honor them, it will be well for us, and we will receive our reward from the Lord. Paul instructed employees, "Whatever you do, work at it with all your heart, as working for the Lord, not for men, since you know that you will receive an inheritance from the Lord as a reward. It is the Lord Christ you are serving. Anyone who does wrong will be repaid for his wrong, and there is no favoritism" (Col. 3:23–25 NIV).

The next chapter will review the far-reaching benefits that are bestowed when we receive His servants in the church and give them due honor. We will also see what we miss when we fail to recognize the ones God sends us.

CHAPTER 10

DOUBLE HONOR

---

*Many times God will send us what we need in a package
we don't want.*

G ive respect and honor to all to whom it is due" (Rom. 13:7). We
will see in this chapter that one primary reason God instructs us to give
honor to the authorities over us is for our sake, not for theirs. It is exciting to note that the adherence to this command from the word of God
brings a blessing. We see an example in 1 Samuel.

AN INSULT TURNED TO A BLESSING

In the days when judges ruled Israel there was a barren woman named
Hannah. She was married to Elkanah, who had taken a second wife
named Peninnah. Hannah was miserable because her rival taunted her
due to her barrenness. More than likely Elkanah took the second wife
because Hannah was barren. Hannah was loved and filled her husband's heart, but Peninnah filled his house. Yearly the family traveled
to worship at Shiloh. There especially Peninnah would provoke
Hannah until she wept. Hannah could not be comforted, even by her
husband.

On one particular visit to Shiloh, she was undone. Out of deep
anguish, Hannah wept before the Lord and made covenant, "If You

will give me a child, then I will give him back to You all the days of his life" (author's paraphrase).

While she prayed, Eli, the head priest and judge of Israel, watched her and: "Seeing her lips moving but hearing no sound, he thought she had been drinking. 'Must you come here drunk?' he demanded. 'Throw away your wine!'" (1 Sam. 1:13–14 NLT).

What an insult! Not only was he insensitive to her pain, but he was so spiritually numb, he thought her travail arose out of a drunken stupor. She had left the presence of her constant adversary to find comfort before the Lord, only to be judged by the highest spiritual authority in the land as wicked. Every year she came to Shiloh empty-handed with no child to present before the Lord. Each year she encountered the looks, the stares, the whispers and jeers of those around her.

How would you have responded if your pastor had accused you of evil at the moment of your greatest pain? Perhaps you would have thought, *This guy is the head pastor? Doesn't he know I am fasting and crying out to God? What an insensitive, unspiritual jerk! This is the last time I will come here to worship!*

These thoughts could have easily produced an outburst, "You call yourself a man of God and can't recognize someone in pain! Can't you recognize someone in deep prayer? What kind of pastor are you? What kind of church is this? I have had it! I'm going to find another church with a pastor who is sensitive to me and the things of God!" This would not be an uncommon response in our churches today—if not brazenly to the pastor's face, then behind his back to congregation members.

But hear Hannah's response when she was severely insulted: "'Oh no, sir!' she replied, 'I'm not drunk! But I am very sad, and I was pouring out my heart to the LORD. Please don't think I am a wicked woman! For I have been praying out of great anguish and sorrow'" (vv. 15–16 NLT). She responded with respect and honor. Even though his actions and assessment far from deserved it, she honored the position of authority on his life. She went so far as to assure him she was not wicked.

In reality the one with excessive behavioral patterns at that time was Eli, and his judgment was hanging over him. Her focus was not on his behavior, but on her own. Hannah was a woman who truly feared the

Lord. If anything was wrong with the leader, God would deal with it. How we need this kind of true submission and humility today.

His response to Hannah changed:

> "In that case," Eli said, "cheer up! May the God of Israel grant the request you have asked of him." "Oh, thank you, sir!" she exclaimed. Then she went back and began to eat again, and she was no longer sad. (vv. 17–18 NLT)

There was no drifting from her submission to him; she honored him as a man of God and even thanked him for his word of blessing.

Watch what happened: "The entire family got up early the next morning and went to worship the LORD once more. Then they returned home to Ramah. When Elkanah slept with Hannah, the LORD remembered her request, and in due time she gave birth to a son" (1 Sam. 1:19–20 NLT).

God used a fleshly, insensitive priest to release the words to bring forth the conception of a promise. A closed womb was opened, and life came out of darkness. The following year she held little Samuel at her breast. The young man consecrated before his conception would bring revival to Israel.

WHO'S THE JUDGE?

There's an amazing principle to glean from this: when God places His authority on a person, no matter his private or personal behavior, we may still receive if we look beyond it and honor him as sent from God. Jesus made it clear that many will receive from corrupt ministers, as Hannah did. He said, "Many will say to Me in that day, 'Lord, Lord, have we not prophesied in Your name, cast out demons in Your name, and done many wonders in Your name?' And then I will declare to them, 'I never knew you; depart from Me, you who practice lawlessness!'" (Matt. 7:22–23).

When we read this scripture, we too often concentrate on the *many* who did miraculous works in Jesus' name but were turned away. This is serious and sobering, indeed, but let's look at the flip side; there were those who received true ministry from these workers of iniquity. They received because they accessed God through them, as Hannah had. The ones Jesus spoke of were similar to Eli, whose house God judged forever!

I have written this book not to corrupt ministers, but to persons under authority. Scripture leaves no doubt that there are corrupt authorities and godly ones. If those under authority take the yoke of judgment upon themselves, they no longer are submitted to established authority, but have elevated themselves as judges over their leaders. Their hearts are lifted up in pride above the ones God placed over them. They have exalted themselves over the ordinance and counsel of God. In essence, they unknowingly say to God, "You are not exercising judgment well, so I will."

Hannah acknowledged the authority on Eli's life and honored it. He judged and insulted her, yet she honored him. If she lived by the seeing of the eye and the hearing of the ear, she might have judged his behavior questionable. However, she lived not by natural reasoning, but by the fear of the Lord and divine authority. She trusted in God who judged righteously.

Hannah knew what Jesus later confirmed, "Most assuredly, I say to you, he who receives whomever I send receives Me; and he who receives Me receives Him who sent Me" (John 13:20). Remember well, Jesus sent Judas equipped with power to do miracles and cast out demons. Yet Jesus knew Judas would eventually be revealed as wicked: "Did I not choose you, the twelve, and one of you is a devil?" (John 6:70). Jesus knew him through the discernment found in the fear of the Lord, even before his sin was evident. Judas did miraculous acts and returned rejoicing with the others that the demons were subject to him in Jesus' name (Mark 6:7–13; Luke 10:17). Did people receive ministry from the hands of Judas? The very same hands that had stolen from the ministry treasury? Absolutely!

WHEN TO LEAVE

Let me make a vital point. If it's revealed that an authority in the church is in blatant corruption or sin, we should not continue to drink from his defiled fountain. We are instructed in no uncertain terms to pull away. If a leader is involved in adultery, homosexuality, extortion, theft, heresy, or some other sin known to you—or exposed publicly— and remains unrepentant, get out from underneath his ministry. Scripture is clear on this matter. We are not even to eat with such a person (1 Cor. 5:9–11). In Eli's case it is unclear whether Hannah was fully aware of Eli's and his sons' corrupt behavior. The people who received from Judas were more than likely unaware he was a thief and potential traitor.

Referring to church leadership, Paul said, "The sins of some men are conspicuous (openly evident to all eyes), going before them to the judgment [seat] and proclaiming their sentence in advance; but the sins of others appear later [following the offender to the bar of judgment and coming into view there]" (1 Tim. 5:24 AMPLIFIED).

The bottom line: if a leader's life is corrupt and the judgment of God is not yet evident, it will come either in this life or in the one to come. You don't have to judge or expose something you're not sure of. Too many operate out of suspicion, and too often they are not accurate in their assessment and bring serious damage to themselves and their peers. Their mouths leak what they incorrectly suspect. They justify their notions as spiritual discernment. They make it difficult for others to receive from ordained leaders, and many miss what God desired to give them. That is why God admonishes, "Do not entertain an accusation against an elder unless it is brought by two or three witnesses" (1 Tim. 5:19 NIV). A witness is one who can produce evidence, not hearsay.

God judges everything in its own time, and if He deems it time or necessary to expose a leader's unrepentant error, you will surely know it, and it will be time to get out from under that authority. Paul declared, "If any of the leaders should keep on sinning, they must be corrected in front of the whole group, as a warning to everyone else" (1 Tim. 5:20 CEV). The warning: don't partake of their sins, and get out from underneath their authority unless they have truly repented.

I once served under a leader who eventually manifested blatant sin. I was not there when it all happened, for we had already moved to another state where I would serve as a youth pastor. A couple of years after we left, he stood up before the body of believers and shared that he was divorcing his wife because he did not want to live with her any longer. A short while later he shared his plans to marry a younger woman. His wife was innocent of any sexual misconduct; he just wanted the other woman.

At that point thousands left his congregation. They did so with good reason. Those who stayed entered into dangerous territory as the doctrine and teaching became increasingly perverted to the leader's and his new wife's purposes. I know many who left and prospered as long as they refused to speak against this pastor. Those who attacked him suffered.

David was an example of proper behavior. Even after being driven from the presence of a demonically tormented king, he honored Saul until the day of his death. David understood Saul was the Lord's anointed servant. To this day I endeavor to honor this man, even though I grieve over the consequences of his choices. Though I honor him, I could not consider his doctrine or ministry safe or sound.

In a different season I'd received richly from his ministry. I found out later his behavior went back to the very time period I had sat under his teachings. There were some vague indications, but nothing was open or manifest. God had rebuked me during that time period for a critical attitude (I will share this in the next chapter); perhaps God was still attempting to reach this man. At that point it was none of my business. God had placed me under his authority, and it was not my place to judge whether he was worthy to be received from. Just as Hannah received from Eli, many received from this man in those times as well.

THE ORDER OF SPIRITUAL AUTHORITY

Let's return to Jesus' words, and view them through a godly leader instead of a man such as Eli. Look at His words in the book of Matthew:

> He who receives you receives Me, and he who receives Me receives Him who sent Me. He who receives a prophet in the name of a prophet shall receive a prophet's reward. And he who receives a right-

eous man in the name of a righteous man shall receive a righteous man's reward. And whoever gives one of these little ones only a cup of cold water in the name of a disciple, assuredly, I say to you, he shall by no means lose his reward. (Matt. 10:40–42)

He was communicating two points in these verses. First and foremost, there is a flow of authority, starting with the Father. He is the One who sent Jesus and gave all authority to Him. In Jesus' own words, "All authority has been given to Me in heaven and on earth" (Matt. 28:18). Jesus is the head of the church, and the day will come when He will turn the kingdom over to His Father, after putting all rebellion under His feet (1 Cor. 15:24–26).

Next in this order of authority is the prophet. Prophets are initially depicted in Scripture as the Lord's spokespersons (Ex. 4:16; 7:1). This would represent one of the fivefold ministry gifts that He gave the church when He was raised from the dead (Eph. 4:8–13). (They are the spokespersons of the Church.) When we receive a ministry gift, we receive from the Lord what He Himself gives through that office of delegated authority.

Then He moved on to the righteous man and did not exclude the babes. I have seen unbelievers blessed because they did something good for even the most infant believers. Although the unbelievers did not serve the Lord, they showed regard for their Master. When receiving and blessing saints, we ultimately receive and bless the Father. Disciples, which include babes, submit to fivefold church authority under the headship of Jesus, who expresses the will of the Father. Therefore, the unsaved come under the blessing of the babe in Christ, for the least in the kingdom has greater spiritual authority than the lost. From Jesus' words we see an order of established authority.

THE REWARD OF RECEIVING SPIRITUAL AUTHORITY

The second point communicated in these verses is found in receiving these servants as ultimately sent by God and receiving the corresponding reward. The ministry of Jesus provides an illustration.

The citizens of one city had a particularly difficult time receiving from Jesus, though they preached the reality of Messiah and knew from the Scripture it was the season of His coming. Jesus said to them, "'Only in his hometown, among his relatives and in his own house is a prophet without honor.' He *could not* do any miracles there, except lay his hands on a few sick people and heal them" (Mark 6:4–5 NIV, emphasis added).

We receive someone as sent by God when we honor his position or office. God told the people through Moses, "I will raise up for them a Prophet like you from among their brethren" (Deut. 18:18). But they didn't honor Jesus as the Spokesperson from the Father or as Messiah.

Why didn't they receive Him? Because He didn't come the way they wanted Him to come. Their expectations were very different from who He actually was. They'd read in Isaiah,

> For to us a child is born,
>> to us a son is given,
>> and the government will be on his shoulders . . .
> Of the increase of his government and peace
>> there will be no end.
> He will reign on David's throne
>> and over his kingdom. (9:6–7 NIV)

So they watched for the arrival of a conquering king who'd set them free from Roman oppression and establish His kingdom in Jerusalem. But instead He came as a carpenter's son accompanied by fishermen and tax collectors. They said among themselves, "This is not the way we want or expect the Messiah!"

Also, note that the scripture tells us, Jesus "could not" do any miracles. It does not say, "He would not," which would deal with His will. It records "could not," which means He was restrained. Think of it. The Son of God, infused with the Spirit of God without measure, was restricted! Why? The answer is twofold: He had not come the way they wanted, so they did not receive or honor Him, and they were too familiar with Him. Listen to their words:

He began to teach in the synagogue. And many hearing Him were astonished, saying, *"Where did this Man get these things? And what wisdom is this which is given to Him, that such mighty works are performed by His hands! Is this not the carpenter, the Son of Mary, and brother of James, Joses, Judas, and Simon? And are not His sisters here with us?"* So they were offended at Him. But Jesus said to them, "A prophet is not without honor except in his own country, among his own relatives, and in his own house." (Mark 6:2–4, emphasis added)

Where is a prophet without honor? Too often it is in his home and among his own. David encountered this situation when he came home to bless his household. His victory was celebrated in the streets but despised under his roof. Michal missed the blessing God had foreordained for her. David had the power to bless his house. How much more Jesus was empowered to bless His own! Though He was unlimited in the power to bless, He could do nothing for them. (See 2 Sam. 6.)

Only those with hungry, teachable, and humble hearts after God could see the hand of God on Jesus and receive from Him. He was the very Sword who divided His people and located the hearts of those who were truly after God, and those who merely had a form of godliness but were blinded by insubordinate hearts. As Simeon said to Mary, His mother, "This child is destined to cause the falling and rising of many in Israel, and to be a sign that will be spoken against, so that the thoughts of many hearts will be revealed. And a sword will pierce your own soul too" (Luke 2:34–35 NIV).

John 1:11–12 delineates these two divided groups: "He came to His own, and His own did not receive Him. But as many as received Him, to them He gave the right to become children of God." This holds a fundamental truth for all of us. *Many times God will send us what we need in a package we don't want.* This very presentation will manifest the true condition of our heart, exposing whether we are submitted to His authority or resistant to it. Jesus said, "You know neither Me nor My Father. If you had known Me, you would have known My Father also" (John 8:19). Those who know the Father recognize His authority manifested in those He sends! It doesn't have to be explained, taught, or proved.

This explains why a minister can go to Africa and see blind eyes opened, the disabled walk, and the deaf hear, then come to America and see only a few headaches or minor back problems healed. I could give numerous examples. In Africa, the man or woman is received as sent by God, no matter the appearance or packaging. Because the person is received and honored this way, the precious African people are blessed by God's power and His presence. In America if the packaging is not just right, honor is withheld. It is proportional. To the degree you receive and honor the messenger as sent by God is the degree you receive from God through the person. Dishonor, and this will be your reception. Give great honor, and honor will be your portion.

WILL YOU BE MY BUDDY?

When I was youth pastor, I had an interesting encounter with a fifteen-year-old named "Tim." Before I joined the ministry, Tim had been involved in the previous youth pastor's group. The pastor had built the group through activities, outings, and sports. Problems among the young people included insubordination, teen pregnancies, and other moral issues. As time passed the senior pastor had to release him, and I was brought on. The former youth pastor went a few miles down the road and started his own church with a handful of young people. Tim was one of those who did not go with him.

Even though most of the young people stayed, I had to lay a new foundation. The Lord instructed me to spend the first six months doing nothing but preaching, praying, and worshiping. In those months I planned no social activities whatsoever. Needless to say, I was a package many were not expecting. As a result, the sword of the Lord passed through. Some left, others stayed out of curiosity, and still others responded enthusiastically; many are in ministry today.

I'd been in that position for approximately four months when I spoke with Tim one evening after service. He asked sincerely, "Pastor

John, will you be my buddy? My last youth pastor was my buddy." I did not fit his desired package.

His question was not to be taken lightly, and I looked inside to hear how I should respond. The answer quickly came in the form of a question: "Tim, Jesus said, 'He who receives a prophet in the name of a prophet shall receive a prophet's reward' (Matt. 10:41). Well, this applies to a youth pastor as well. If you receive a pastor in the name of a pastor, you'll receive a pastor's reward."

I continued, "Tim, you have a lot of buddies, don't you?"

He responded, "Yes, sir."

"But you have only one youth pastor, right?"

He responded, "Yes, sir."

I asked, "What do you want: a buddy's reward, or a youth pastor's reward? Because the way you receive me is what you get from God."

It was as though a light went on inside him. I saw his eyes register the revelation, and he quickly answered, "I want a youth pastor's reward. I see what you're saying." He flourished from that point forward. He moved a few years later, but he still sought me out whenever I came through his city.

MY OWN EXPERIENCE

I could write an entire book on this subject alone. My heart breaks when I see the way people have not received from God because they do not honor His servants by receiving them. In the ministry I've seen this countless times: those hardest to reach are those who take God's servants for granted. I have found them often in churches and Christian schools in the United States. They are already filled to a level of drowsiness from a constant buffet of ministries passing through, and I am but one entrée in their long line of choices.

Quite possibly the easiest people to preach to are those in the military with an understanding of authority. Next would be prisoners or people in developing nations because they are desperate and hungry. God spoke to Ezekiel in similar terms:

You are not being sent to a people of obscure speech and difficult language, but to the house of Israel . . . Surely if I had sent you to them, they would have listened to you. But the house of Israel is not willing to listen to you because they are not willing to listen to me, for the whole house of Israel is hardened and obstinate.(Ezek. 3:5–7 NIV)

To Israel, Ezekiel was yet another prophet, and he was sterner than the others, who preached what the people wanted to hear, so they did not receive him.

God confused me one day with this declaration: *I am going to send you to places that will not receive you.*

I questioned, "Wait a minute. You're going to send me to places that before You send me, You already know they will not receive what I have to say. Why?"

The Lord responded, *They will never be able to say I did not give them a chance.*

I have gone to those places, and while I was there I thought, *Why did they even invite me? They are acting as if they don't want me here.* Other times I have gone to places where—from the moment I was picked up at the airport until the time I was dropped off again—I was met with excitement and treated with kindness and honor, both before and after the services. I was welcomed to my hotel room with a beautiful basket filled with fruit and snacks, and I was constantly asked, "Do you need anything?" I often felt like a broken record, "I'm fine. I'm fine." Looking back, I see that the greatest testimonies of lives or churches being changed came from such places. At first I was uncomfortable when I was treated so well, or applauded when I was introduced. I thought, *I am just like the rest of you. Don't do this.* But I soon learned it was not about me.

Bit by bit, God showed me, *Allow them to honor you for their sake, not yours.* It became easier when I realized they were honoring not me, but the gift of God on my life. Their positive response opened their hearts to receive from Jesus what He had to give them through me as a vessel. Instead of pride I felt a deepening sense of humility and dependence developing within me. I knew it was His choosing, not my ability.

I would direct their honor to Him and acknowledge my dependence on Him immediately. The ones who gave honor received easily; those who didn't were harder to reach.

DOUBLE HONOR

Paul instructed, "Let the elders who rule well be counted worthy of double honor, especially those who labor in the word and doctrine" (1 Tim. 5:17). Paul said "double honor," in other words, twice the honor you'd give someone in a place of secular authority.

If this scripture is read in context, it actually includes the way we financially honor ministers. He continued, "The laborer is worthy of his wages" (v. 18). The Amplified Bible brings this out in no uncertain terms: "Let the elders who perform the duties of their office well be considered doubly worthy of honor [and of adequate financial support], especially those who labor faithfully in preaching and teaching. For the Scripture says . . . The laborer is worthy of his hire" (1 Tim. 5:17–18).

This principle doesn't fail. If church members take care of their pastors and leaders who serve them, businessmen and other members prosper and are blessed. They enjoy heaven's economy. But if they are stingy, I have found these people complaining of theft and lack, or the bad conditions of this present world's economy.

I realize this truth has been abused, especially by ministers in America. I grieve when ministers constantly talk about money and material things. They have a truth, but have lost the heartbeat of ministry and have veered to the path of hirelings. That was how the Pharisees lived. They caused many to draw back from honoring principles in which God desired them to walk because they saw the abuse. This in turn hurts the people under their care who need the truth presented in a healthy manner.

I saw this harm the first year I traveled. I was at a small church of a little over one hundred members. The meetings went well, and the people were precious. We stayed with the pastor and his wife and realized things were tight. She worked full-time as a flight attendant and was not able to minister to the people as she desired. She didn't want to quit and draw a salary she felt would be too much from the church. I understood where they were coming from. The pastor and I were formerly employed by the church I mentioned earlier. Our pastor there was exorbitant with teaching on finances and offerings. Both of us were cautious, not wanting to do the same, and without realizing it we leaned too heavily in the other direction. However, God was teaching me that extremes either way were not good. He wanted a truer balance.

The meetings had begun Sunday morning and continued through Wednesday night. The first three were good, but something seemed to be holding the church back. All day Tuesday the Lord dealt with my heart about this man and the way finances were being handled. I couldn't shake it, yet I wondered what I could possibly do.

Right before the service the pastor told me he wanted me to receive our ministry's offering that night. His exact words as he turned over the service were, "I give you liberty in the offering."

I was delighted. I realized God had opened this door so I could do what He had dealt with me about. That night I ministered along the lines of what I've been writing. We read the scripture in 1 Timothy, and I told them this pastor and his wife were not being properly cared for financially. I made it clear to the church that the time had come when it was wrong for her to fly out every three or four days in order to support their family. I shared how the pastor had given me liberty in the offering, but we would not be receiving it for our ministry. We wanted the offering to go to the pastor and his wife instead. The people became really excited about this opportunity to bless their pastor and responded in turn. The offering that night was three times the largest one ever received! The pastor's wife was in tears, and he was stunned.

You'd be amazed if I wrote all the breakthroughs that happened over the next twenty-four hours. One couple received a ten-thousand-dollar check the following day; another found an envelope in his door with a fifteen-hundred-dollar check in it. That was only the beginning. By the next Sunday morning, the testimonies were so great and numerous, the pastor never preached. The entire service consisted of people testifying what God had done in their businesses or personal lives that week financially. The pastor later sent me the tape of the unplanned service.

The church exploded with growth the next two years. They bought a new building and grew to five hundred. They had hovered around the one-hundred mark for several years. This and countless other examples have taught me that God wants us to honor those who labor among us for our sake.

I have been in developing world nations and nearly wept when I saw the way the churches treated me. Monetarily, it may have been small by American standards, for I'd received much larger offerings at some of the churches that were indifferent in America. What touched me the most was the love behind the gift of these grateful people. It was no different from the widow Jesus said gave more than all the rest, even though the amount she gave was the least. She honored God with her gift. These precious saints honor and appreciate the servants God sends to them. Let this permeate your heart. Seek to honor the men and women who labor among you in the Word of God.

THOSE WHOM LEADERS APPOINT

Let's look again at Jesus' words: "Most assuredly, I say to you, he who receives whomever I send receives Me" (John 13:20). In the book of Matthew, Jesus actually described the chain of order: the Father sent Jesus, and Jesus sends the fivefold ministers. If we receive His appointed ministers, we receive Him, and by receiving Him, we receive the Father.

The chain of order does not stop with the fivefold ministers. It continues to those appointed by the ministers. I'll never forget what came out of my mouth while preaching in the South. The church had a good pastor. He walked in his authority to protect the people, and they respected him. However, this respect did not continue down through the rest of the staff and workers. I observed those who did not honor persons he appointed, such as ushers, secretaries, greeters, and associate pastors.

At the service I was ministering in a prophetic mode. When I preach this way, many times I hear the words as they come out of my mouth. I pointed to one church worker and sternly said, "How you treat this person is how you treat this pastor. The way you treat him is the way you actually respond to Jesus."

You should have seen the eyes of some church members. The light of revelation went on and exposed their attitudes. It was a healthy church, and the people gladly received correction. The words actually ministered to me as well. When I minister at a church or attend my home church, I give honor to those the pastor appoints, including ushers, staff, secretaries, associate pastors, and parking lot attendants. They have been appointed by the pastor, who has been appointed by Jesus, who is appointed by the Father. It is all about seeing God's authority in the people we encounter.

An excellent scriptural example is the story of Naaman, commander of the Syrian army. He had leprosy and had no hope of a cure. His Hebrew servant girl told him there was a prophet in Israel who could heal him by the power of the Lord God of Israel.

The king of Syria gave him permission and sent Naaman to the king of Israel, who directed him to Elisha's house: "Then Naaman went with his horses and chariot, and he stood at the door of Elisha's house. And Elisha sent a messenger to him, saying, 'Go and wash in the Jordan seven times, and your flesh shall be restored to you, and you shall be clean'" (2 Kings 5:9–10).

When he heard that, Naaman became furious. He said, "Indeed, I said to myself, 'He will surely come out to me, and stand and call on the name of the Lord his God, and wave his hand over the place, and heal the leprosy'" (v. 11).

His wrong expectation caused him to almost reason away what God was willing to provide. He would have gladly received Elisha if he had come out, but not a mere servant or employee; after all, Naaman was an important man. He was insulted by the lack of direct contact with Elisha. Yet as a commander, he should have understood delegated authority. The good news is, his servant convinced him otherwise, and he went and washed seven times in the River Jordan and was made perfectly whole. It happened exactly as the servant-employee said. After all he was under the man of God's authority.

I become sad when I hear of churches where attendance drops any-time the pastor is away. These people show their lack of understanding of true authority. If hearts are right, the people will receive just as effec-tively from an associate or traveling minister because each was appointed by the pastor. The pastor stands in Jesus' stead. If we under-stand kingdom authority, we realize it is not a personality contest, but the authority vested in the man, which traces back to Jesus.

As believers, we should honor civil leaders, employers, teachers, and others who are appointed. We should honor parents or husbands, and when we do, we are promised a reward. Finally, let us give double honor to those who serve in the ministry, especially those who labor in teaching and ministering the Word of God.

CHAPTER 11

OBEDIENCE AND SUBMISSION

We can obey and not necessarily be submissive.

Submission quite possibly causes the greatest number of misunderstandings among believers. We will address difficult issues in these next three chapters. Over the past ten years as I taught on being under cover, I repeatedly heard questions like these:

- Is obedience unconditional?

- What if I don't agree with my leader's decisions?

- What if authority is making bad decisions?

- What if authority tells me to do something wrong?

- Where do I draw the line?

These are excellent questions that must be answered if we are to confidently submit to authority. To begin, let's look to the book of Hebrews:

"Obey those who rule over you, and be submissive, for they watch
out for your souls, as those who must give account. Let them do so
with joy and not with grief, for that would be unprofitable for you"
(Heb. 13:17).

The writer distinctly exhorted us to do two things: (1) to obey those who rule over us; and (2) to be submissive to those who rule over us. These are different directives, and this is where many get confused. We can obey and not necessarily be submissive. To explain, allow me to share a personal example.

NOT BEING FED

As I mentioned in an earlier chapter, I worked for a large church in the southern part of the United States after a short career in my engineering field. I served there four and a half years as a personal assistant to the pastor. It was a wonderful learning position, and the first year I was often overwhelmed that God would allow me to serve in this capacity in His kingdom. I remember thinking, *I should pay Him for letting me do this*. This honeymoon phase lasted for about a year before it began to fade, at first subtly, then it turned into a rapid decline.

The closer I got, the more flaws I saw. The newness and excitement no longer worked as camouflage. I was having a hard time reasoning away some of what I witnessed. It wasn't long before these images began to overwhelm me. I was disagreeing more often than not with the way things were being done, the way problems were handled and the decisions that were made.

Comments were made that seemed no different from the cutting remarks I'd heard in corporate America. If those mentioned were employees, I knew it was but a matter of time before they'd be fired or forced to leave on their own. Too often they were replaced by those I considered to be smooth-talking, deceptive people. Most of the newcomers seemed to be slipping into management or other key positions. My pastor seemed to enjoy being around these people more than the godly ones. He laughed and giggled at their off-color comments, yet acted disinterested and distracted in the company of sincere believers. I was baffled by his behavior, and I soon became critical.

There were other discrepancies, and I focused on all of them. It was an international ministry, which was highly visible in the United States. All of the programs required a lot of manpower and money to keep the machines rolling. We had a staff of more than 250, and we possessed state-of-the-art everything. Consultants were brought in to help raise more money for the existing programs and for future ideas. I was responsible for hosting them. Alone in their company, I heard discussions of their meetings with my pastor. I would question within myself, *Is this big business or ministry?* The more I heard, the more I thought, *This is deceptive. Do these guys really care about people, or are they just in this for the money? Why would my pastor surround himself with these men?*

The whole time, I was surrounded by friends who were as critical as I was. I distinctly remember dinner at one couple's house. Both of us guys reported directly to the pastor and his wife. We discussed how we were not receiving any longer from the ministry. I remember saying, "For the last six months I haven't gotten anything out of what is being preached from the pulpit." We all agreed, except my wife, who kept quiet.

I repeatedly heard the statement, "We just aren't getting *fed* any longer." We agreed our time of serving in this ministry was coming to a close. We felt very spiritual about the whole issue and were convinced God was preparing to release us into the ministries He'd ordained for us. There was a confident sense among us that our days were coming to a close at our posts, and we were on the verge of promotion.

THE PROBLEM WAS WITH ME

A few days later while I was in prayer, God in His mercy brought to mind the issue we'd discussed at the couple's house. The phrase "not being fed" was not isolated to that evening, but continued to loudly frequent my thoughts, even as I sat under my pastor's preaching at each service. As I was pondering my present starvation from *not being fed*, the Holy Spirit firmly informed me, *The problem is not with your pastor. The problem is with you!*

I was stunned and almost in disbelief: Would God say this to me? In the past when I experienced this type of correction, many times I would hesitate a moment and challenge the accuracy of what I had heard. My mind questioned, *Are You sure You have the right person?* (As we mature, this questioning should happen less frequently because we come to realize just how little we *really* know.)

I questioned aloud, "Why is the problem with me?"

The Lord responded, *You keep bringing up the lack of being fed. The book of Isaiah states, "If you are willing and obedient, you shall eat the good of the land; but if you refuse and rebel, you shall be devoured by the sword"* (1:19–20).

I knew this scripture quite well and thought, *I have been very obedient.* But the Holy Spirit continued, *You obey everything you're told to do in this ministry, but I did not say, "If you are obedient, you shall eat the good of the land;" I said, "If you are* willing *and obedient . . . ," and willingness deals with your attitude. And your attitude stinks!*

Then He reminded me that when I was in high school, before I was born again, my favorite Wednesday night TV show was *Baretta*. Garbage day was Thursday, and the pickup was very early. The trash had to be taken out the night before, and that was my responsibility. It seemed that each week my mom would come in right at the climax of the program and ask, "Son, did you take out the garbage yet?"

My response would be, "Not yet."

My mom would say, "I want you to get up and take it out this moment."

I would respond, "Yes, ma'am," and do it.

If anyone observed my behavior, he might have commented on my obedience and been accurate. Yet under my breath I was sharply complaining, "I can't believe she always tells me to do this right in the middle of my favorite TV show. Why can't she wait ten minutes until the program's over?

The Holy Spirit said, *You were obedient, but you were not willing. Your attitude toward your mother was not right. The reason you are not being fed (eating of the good of My kingdom) in this church is that though you are obedient, you are not willing!*

I saw how my attitude toward my pastor had brought me to this place of not receiving from God as well as leading me into dangerous territory. Hebrews 13:17 concludes with these words: "For that would be unprofitable for you."

My eyes were open. I repented right away. The following Sunday I attended the same church, sat in the same seat, and listened to the same pastor teach the same series. But that morning everything was different. The heavens opened up, and I was astounded by the revelation God gave me through my pastor's teaching. I sat almost in tears, wondering what I'd missed the previous six months because of my bad attitude toward the authority that God had put me under.

When we are not submissive to our delegated authorities, we resist God's authority because they are appointed by Him! God wants us to be able to freely enjoy and benefit from the banqueting table He prepares for us through those He provides for us.

Obedience deals with our responsive *actions* toward authority. Submission deals with our *attitude* toward authority. This is where most of us miss it. God looks at our outward actions and at the hidden attitude of our hearts. David spoke these words to his son Solomon when transferring the throne to him: "As for you, my son Solomon, know the God of your father, and serve Him with a loyal heart and with a *willing mind*; for the LORD searches all hearts and understands all *the intent of the thoughts*" (1 Chron. 28:9, emphasis added).

For this reason the writer of Hebrews exhorted us not only to obey those over us, but also to be submissive. When Paul said, "Let every soul be subject to the governing authorities," obedience was coupled with a willing attitude.

SUBMISSIVE ATTITUDE BUT NOT OBEDIENT

Let's examine the words of the writer of Hebrews from another translation: "Obey your leaders and submit to their authority" (13:17 NIV). I illustrated how we can be obedient, but not be submissive. However, the converse is true. We can be submissive in attitude, but not obedient. A good example is the parable Jesus told of two sons, discussed in Chapter 3. The one son had a willing attitude: "Yes, sir, I will go and work in your vineyard." However, he did not obey. Jesus made it clear he did not do the will of his father, even though he mentally assented to it.

This is often the case in churches today. We have great intentions, nod, smile, and agree with the authorities over us: "I'll do it!" Then we don't because it just isn't important to us. I like to call it *nice rebellion*. Don't be fooled: nice rebellion is as deadly as blatant rebellion with an attitude. Neither is honored in the kingdom of God.

Jesus' riveting words to the churches in the book of Revelation confirm this. He greeted each church, "I know your deeds," or "I know your works" (Rev. 2–3). The churches had good intentions and one church called itself *alive*, but Jesus said because of their disobedience in works, they were *dead*. Remember He is the One who will "render to each one according to his deeds" (Rom. 2:6). Good intentions will not stand the judgment of God. Only true faith, which is evidenced by corresponding works of obedience, will stand.

WHERE DO WE DRAW THE LINE

Again the command of God reads, "Obey those who rule over you, and be submissive." As I previously stated, people often ask me with all sincerity, "Where do we draw the line? Does God expect us to obey authorities, no matter what they tell us to do? What if I am told to do something that is sin?" The Bible teaches unconditional submission to authorities, but the Bible does not teach unconditional obedience. Remember, submission deals with attitude, and obedience deals with fulfillment of what we are told.

The only time—and I want to emphasize the *only* exception in which we are not to obey authorities—is when they tell us to do something that directly contradicts what God has stated in His Word. In other words, we are released from obedience only when leaders tell us to sin. However, even in those cases we are to keep a humble and submitted attitude.

Nebuchadnezzar, the king of Babylon, was brutal and destroyed many descendants of Israel and their homeland. Yet God called him His servant (Jer. 25:9; 27:5–7), again confirming that God is the One who gives authority to man. This king brought back a remnant of God's people captive to Babylon. Among them were Daniel, Shadrach, Meshach, and Abed-Nego.

This king issued a decree that required all the people to bow and worship a golden image when they heard the sound of musical instruments. The decree held consequences for those who refused: they would be thrown into a blazing furnace. The Hebrew men feared God more than the furnace and did not obey this decree, for it directly violated the second commandment God gave through Moses recorded in the Torah. They disobeyed the ordinance of man in order to obey the ordinance of God.

It was only a matter of time before their disobedience came to the attention of King Nebuchadnezzar. He was furious with Shadrach, Meshach, and Abed-Nego and had them brought before him for questioning. Listen to their reply: "O Nebuchadnezzar, we do not need to defend ourselves before you. If we are thrown into the blazing furnace, the God whom we serve is able to save us. He will rescue us from your power, Your Majesty. But even if he doesn't, Your Majesty can be sure that we will never serve your gods or worship the gold statue you have set up" (Dan. 3:16–18 NLT).

They stood firm in obedience to God's command, yet spoke to the king with respect. They addressed him as "Your Majesty"; they didn't say, "You jerk, we'll never do what you say!" To speak in this manner of disrespect would have been rebellious. We are to submit to authority, even when we must disobey their command.

We see this brought out in Peter's instructions to wives: "Wives, in the same way be submissive to your husbands so that, if any of them do not believe the word, they may be won over without words by the behavior of their wives, when they see the purity and *reverence* of your lives" (1 Peter 3:1–2 NIV, emphasis added). A wife is to obey (Titus 2:5) as well as honor her husband with a submissive attitude. Peter drew again the parallel between behavior and submission. These are then coupled with the lifestyle of purity and reverence. A wife is admonished to maintain an attitude of *reverence* toward her husband's position of authority, even though he is not a believer. She would not be required to unconditionally obey if asked to sin, but she is called to unconditional submission and honor of his authority position.

A possible example would be a believing wife who answers the phone, but her husband doesn't want to speak to the caller and instructs her, "Tell him I am not here."

An appropriate response would be, "Honey, I'm not going to lie. Would you like me to tell him you're not available?" She maintains her reverence for his position of authority, but does not obey his request for her to lie.

Peter went on to say,

> Your beauty should not come from outward adornment, such as braided hair and the wearing of gold jewelry and fine clothes. Instead, it should be that of your inner self, the unfading beauty of a gentle and quiet spirit, which is of great worth in God's sight. For this is the way the holy women of the past who put their hope in God used to make themselves beautiful. They were submissive to their own husbands, like Sarah, who obeyed Abraham and called him her master. You are her daughters if you do what is right and do not give way to fear. (1 Peter 3:3–6 NIV)

Sarah's reverence was evident in the way she honored Abraham as her master and obeyed. *Master* reflected her submissive attitude, and obedience showed she did not yield to fear. Fear is a terrible taskmaster. Fear taunts, "I cannot trust God in submitting to my husband or any other authority. I must protect myself!" Let's remember, God, not some power-hungry man, is the One who said to submit. As we obey Him, His protection becomes ours.

PERVERTING THE COMMAND

I have grieved upon hearing stories of women who took the command of unconditional submission and applied it to encompass unconditional obedience as well. I've heard cases as perverse as believing husbands who demanded their wives to watch lewd adult videos with them to provide sexual excitement, and the wives yielded because they thought they didn't have scriptural recourse. I know of husbands who demanded their wives be dishonest for them, and they did. I've heard of husbands who forbade their wives from attending any church service, and the wives actually stopped attending. These directives are not to be obeyed because they violate scripture.

Let's go further. I know of cases of husbands beating their children or wives, and the wives covering for their abuse. In other instances children were sexually molested, and the wives did nothing. This is a violation of every premise on which God establishes authority, and women in these situations need to understand that God would never want them to stand back and do nothing. If a husband is involved in life-threatening behavior, a wife should separate herself and the children from him and not return until she is sure there has been complete repentance.

Even David, a warrior and man of strength, did not hang around the palace when Saul was throwing javelins. He left and lived in the wilderness, but never lost his reverential attitude toward Saul's authority. David's submission to Saul's authority did not cease, though he fled Saul's presence and awaited either true repentance or the righteous judgment of God.

GOD BLESSES THOSE WHO WILL NOT OBEY COMMANDS TO SIN

There are other cases where authority was disobeyed. Pharaoh commanded the Hebrew midwives to kill the baby boys born to the Hebrew women. However, the Bible notes, "But the midwives feared God, and did not do as the king of Egypt commanded them, but saved the male children alive" (Ex. 1:17). God was so pleased with their behavior that Scripture records, "Because the midwives feared God, . . . He provided households for them" (v. 21). The Lord rewarded them for disobeying the command to sin.

The Sanhedrin commanded the disciples "not to speak or teach at all in the name of Jesus. But Peter and John replied, 'Judge for yourselves whether it is right in God's sight to obey you rather than God. For we cannot help speaking about what we have seen and heard'" (Acts 4:18–20 NIV). How could they obey those leaders when Jesus had already told them, "Go into all the world and preach the gospel to every creature" (Mark 16:15)? They could not! The Sanhedrin had commanded the disciples to do something against the command of Jesus, so they respectfully refused. Hear what Scripture records resulted from their decision: "And with great power the apostles gave witness to the resurrection of the Lord Jesus. And great grace was upon them all" (Acts 4:33). Their fear of God brought great blessing and power.

Yet we see the disciple's attitude of reverence or submission in Paul's response toward the same Sanhedrin. When he was brought before them, his first words of defense were, "I have lived in all good conscience before God until this day" (Acts 23:1). Upon hearing these words, the high priest Ananias commanded those who stood near Paul to strike him on the mouth. Paul then said, "God will strike you, you whitewashed wall!" We then read: "And those who stood by said, 'Do you revile God's high priest?' Then Paul said, 'I did not know, brethren, that he was the high priest; for it is written, "You shall not speak evil of a ruler of your people."'" (Acts 23:4–5).

Upon learning Ananias was a man in authority, Paul repented of his attitude and words. The disciples did not obey commands that contradicted scriptures, but they maintained a submitted attitude, for they knew, "The authorities that exist are appointed by God."

DANIEL'S DECISION TO OBEY A HIGHER LAW

In Daniel's day a law was passed that anyone who petitioned any god or man other than the king would be cast into a den of lions. Envious governors initiated the law in order to destroy Daniel. The corrupt leaders tricked King Darius into signing the law. Daniel did not even consider obedience to that law; he chose to obey God. He adhered to the psalmist's plan: "Evening and morning and at noon I will pray, and cry aloud, and He shall hear my voice" (Ps. 55:17).

Read of Daniel's actions: "Now when Daniel knew that the writing was signed, he went home. And in his upper room, with his windows open toward Jerusalem, he knelt down on his knees three times that day, and prayed and gave thanks before his God, as was his custom since early days" (Dan. 6:10).

Daniel's disobedience was reported to the king, who was forced to deliver Daniel to the lions' den. Yet Daniel's submitted attitude never wavered, even in the face of injustice. God delivered him and shut the mouth of hungry lions as he slept unharmed. When the king saw what happened, he had those who had plotted against Daniel thrown to the ravenous lions, which devoured them.

NOT ALWAYS A PLEASANT OUTCOME

God delivered these saints, but that is not always the case. We read in Hebrews,

> Others were tortured, not accepting deliverance, that they might obtain a better resurrection. Still others had trial of mockings and scourgings, yes, and of chains and imprisonment. They were stoned, they were sawn in two, were tempted, were slain with the sword. They wandered about in sheepskins and goatskins, being destitute, afflicted, tormented—of whom the world was not worthy. (11:35–38)

Those men and women received harsh and unfair treatment from leaders.

Tertullian, who was a teacher in the early church and lived from A.D. 140 to 230, reminded the Roman leaders and citizens that their persecution only strengthened the cause of Christianity. He wrote, "The more you cut us down, the more in number we grow. The blood of Christians is seed" (*Apology*, chapter 50).

Allow me to repeat the words of this unknown Roman who described the persecuted believers,

> They dwell in their own countries simply as sojourners. They are in the flesh, but they do not live after the flesh. They pass their days on earth, but they are citizens of heaven. They obey the prescribed laws, and at the same time, they surpass the laws by their lives. Those who hate them are unable to give any reason for their hatred. (*Letter to Diognetus*, chapter 5)

They obeyed and submitted, yet surpassed mere obedience with their reverential or submitted behavior. Again, as we saw in Peter's exhortation, the behavioral response of those believers toward unfair leaders baffled them and caused some to be won to the Lord.

No Gray Areas

Whether the authority is civil, family, church, or social, God admonishes a submissive regard to be our attitude, and we are to obey in action, unless authority tells us to do what is *clearly* seen in Scripture as sin. Let me emphasize the word *clearly*. In the cases noted the believers did not obey when commanded to deny Christ, murder, worship other gods, or directly subvert a command of Jesus. They were not gray areas or judgment calls.

Here is an example of a gray area I've heard from people who work on ministry staffs: "My pastor told me not to counsel and pray for people during office hours, but that is not the love of God, and to not walk in love is sin, so I have to do it." This is a judgment call from the people under authority. It is their interpretation. The pastor is not asking them to violate the word of God. Furthermore, they are paid to type, file, do data processing, or some other form of labor, not pray.

In essence these people, because of insubordination, would actually end up stealing. If they really have hearts to pray for others, they should ask for permission from the pastor to call those who need prayer on their own time or after hours. If the pastor still is not comfortable with this idea, he may feel the employees are not properly trained to counsel the people who call the ministry for help. If the pastor has made a bad decision with this policy, he will answer to God for it, but it is not a judgment call for those under his authority. This is merely one example of hundreds, but the point remains the same: we are to disobey authority only when there is a clear violation of the Word.

You may still question, "But what if the authority in my life tells me to do something I don't agree with? Or what if my authority tells me to do something clearly foolish? Or what if authority tells me to do the opposite of what I was shown in prayer?" I will give scriptural answers to these questions in the next chapter.

CHAPTER 12

WHAT IF AUTHORITY TELLS ME . . . ?

What we are after is a revelation of authority, which is a revelation
of God Himself, for He and His authority are inseparable.

We've all encountered people who are dissatisfied with the leaders
over them. They complain about ineffective techniques or unwise decisions and how they negatively affected their lives. They complain they
were promised certain things by leaders, but they are still waiting for
those things to happen. In fact, things seem to be going backward.
They are certain their pastor has missed it and now reason that his
authority is separate from God's. This reasoning opens the door to
complaining, which eventually manifests itself as insubordinate behavior. It is only a matter of time before they're flirting with deception and
they're lured away from the authority God placed over them for growth
and protection.

WE WERE BETTER OFF WITHOUT YOU!

The children of Israel followed this pattern. There was a time when
they regarded Moses' leadership as ineffective and even detrimental to
them. However, it didn't start off that way. When Moses arrived on the
scene after his desert trek, he met with the leaders of Israel before meeting with Pharaoh. He shared how the Lord had sent him to deliver

them and bring them "up from that land to a good and large land, to a land flowing with milk and honey" (Ex. 3:8). When they heard the wonderful news, they believed Moses and worshiped God. There was an overwhelming sense of joy as they were beholding God's promised leader who would lead them out of their bondage.

Moses left the meeting, went to Pharaoh, and proclaimed the exact message God gave him on the mountain: "Thus says the LORD God of Israel: 'Let My people go'" (Ex. 5:1).

Pharaoh responded, "'Who is the LORD, that I should obey His voice to let Israel go? I do not know the LORD, nor will I let Israel go. Why do you take the people from their work?' So the same day Pharaoh increased their hardship. He angrily declared to his slave drivers, 'Load them down with more work. Make them sweat!'" (vv. 2–9 adapted from NLT).

No longer would straw be provided for the already overwhelming tally of bricks the Israelites were required to produce each day. They would have to glean by night and labor by day. The total number of bricks would not diminish, even though the straw could no longer be provided.

The Israelites scattered throughout the land searching for straw. The slave drivers were brutal. Backed by their whips, they harshly ordered, "Meet your daily quota of bricks, just as you did before!"

They beat the Israelite foremen in charge of work crews. "Why haven't you met your quotas either yesterday or today?" they demanded.

So the Israelite foremen went to Pharaoh and pleaded with him. "Please don't treat us like this," they begged. "We are given no straw, but we are still told to make as many bricks as before. We are beaten for something that isn't our fault! It is the fault of your slave drivers for making such unreasonable demands."

But Pharaoh replied, "You're just lazy! You obviously don't have enough to do. If you did, you wouldn't be saying, 'Let us go, so we can offer sacrifices to the LORD.' Now, get back to work! No straw will be given to you, but you must still deliver the regular quota of bricks."

Since Pharaoh would not let up on his demands, the Israelite foremen could see that they were in serious trouble. As they left Pharaoh's court, they met Moses and Aaron, who were waiting outside for them.

"May the LORD judge you for getting us into this terrible situation with Pharaoh and his officials. You have given them an excuse to kill us!" (Ex. 5:13–21 adapted from NLT)

The people of Israel were now upset with Moses' leadership. His preaching and directives had brought affliction and hardship on them. They began to separate his authority from God's authority as evidenced by their calling down divine judgment on him.

It was Moses' fault. If he had let them alone, Pharaoh wouldn't have dealt with them so severely. They failed to realize that God, not the devil or some confused leader, orchestrated the turn of events. Nothing had transpired outside His master plan or foreknowledge. The Lord commanded Moses to speak to Pharaoh. God, not the devil or even Moses, hardened Pharaoh's heart! This is clear as we read in several passages, "The LORD hardened Pharaoh's heart, and he did not let the children of Israel go out of his land" (Ex. 11:10; see also Ex. 9:12; 10:1, 20, 27). The harder Pharaoh's heart became, the more miserable life was for the descendants of Abraham.

After much tribulation, the Israelites were freed from Egypt, only to wander in a vast desert. Without water and with the supplies of food dwindling, they again began to wonder: Hadn't Moses promised them liberty and abundance? "A good and large land, a land flowing with milk and honey." It was large all right, but as far from good as you could get, with no milk or honey in sight! Was that his idea of freedom and provision? Was he really sent by God?

After three days of lack, Moses led them to a place called Marah where they found water. They probably thought, *okay, maybe things will start turning around.* However, they soon discovered they could not drink the waters for they were bad. They couldn't believe it, and an uproar of disbelief arose from the followers. Their criticisms became sharper as they murmured to one another and to Moses. Discontent-ment spread unchecked like a cancer that infected the entire congregation. Maybe Moses knew enough only to get the people out, but not enough to get them in.

The people complained to Moses and Aaron, "If only we had died by the LORD's hand in Egypt! There we sat around pots of meat and ate all the food we wanted, but you have brought us out into this desert to starve this entire assembly to death" (Ex. 16:3 NIV).

They'd had it. Moses' leadership skills were proving to be futile in many ways. Wasn't life better for them before he'd come into authority? All they'd known was tremendous stress and hardship from his preaching in Egypt. Would it ever end? They escaped one hardship only to be overtaken by the next. Their leader promised land flowing with milk and honey, but they saw only parched ground, snakes, and scorpions in the desert. Their leader must have missed a turn somewhere, or possibly he was evil. At least under Pharaoh they had food. Moses seemed intent on torture and starvation. Life had been better in Egypt! Their complaining escalated to the point that they said to one another, "Let us select a leader and return to Egypt" (Num. 14:4).

But hear the word that Moses delivered to those who were fed up with the God-appointed leader: "The LORD hears your complaints which you make against Him. And what are we? Your complaints are not against us but against the LORD" (Ex. 16:8).

Those men and women thought their insubordination was against Moses and not in any way connected to God. They thought they had successfully separated the two. They lived by reasoning instead of by the principle of obedience. Those who walk by the limited reasoning produced by sight and circumstances find themselves on the path of folly. They will not fulfill their destiny whereas those who recognize and obey authority enter the promises, just as Joshua and Caleb did.

What If I Discern . . . ?

You may consider yourself wiser than the children of Israel who judged by the obvious and the immediate effects of their leader's decisions. You may fancy yourself more spiritual, like Joshua. You would have discerned Moses was right and never responded as the children of Israel did; you would have been right there with Joshua.

That may be true, but we must be cautious before making such assumptions. The Pharisees adamantly insisted, "If we had lived in the days of our forefathers, we would not have taken part with them"

(Matt. 23:30 NIV), yet Jesus said they had the same spirit of their forefathers. It is always easy to see right from wrong when the whole matter has been played out and books have been written. What separated Joshua from the rest of his peers was not his discernment, but his ability to recognize and submit to true authority. Out of that came true discernment.

I hear disapproving tones echoed in the voices of many who claim to be discerning, yet have insubordinate hearts. Even as I write this book, I've just received a letter in the past twenty-four hours in which I had to deal with an "I'll submit as long as I agree" attitude coupled with the "ability to discern." Those who think like this mistakenly believe they have a sure way out of true submission.

WHO PUT HIM IN THAT POSITION?

You may question, "What if I discern that my leader is not making a very good choice? Should I still obey him, knowing he is headed for misfortune?" As I look back at my serving years, I remember many times when I felt this frustration: "They're making a bad decision! They're missing God! They've been negatively influenced. I just can't submit to this!" Yet more often than not, my unbroken heart was manifesting its independence.

I'd served as an administrative assistant to my pastor for a year and found myself questioning many decisions. I saw his directives as they crossed my desk before being distributed to the department heads. Countless times I thought his decisions unwise and murmured in my heart against them. One day the Spirit spoke to me, *I have a question for you.*

Experience has taught me, when God questions me, He is about to expose my faulty wisdom. I responded, "Yes, Lord?"

Did I put you in the position of pastor, or did I put him in the position of pastor?

I said, "You put him in the position."

The Lord quickly said, *That is right. Therefore, I will show him things I don't need to show you, and many times I will keep the wisdom of his decision from you on purpose, to see if you will follow him as he follows Me.*

Usually months later, the wisdom of the pastor's decision would surface. I'd see it, lights would go on, and I'd realize once again I'd been led astray by my reasoning, by exalting it higher than the principle of obedience. This very thing causes splits in churches, homes, and businesses. God did not limit our submission to authorities to the times when we see their wisdom, agree with them, or like what they tell us. He just said, "Obey!"

Later the Lord spoke to my heart, *John, if I intended for every believer to get all his information, wisdom, and direction only from prayer and communion with Me, then I'd never have instituted authority in the church. I placed authorities in the church with the full intent that My children could not get all they needed just from their prayer life. They would have to learn to recognize and hear My voice through their leaders as well.*

It's not our responsibility to make calls on leadership decisions or even to judge the results after the fact. The One who put that person in authority will. If the Israelites had been allowed to judge Moses' decisions, he would have come out on the short end of the stick, and they would have returned to Egypt.

Leaders will be judged, and we will be judged. Leaders will be judged for their decisions, and their judgment will be more severe than ours. For this reason Jesus warned, "For everyone to whom much is given, from him much will be required; and to whom much has been committed, of him they will ask the more" (Luke 12:48). And James warned as well, "Dear brothers and sisters, not many of you should become teachers in the church, for we who teach will be judged by God with greater strictness" (3:1 NLT).

On the other hand, our judgment will be relative to our submission, for authority is of God. To resist delegated authority is to resist God's authority. We should not take upon ourselves the pressure to discern beforehand whether leaders are right or not. Nor should we judge after the fact. This is not our burden, but God's. He alone knows and can change hearts as He so desires.

THE LEADER'S HEART IS IN GOD'S HANDS

Returning to the testimony I gave in Chapter 2, when my pastor announced the cancellation of home fellowships for the church, not only did I believe he was wrong, but I also believed he was influenced to make this decision against me. There was another dynamic I haven't mentioned that revolved around my superior, the office manager. He did not like me and was building a case to see me fired.

To accomplish this, he erected a wall of separation between me and the senior pastor by giving negative reports to each of us about the other. Most were blatantly not true. In addition, he had launched a memo campaign of sorts to the entire staff that specifically targeted me. Employees would say to my wife, who also was on staff, "why doesn't he just put your husband's name on this?" I knew what he was doing, but my hands were tied.

When the senior pastor canceled the home cells, I saw it as yet another attack against me because of the lies and suspicion sown by this manager. I was certain I was "discerning" accurately. I felt further justified and more unwilling to yield to the senior pastor's authority. After all he had been misled and was making a bad decision, I reasoned. How could God want eight months of hard work washed down the drain along with the potential of many salvations? For all these reasons I was relentless as I challenged the senior pastor for twenty minutes in that meeting. I left feeling righteous and justified—only to be rebuked by the Holy Spirit when I reached my home. Then the deep realization came to me: I was dealing not with a man's authority, but with God's.

Shortly afterward the Lord burned a scripture into my heart. It brought clarity to similar situations, and direction in the midst of difficulty:

The king's heart is in the hand of the LORD,
Like the rivers of water;
He turns it wherever He wishes. (Prov. 21:1)

The king represents one in authority over you. Whether he is godly or harsh, his heart is still in the hand of the Lord. The verse doesn't say, "The good king's heart is in the hand of the Lord." It doesn't matter how he has been influenced; his heart remains in the hand of the Lord. For it doesn't say, "As long as the king has not been wrongly influenced, his heart can be turned by the Lord."

WHAT IF WE *KNOW* IT IS A BAD DECISION?

What if we aren't discerning, but are sure that authority is making a bad decision? What if we have concrete evidence the leader was influenced by an evil report? Is there no recourse? Can't we do something to help our leader? The answer is yes.

Esther is a good example of these situations. Abraham's children were captive under Persian rule. An evil plan was hatched by the wicked Haman, who influenced the Persian king Xerxes to sign a decree to kill all the Jews. The king himself set the day.

Queen Esther was a descendant of Abraham but had not acknowledged the fact at her uncle Mordecai's urging. But Mordecai went to Esther and asked her to go before the king on her people's behalf. He understood that for her to do so might mean her death. She had everything to lose and nothing to gain; she was queen and her secret was safe.

Esther made the decision to appeal to the king. After fasting three days, she approached King Xerxes' inner court, and God caused the king to look favorably upon her. He asked her request, and she petitioned the king to attend a banquet she would hold for both the king and Haman. He consented and he and Haman joined her for a meal.

Later that evening, the king could not sleep. He ordered his servants to read the chronicles to him. From the readings he remembered Mordecai the Jew had saved his life, and yet was never rewarded. The king was contemplating a manner in which to honor him and consulted Haman for advice. Haman mistakenly imagined the king was referring to him and came up with an elaborate way to honor the unidentified man. The king then revealed it was Mordecai and had Haman carry out the honor on his behalf, much to Haman's displeasure. God was already at work preparing this king's heart for the words Esther would bring at the banquet.

Once Esther had the king and Haman together at another banquet, the king asked again her request.

> "If Your Majesty is pleased with me and wants to grant my request, my petition is that my life and the lives of my people will be spared. For my people and I have been sold to those who would kill, slaughter, and annihilate us. If we had only been sold as slaves, I could remain quiet, for that would have been a matter too trivial to warrant disturbing the king." (Est. 7:3–4 NLT)

There are a couple of things to note. First, the king had made an obvious terrible and uninformed decision, yet she still spoke to him with respect, maintaining a submitted heart. Second, she gave her wisdom with great humility and in the light of his good, not just hers. She petitioned, but allowed him to make the final decision. She did not say, "You foolish husband, you have listened to a murderer. Don't you realize all you will lose by this command you have given?" She counted on one thing: that God would turn his heart. The Lord did turn his counsel, and the king hanged the wicked man Haman. The Jewish people were spared from being slaughtered.

Esther had concrete evidence, not just discernment, that her leader lacked the true facts. She went to him in humility and made her presentation in such a way the king was in position to make the decision. She did not belittle, force, or manipulate him. She just trusted in the power of the Holy Spirit to direct her lord's heart.

Not Having All the Facts

We see this in Scripture not only when a leader is wrongly influenced, but if a leader actually makes a decision before having all the facts or before hearing the whole matter. We have an example in David and King Saul. The Philistine giant defied the armies of God repeatedly for forty days. He challenged Israel to send out a champion to fight, so the matter could be settled by one fight. David saw all the soldiers terrified and not able to respond to the giant's threats. God put it in his heart to fight. But King Saul looked at him and said, "No way. You're just a kid and when you lose, we will all have to serve this army!" (author's paraphrase).

When David heard that, he did not argue, but entreated him,

> Your servant used to keep his father's sheep, and when a lion or a bear came and took a lamb out of the flock, I went out after it and struck it, and delivered the lamb from its mouth; and when it arose against me, I caught it by its beard, and struck and killed it. Your servant has killed both lion and bear; and this uncircumcised Philistine will be like one of them, seeing he has defied the armies of the living God . . . The LORD, who delivered me from the paw of the lion and from the paw of the bear, He will deliver me from the hand of this Philistine. (1 Sam. 17:34–37)

There was respect in his manner when he presented the information to authority. He presented what he knew the king lacked in his initial decision. After that, David trusted in God's ability to turn his leader's heart. He trusted that what God placed in his heart would come to pass through the king's decision. By remaining humble and submissive, he kept God actively involved. The Lord turned Saul's heart and he said, "Go, and the LORD be with you!" (1 Sam 17:34–37).

TRUE INTERCESSION

Another scriptural example of petitioning a leader after he made his decision is found with Abigail. She was married to a harsh and evil rich man named Nabal. David was in need of food because Saul continued to threaten his life. David sent a request to Nabal for supplies; he knew it was festival time, and there would be abundance. David had previously protected Nabal's servants and never taken anything from him.

Not only did Nabal deny David's request, but he insulted him as well. Nabal's behavior infuriated David, and he rallied four hundred of his men to take revenge. He was going to destroy Nabal and all who were his.

Word reached Abigail, Nabal's wife, and she hurriedly prepared a gift offering of bread, wine, meat, grain, raisins, and figs. She then rode out in the direction of David to intercept him and his men. When she saw them, she dismounted and fell on her face before David. Then she made this plea:

> On me, my lord, on me let this iniquity be! And please let your maid-servant speak in your ears, and hear the words of your maidservant. Please, let not my lord regard this scoundrel Nabal. For as his name is, so is he: Nabal is his name, and folly is with him. But I, your maid-servant, did not see the young men of my lord whom you sent. Now therefore, my lord, as the LORD lives and as your soul lives, since the LORD has held you back from coming to bloodshed and from aveng-ing yourself with your own hand, now then, let your enemies and those who seek harm for my lord be as Nabal. And now this present which your maidservant has brought to my lord, let it be given to the young men who follow my lord. Please forgive the trespass of your maidservant. For the LORD will certainly make for my lord an endur-ing house, because my lord fights the battles of the LORD, and evil is not found in you throughout your days . . . But when the LORD has dealt well with my lord, then remember your maidservant. (1 Sam. 25:24–31)

Allow me to bring out point by point all this woman did for her husband, for her household, and for David:

1. She addressed David with great respect, representing herself repeatedly as his servant.

2. She took David and his men a generous gift, reflecting her care and regard for their welfare.

3. She interceded for her household by taking on the

responsibility as her own. She actually called it her "trespass."

4. She pointed out to David with fear and trembling that for him to bring such bloodshed would be sin.

5. She reminded David it was God who avenged him and fulfilled the promises made to him.

6. She asked David to remember her when he was promoted.

You may question, "How did this woman honor her husband?" She spared him from slaughter. Her husband sinned against those men and the Lord's anointed. To justify his behavior would have given David all the more reason to take vengeance. She would have added fuel to his fire and encouraged his doom. What good is superficial honor that ends in the death of your husband?

For her to truly dishonor Nabal would have been for her to say, "I'm getting out of here and letting my husband get what he deserves because he is a jerk." Or if she had gone to David and said, "Listen, I had nothing to do with this. I would have given you what you needed. When I heard what my unreasonable husband did, I came with some food for you and your men, but go ahead with your plans to kill him, for he is a jerk and scoundrel. He deserves whatever you do to him." Those actions would have dishonored her husband.

Intercession on someone's behalf does not mean you ignore the transgression; rather you acknowledge it. Then you place yourself in between him and judgment. You say, in essence, "I know he deserves judgment, but I plead for mercy. I'll take it upon myself and stand in his stead."

That was exactly what Abigail did. David came to bring judgment, and Abigail came to plead mercy. In her exact words, "Please forgive the trespass of your maidservant."

She spoke in this manner to prevent David from committing the sin of taking revenge for himself. God's Word commands, "You shall not take vengeance, nor bear any grudge against . . . your people" (Lev. 19:18). She sought mercy as she stood in the gap, and she sought righteousness for David.

Abigail wasn't gossiping to the neighbors or her friends, "You know I am married to a scoundrel. He is the biggest loser I have ever known." Nor did she speak to David about her husband out of spite, anger, disgust, disrespect, or revenge. She spoke to save lives. Hear what her intercession accomplished:

> Then David said to Abigail: "Blessed is the LORD God of Israel, who sent you this day to meet me! And blessed is your advice and blessed are you, because you have kept me this day from coming to blood-shed and from avenging myself with my own hand. For indeed, as the LORD God of Israel lives, who has kept me back from hurting you, unless you had hurried and come to meet me, surely by morning light no males would have been left to Nabal!" So David received from her hand what she had brought him, and said to her, "Go up in peace to your house. See, I have heeded your voice and respected your person." (1 Sam. 25:32–35)

When Abigail returned home, her husband was holding a feast for himself. He had no idea what had almost happened. She chose to say nothing to him that evening. The next morning she told him how she had saved his life. His heart turned to stone when he heard. Ten days later the Lord killed Nabal. It was not at the hands of David or Abigail, but by God's hand that vengeance was taken on the wicked man.

FOR THE SAKE OF THE ONE IN AUTHORITY

Moses found himself in a position where he was compelled to question an Authority's decision—God's! That happened more than once. Let's look at the first account. Israel had sinned by building a golden calf, then worshiping it. God was so angry, He told Moses He would kill them all and make a nation out of Moses. Listen to Moses' entreaty:

> Then Moses pleaded with the LORD his God, and said: "LORD, why does Your wrath burn hot against Your people whom You have brought out of the land of Egypt with great power and with a mighty hand? Why should the Egyptians speak, and say, 'He brought them out to harm them, to kill them in the mountains, and to consume them from the face of the earth'? Turn from Your fierce wrath, and relent from this harm to Your people. Remember Abraham, Isaac, and Israel, Your servants, to whom You swore by Your own self, and said to them, 'I will multiply your descendants as the stars of heaven; and all this land that I have spoken of I give to your descendants, and they shall inherit it forever.'" (Ex. 32:11–13)

There are several things to point out. First, Moses spoke in complete submission and with fear and trembling. Second, Moses pleaded passionately or petitioned God; he never commanded. Third, he spoke on God's behalf, first and foremost, not the people's. In essence Moses was communicating, "What about Your reputation that You worked four hundred years to establish? Your name is now known all over the earth, but You will tarnish it by not being able to finish what You began." Since Moses did it primarily for the Lord's sake, he could challenge God's decision. His motive was not for himself but for others.

We must ask ourselves before petitioning a leader, "Who is this primarily for?" Even when Moses reminded God of His promise to Abraham, it was still primarily for the Lord's sake. He reminded God of the importance of His word. Moses had the right focus because his heart was right. He was God's servant, so he thought first of Him before thinking of himself or the children of Israel. Here is God's response: "So the LORD relented from the harm which He said He would do to His people" (Ex. 32:14).

God changed His mind! The decision was reversed. I would like to make another important point. Moses could speak in such a direct manner to God because he had proved again and again his loyalty. To bring the principle to our day, there are staff members who've proved their faithfulness to Lisa and me over the years. They have greater favor and an ability to petition us more quickly than others who just started working for us. You have to earn the right to speak into a leader's life. You accomplish this through loyalty, integrity, and faithfulness. Not everyone has the ability to speak into a leader's life in this manner.

Another significant point is that Moses did not talk about God's decision to others, he talked to God about His decision. The Lord was repeatedly angered by the children of Israel because they constantly murmured their disagreement with His ways among themselves. This is also called complaining, and God hates it! This behavior is very dangerous and should be avoided at all cost. When we murmur among ourselves and complain against the decision made by our authorities, we are sowing dissension and rebellion. We will see in another chapter that this brings certain judgment.

I have an agreement with the people who work for me. If I make a decision they believe is uninformed, they can petition me once, or if new facts surface that may aid in the decision, they can petition me again. When they petition, it is important that they have carefully thought it through and they present it in such a way that helps me see what they wish to communicate. I have often changed a decision when I've seen new information. However, if they petition me, and I stay with the original decision, then we move forward in agreement. If we move forward in unity, and I am wrong, God still protects us. He will protect me as well as those under me if we acted out of integrity of heart. David said, "Let integrity and uprightness preserve me, for I wait for You" (Ps. 25:21).

WHAT IF IT GOES AGAINST WHAT GOD SHOWED ME?

You may still question, "What if authority tells me the opposite of what I felt to do in prayer?" This is a good question and needs to be addressed. To answer, let me return to the example I gave in the second chapter. Before starting the entire "party" program, I earnestly sought the Lord in prayer, and I was sure He instructed me to do so. To this day, I still fully believe He told me to do the home groups because the whole episode proved to be a test for me to see whether I would obey the authority He placed over me.

Scripture is full of examples of God testing His people. When God told Abraham to offer Isaac as a burnt offering, Scripture specifically states, "God tested Abraham" (Gen. 22:1). The Lord never intended for Abraham to kill his son, yet He allowed Abraham to head toward the mountain for three days and did not stop him until he raised the knife. God saw Abraham's unwavering faithfulness in his actions of obedience. Does He see the same in us today?

The apostle Paul told the Corinthian church to do something in his first letter that he altered in his second one. Once he changed his orders to the church, he made this remarkable statement:

> "For this was my purpose in writing you, to test your attitude and see if you would stand the test, whether you are obedient and altogether agreeable [to following my orders] in everything" (2 Cor. 2:9 AMPLIFIED).

Paul gave them the orders for one purpose: to see whether they would submit to his authority. I have a very wise friend who has been a pastor for years. He told me the way he finds insubordination among his workers is to give a directive that makes no sense. He said, "John, I'll soon hear the gripes and complaints of the rebellious. I deal with it, then change the directive back to normal operations."

Paul gave the command to see whether they would follow his orders in *everything*. The key word is *everything*. His command was difficult, which in itself carried a purpose as well. The purpose: if they followed this directive, they would follow anything else.

That was exactly what God did with Abraham. He found the most difficult thing for Abraham to submit to: he was to give up what was most important in his life, the promise he waited twenty-five years for. It wasn't Abraham's doing; rather, one that God promised him in prayer. It would have been easier for Abraham to put himself on that altar, but God wanted the most important thing. If Abraham was obedient in that matter, he would be obedient in all things!

My senior pastor told me to give up what was the most difficult. I had worked on it for months, and everyone knew it. In my eyes it seemed to hold the promise of lost souls coming into the kingdom. It was my key to whether I'd have a successful youth ministry. My reputation was at stake because I told everyone it was God's will. I had heard that I was to go forward with the program in prayer. I didn't know it was a test, and often God's tests are never recognized until after the fact since they always expose our hearts.

My parties might have brought many souls into the kingdom, but God is more concerned that His authority is manifested in our hearts than that of our own methods accomplish His work. He is God; He has many other fresh ideas of how to reach lost souls. What cannot be done differently is the principle of submission in a man's heart, for apart from this a man cannot enter the kingdom, and there is no other alternative for an unsubmitted heart.

We must establish a critical and difficult principle within our hearts. Once God delegates His authority to men, He does not override it. The only exception occurs when a leader directly violates the written Word or laws of God. God Himself will not supersede the delegated authority He establishes. We cannot bypass delegated authority and declare ourselves subject only to God's. Moses spoke of this principle to the heads of the tribes of Israel:

> This is what the LORD commands: . . . "When a young woman still living in her father's house makes a vow to the LORD or obligates herself by a pledge and her father hears about her vow or pledge but says nothing to her, then all her vows and every pledge by which she obligated herself will stand. *But if her father forbids her when he hears about it, none of her vows or the pledges by which she obligated herself will stand; the LORD will release her because her father has forbidden her."* (Num. 30:1–5 NIV, emphasis added)

Moses further enforced this principle by applying it to a wife and her husband. God, the supreme or direct authority, upholds what delegated authority has consented to. He also annuls what delegated authority has canceled. The Lord respects His delegated authority. Since a young woman is under her father's authority, or a wife her husband's authority, God would deal with the father or the husband, but release the woman.

This principle is found in the overall counsel of the Scriptures, not just within the family unit, but in other areas of delegated authority as well. Again, I want to emphasize, the exception occurs when authorities tell us to do something that directly contradicts the commands of God. I grieve when I hear people in ministry say, "My pastor told me not to do this, but he is not hearing from God, so I am still going to do it—but in a roundabout way." It doesn't matter what you believe you've heard in prayer; you are rebelling against God's authority if it goes against the directives of authorities in your life!

The examples I could give are endless. I have discovered when revelation knowledge is burned in our hearts, many questions are answered, and numerous problems solved. This cannot be an exhaustive book of examples and explanations. What we are after is a revelation of authority, which is a revelation of God Himself, for He and His authority are inseparable. As I encouraged you in the introduction, cry out to God, and ask Him to burn the principle of godly submission in your heart as you read. If not, you'll end up with more questions than when we started.

In the next chapter we'll discover how to handle unfair treatment and how to respond to authority who is harsh with us. We'll see that God has a glorious plan for us in these situations.

CHAPTER 13

UNFAIR TREATMENT

To be broken does not mean to be weakened.
It has to do with submission to authority.

God our Father has a certain goal to accomplish in each of us. Let me warn you, it may not sound delightful, popular, or pain free, but it is what's best for us. His desire is to break us. Scripture makes this plain:

> For You do not desire sacrifice, or else I would give it;
> You do not delight in burnt offering.
> The sacrifices of God are a broken spirit,
> A broken and a contrite heart—
> These, O God, You will not despise. (Ps. 51:16–17)

> The LORD is near to those who have a broken heart,
> And saves such as have a contrite spirit. (Ps. 34:18)

A prerequisite for intimacy with the Lord is a broken heart. Even though the process is not pleasant, the closeness of His presence far outweighs the hardship involved. David learned that as a young man. You can glimpse his broken heart and what it entails throughout his psalms. It's attained not through sacrificial living or offerings, but through obedience.

BROKENNESS DEALS WITH AUTHORITY

Allow me to illustrate. A warhorse is not fit for service until his will is broken. Though he may be stronger, swifter, and more gifted than all the other horses in the stables, he cannot serve until he's broken. He will stay in the stables while less gifted horses go to war. To be broken does not mean to be weakened. It has to do with submission to authority.

In the horse's case, his master is the rider. If the horse is successfully broken and trained, he can be trusted in any and all circumstances. In the heat of the battle as the bullets or arrows fly, he will not flinch. While swords and axes are wielded, he will not retreat. While guns are raised and cannons shot, he will not deviate from his master's desires. He will stay in firm submission to his master, no matter who he is. He will bypass any attempt to protect or benefit himself in order to fulfill the commands of his rider.

This breaking process is uniquely accomplished in each individual in accordance with the prescription of the Lord Himself. He is the only One who knows when the process is truly complete, and you are prepared for the manner of service He desires to bring through you. Each new level brings another round of breaking.

I remember well the past processes I've been through. All too often I fully believed I was ready and fit for the next level of service, long before I actually was. I confidently declared, "I am fully submitted to Your Authority. I know I am ready for the ministry You have called me to." Yet the mature believers who surrounded me knew I was far from broken. Sure enough, I'd head into another round, kicking, squirming, and fighting for my rights.

WHAT ABOUT HARSH LEADERS?

As with horses, our breaking process deals with our response to authority. God customizes the perfect process for each of us, and this always entails some form of leadership. For this reason Peter wrote,

"Therefore submit yourselves to every ordinance of man for the Lord's sake . . . Servants, be submissive to your masters with all fear, not only to the good and gentle, but also to the harsh" (1 Peter 2:13, 18).

Let's put this in modern vernacular. Servants could be identified as employees, students, church members, or civilians. Masters could be employers, teachers, church leaders, or governmental leaders. Most of us have had good and gentle leaders, and we loved them. They were easy to submit to. However, God commands us to be submissive not only to the good and gentle, but also to the harsh!

The Greek word for "harsh" is *skolios*. Thayer's Greek dictionary defines the word as "crooked, perverse, wicked, unfair, and forward." Vine's dictionary defines the word as related to "tyrannical or unjust masters." Is the Lord telling us to submit to these kinds of leaders?

Let's reference a few other translations. The New Century Version reads, "Not only those who are good and kind, but also those who are dishonest." The Contemporary English Version declares, "Do this, not only to those who are kind and thoughtful, but also to those who are cruel." The New American Standard Bible states, "Not only to those who are good and gentle, but also to those who are unreasonable." We cannot overlook this command, so let's seek the wisdom of God in it.

Actually Peter's words become more uncomfortable before they get easier. He continued, "God is pleased with you when, for the sake of your conscience, you patiently endure *unfair treatment*" (1 Peter 2:19 NLT, emphasis added).

I remember an incident that happened with my wife and one of my older sons. He felt his brother got more than he did, and the treatment was unfair. He protested, "Mom, that's not fair!"

My wife calmly responded, "Son, life is not fair!"

He looked at her as if to say, "How can you say this? You're my mom."

Lisa questioned him, "Was it fair that Jesus took our punishment and died on the cross when He did nothing wrong?"

My son's eyes registered the wisdom, and he was silenced.

CHRIST'S PERSONAL EXAMPLE

Peter went on to say, "For even to this *you were called*." Whenever I am preaching from this scripture, I usually ask the people to look up from their Bibles, and I say with enthusiasm, "Everyone say these words, 'This is my calling!'" We are always talking about our call in life. Well, this is one of them. Hear what Peter said: "For even to this you were called [it is inseparable from your vocation]. For Christ also suffered for you, leaving you [His personal] example, so that you should follow in His footsteps" (1 Peter 2:21 AMPLIFIED).

How did He suffer? Peter had explained in the previous verse: unfair treatment from delegated authorities. At times, God places us in situations where we receive unreasonable treatment from authorities, as He did with David, Joseph, Daniel, the apostle Paul, and others. Our calling is to handle it correctly, and Jesus left us His personal example of how to do it.

You may now wonder, "What good does suffering harsh treatment from leaders accomplish?" The idea was against our natural minds since its logic appears absurd. However, the wisdom of God molds a submitted heart through this kind of treatment in three ways. First, it makes room for God's righteous judgment. Second, it develops in us the character of Christ. Third, our submission under this treatment glorifies God.

Paul prefaced his discussion of submission to governing authorities: "Beloved, do not avenge yourselves, but rather give place to wrath; for it is written, 'Vengeance is Mine, I will repay,' says the Lord" (Rom. 12:19). Defense, correction, vindication, or other appropriate responses should proceed from the hand of God, not man. An individual who vindicates himself lacks the humility of Christ.

No one on earth possesses more authority than Jesus, yet He never defended Himself before authorities. Let's go to the exact situation Peter referenced, which was Jesus standing trial: "And the chief priests accused Him of many things, but He answered nothing" (Mark 15:3).

Picture a court of law where everything spoken by the witness would be officially used against Jesus. The men testifying were the religious and political leaders of His nation. They were men of influence whose words carried great weight, but there was not a shred of truth to what they said. They spoke complete lies, yet Jesus was silent before His accusers and didn't defend Himself! "Then Pilate asked Him again, saying, 'Do You answer nothing? See how many things they testify against You!' But Jesus still answered nothing, so that Pilate marveled" (Mark 15:4–5).

Pilate sat as judge in the highest seat in the land. Countless times he witnessed men under trial and watched them frantically defend themselves to avoid judgment. If convicted, they were imprisoned, exiled, or executed. There was no higher court of appeal. He'd never seen an accused man stand silent. Pilate knew the leaders had delivered Jesus to trial out of envy, and they wanted the severest punishment, death by crucifixion. He also knew Jesus was not who they made Him out to be. Yet Jesus refused to defend Himself. His behavior caused the governor to marvel at His composure.

Why didn't Jesus defend Himself? The reason: to remain under His Father's judgment and thus His protection. Peter said, "He did not retaliate when he was insulted. When he suffered, he did not threaten to get even. He left his case in the hands of God, who always judges fairly" (1 Peter 2:23 NLT).

When we refuse to defend ourselves, we are hidden under the hand of God's grace and judgment. There is no safer place: "Who shall bring a charge against God's elect? It is God who justifies" (Rom. 8:33).

In contrast, those who defend themselves come under the jurisdiction of their accusers and their judgment and thus forfeit divine intervention. I recall a situation where I defended myself with one in authority over me. God afterward showed me a brief vision in my heart. I saw the Lord standing by me with His hands behind His back. He was refrained from bringing the aid I needed. Once I stopped justifying myself, He was at work on my behalf.

Jesus never lost sight of His ultimate Judge, even when He stood before delegated authority. Remember, the heart of the king is in the hand of the Lord. By refraining from self-defense, He remained under God's defense throughout the process. The moment you justify and

164

defend yourself, you yield to your accuser as judge. You forfeit your spiritual right of protection, for he rises above you in the realm of the spirit as you answer his criticism. His influence is elevated by your self-defense. Attempting to prove your innocence, you are at the mercy of your accuser. For this reason Jesus exhorted us:

> Agree with your adversary quickly, while you are on the way with him,
> lest your adversary deliver you to the judge, the judge hand you over
> to the officer, and you be thrown into prison. Assuredly, I say to you,
> you will by no means get out of there till you have paid the last penny.
> (Matt 5:25–26).

According to this parable, you will be made to pay what your accuser demands as restitution. The greater the offense he has against you, the less mercy he extends. He will exact every last penny of your debt, in his eyes whether it is just or not.

THE FAITH OF A CHILD

When our oldest son, Addison, was in third grade, he shared over dinner with Lisa and me a problem he faced at school. He felt one of his instructors had it out for him. Addison felt the teacher disliked and blamed him whenever there was talking or disorder in class. This had gone on for a while, and the teacher had sent home a note to be placed on the record against him. Addison is extremely conscientious, and the thought of having a negative report was too much for him to bear. As he shared his frustration and fears, he broke down in tears.

We assured him we believed the best of him and asked him to relay the details. He moaned, "I get blamed for everything. Even if there is more than one person involved, I still get all the blame. I get blamed for things I haven't done. Like today, the two boys next to me were laughing and giggling, and I was quiet. The teacher turned around and yelled at me." His lip quivered at the injustice. To a nine-year-old, it was a hopeless crisis.

Addison's other teachers had reported his conduct was excellent, so we knew it was an isolated situation. While Lisa tried to comfort him, I probed, "What did you say when he corrected you today?"

Addison answered, "I told him, 'It wasn't me who was talking. It was those two boys!'"

I asked, "Is this the way you usually respond when he corrects you?"

Addison replied, "Yes, if I know I wasn't doing anything."

I looked at him, "Well, son, this is where the problem lies. You are justifying yourself before your authority, and when you defend yourself, God will not."

I shared with him the scriptures presented in this chapter. To further help him understand, I shared with him the following trial I experienced with the office manager mentioned in the last chapter.

A Boss Determined to Harm

This man had a son in our youth group. I'd been preaching strong messages on holiness, prayer, and lordship. Many young people were being transformed. At one point, this son came to my wife in tears and asked her how it was possible to live a pure and holy life when so much ungodly behavior went on at home. Then he shared details, which helped me understand why his father was against me.

A few months later, four different young people told me how sad they were that I was to be fired. I traced this information back to the son, and he told me that he had heard it from his dad.

I went to his father, and he admitted it, but blamed the senior pastor, saying it was his intention to let me go. Weeks went by, and the situation escalated. My family was under the constant tension of never knowing whether we'd remain or be let go. We'd bought a house, my wife was pregnant, and we had no money and nowhere to go. I did not want to send out résumés. I believed God had brought me, and I was staying with no alternate plan. My wife was nervous and worried and encouraged me to do something, "Honey, I know they are going to fire you. Everyone is telling me they are."

She was right. The senior pastor finally agreed to fire me. In a Sunday morning service he announced that major changes were coming to the youth group. I still had not spoken with him. I was scheduled to meet with him and the manager the next day. God told me not to defend myself.

When I walked into the senior pastor's office the next day, he was alone. He said, "John, God sent you here. I am not letting you go." He had changed his mind. I was relieved, God had protected me at the last moment. The pastor then said, "Why does the office manager want you fired?" I responded that I didn't know, and at his request I agreed to do everything possible to bring peace.

Shortly after the meeting I received written evidence of a decision this manager had made that exposed his motives. I was ready to take it to the senior pastor. I wanted him to see what was going on behind his back. I paced the floor praying for forty-five minutes, trying to overcome the uncomfortable feeling I had. I kept arguing, "God, this man has been dishonest. He must be exposed. He is a destructive force in this ministry. I must tell the senior pastor the way he really is!" I further justified my intentions to expose him, "Everything I am reporting is fact and documented. It's not emotional. If he is not stopped, his corrupt behavior will infiltrate this entire church."

Finally in frustration I blurted, "God, You don't want me to expose him, do You?" When I said that, the peace of God flooded my heart. I shook my head in amazement. I knew God did not want me to do anything, so I threw away the evidence. Later when I could look at the situation objectively, I realized I had really wanted to defend and avenge myself more than protect anyone else. I reasoned myself into believing my motives were unselfish. My information was accurate, but my motives were impure.

Time passed, and one day while I was praying outside on the church grounds before office hours, this man pulled up. God told me to go and humble myself. Immediately I was defensive: "No, Lord, he needs to come to me. He is the one causing all the problem." I continued to pray, but God was silent. After twenty minutes, again the Lord insisted I go immediately to him and humble myself. I knew it was God. I called this man and went to his office. However, what I said, and how I said it, was very different from what it would have been before God dealt with me. With all sincerity I asked his forgiveness. I told him I'd been critical and judgmental of him. He softened, and we talked for a while. From that day his attacks against me stopped.

Six months later, while I was out of town, all the wrong he'd done was exposed to the senior pastor. What he was doing was much worse than even I knew. He was fired immediately. Judgment came, but not by my hand. The very thing he tried to do to me happened to him. However, when it did, I was not happy. I grieved for him and his family. I understood his pain; I'd been through it myself at his hands. Because I'd released him six months earlier, I loved him and did not wish the circumstances on him.

I attended that church eleven more years and was asked often to minister. The shame he'd brought to my name was removed and was replaced with honor. I look back and realize I grew during that time of hardship, and later God promoted me before the very people who'd heard so many false reports. Just as the Father highly exalted Jesus for His obedience and for His willingness not to defend Himself, so He honors His children who follow the example Jesus left us.

STUDENT OF THE YEAR

After sharing the scriptures and this incident with Addison, I said, "Son, you have a choice. You can continue to stand up for yourself and remain under your teacher's judgment, or you can realize you have not responded to his accusations in a godly manner. Then you can go to your teacher, humble yourself, and apologize for being disrespectful and resisting his authority, and God will get involved."

Addison questioned, "Then what do I do when I'm blamed for something I didn't do?"

"Let God defend you. Has it worked to defend yourself?"

Addison responded, "No, I want God to defend me."

The next day he went to his teacher and humbled himself. He asked the teacher to forgive him for challenging him when corrected.

The teacher forgave him, and the next week Addison was honored as the student of the week in that class. Addison never had another problem. He ended the year by receiving from the instructor the highest honor in the awards ceremony.

If a nine-year-old can humble himself and prove God's Word in a crisis, how much more should we? I think this illustrates why Jesus said, "Therefore whoever humbles himself as this little child is the greatest in the kingdom of heaven" (Matt. 18:4).

DAVID'S ENCOUNTER WITH UNREASONABLE AUTHORITY

Addison learned what David, son of Jesse, had learned. God is the just Judge, and if we leave our unfair treatment from authority in His hands, He will always judge rightly. When speaking of David, we must remember that God, not the devil, placed David under the unreasonable and eventually cruel leader named Saul.

It began even before they met when Samuel, the senior prophet in Israel, anointed David the next king over God's people. David must have been overwhelmed with excitement, thinking, *This is the man who anointed the current king. I am going to be king!*

Saul had disobeyed God and was tormented by an evil spirit. His only relief came as someone played the harp. His attendants began to look for a young man who could sit in his presence and minister to him. One of the king's servants suggested David, the son of Jesse. King Saul sent for David and requested he come to the palace and minister to him. David must have thought, *God is already bringing to pass His promise through the prophet.* He said to himself, *This must be my entry-level position.*

Time passed, and he was asked to take refreshments to his older brothers who were at war with the Philistines. Upon arrival at the battle lines he saw the Philistine champion, Goliath, mock the army of God and learned the taunting had gone on for forty days. He found out the king had offered his daughter's hand in marriage to the man who would defeat the giant. David went before the king and requested permission to fight. He killed Goliath and won Saul's daughter. He had won Saul's favor and was engaged to become the king's son-in-law.

Jonathan, Saul's oldest son, made a covenant of everlasting friendship with David. Everything Saul gave David to do, the hand of God was on him, and it prospered. The king requested that he sit at the table with his own sons. Everything was going well, and David was thrilled. He lived in the palace, ate at the king's table, was married to the king's daughter, was friends with Jonathan, and was successful in all his campaigns. He was even winning the favor of the people. He could see the prophecy unfolding before his very eyes. Saul favored David over all his other servants and made him his armor bearer. Saul had become a father to David, who was sure Saul would mentor and train him, and one day with great honor put him on the throne. David rejoiced in God's goodness and faithfulness.

AN ABRUPT CHANGE

But in one day everything changed. Saul and David were returning from battle, side by side, when the women from all the cities of Israel came out dancing and singing, "Saul has slain his thousands, and David his ten thousands." This infuriated Saul and from that day on he despised David. Saul began to throw spears at David and conspires to kill him. The Bible said Saul hated David for he knew God was with him. Saul knew God had departed from him. David is forced to run for his life. With no where else to go he runs to the wilderness. "What is happening," David thinks, "The promise was unfolding and now it is shattered. The man who is my mentor and leader is trying to kill me. What can I do? Saul, is God's anointed servant. With him against me what chance do I have? He's the king, God's man, over God's nation. Why is God allowing this?"

Now Saul chases David from wilderness to wilderness, cave to cave, accompanied by three thousand of Israel's finest warriors, with one purpose, to destroy David. At this point the promise was just a shadow as David ran to survive. David was no longer living at the palace or eating at the king's table. His habitation was damp caves, he ate the scraps of wilderness beasts. He no longer rode at the king's side but was hunted by the men he once fought with. There was no warm bed, no servants to attend him, no compliments in the royal court. His bride was given to another.

How could the leader under whom God placed him be doing this?

David was most likely fighting thoughts of anger, disappointment, and disillusionment. *Why isn't God doing anything about this? Does He care for me? What about His promises? Why would He place His hand on such a cruel man to lead His congregation of covenant people?*

Saul was so determined to kill the young man, at any cost, that his madness increased. There were priests in the city of Nob who provided David with shelter, food, and Goliath's sword. They knew nothing about David running from Saul and thought he was on a mission for the king. They inquired of the Lord for him and sent him on his way.

When Saul found out, he was furious. He killed eighty-five innocent priests of the Lord and put the entire city of Nob to the sword—every man, woman, child, nursing infant, and animal. He carried the judgment against them, the innocent, that he was supposed to carry against the Amalekites. To make sense of God's pick for leader became almost impossible to reason. Saul was a murderer. How could God have ever put His Spirit on such a man?

Many say Saul was the people's choice, and David was God's choice. This misleading statement is taught by people who can't imagine God placing a harsh man in leadership. It is true the people wanted a king; however, God chose both Saul and David. God said, "I have set up Saul as king" (1 Sam. 15:11).

At one point Saul learned David was in the wilderness of En Gedi, and he set out with three thousand warriors. During their journey, they rested at a cave in which David was hiding. After Saul and his soldiers undressed to bathe, the Scripture tells us that David's men prompted him, "This is the day the LORD spoke of when he said to you, 'I will give your enemy into your hands for you to deal with as you wish.'"

Then David crept up unnoticed and cut off a corner of Saul's robe. Afterward, David was conscience-stricken for having done that: "He said to his men, 'The LORD forbid that I should do such a thing to my master, the LORD's anointed, or lift my hand against him; for he is the anointed of the LORD.' With these words David rebuked his men and did not allow them to attack Saul. And Saul left the cave and went his way" (1 Sam. 24:4–7 NIV). In regard to his conscience, the King James Version says that, "David's heart smote him." He was still tender in heart toward the leader who had brought such hardship into his life. He obviously had resisted and brought into submission the thoughts of anger, fear, and frustration.

Since he had already taken a corner of the king's robe, he chose to use it to prove his innocence to Saul. From a distance David bowed himself to the ground and cried out to Saul, "My *father*, see! Yes, see the corner of your robe in my hand! . . . Know and see that there is *neither evil nor rebellion* in my hand, and I have not sinned against you. Yet you hunt my life to take it" (1 Sam. 24:11, emphasis added).

David was concerned that Saul believed he was rebellious and evil. David must have searched his heart, "Where have I gone wrong? How was Saul's heart turned against me so quickly?" That was why he cried out, "Someone urged me to kill you . . . For in that I cut off the corner of your robe, and did not kill you. Know and see that there is neither evil nor rebellion in my hand." He couldn't believe Saul would think this on his own. Someone must have poisoned his heart toward David, so he wanted to prove his loyalty for Saul. He thought if he could, Saul would restore him to favor, behave kindly toward him, and the prophecy would be fulfilled.

Those who have been rejected by a father or leader tend to take all the blame on themselves. They are imprisoned by tormenting thoughts: *What did I do?* and, *Was my heart impure?* They carry the burden of constantly trying to prove their innocence to their leaders. They believe if they could only show their loyalty and value, they would be accepted. But the more they try, the more rejected they feel.

Saul acknowledged David's goodness when he saw David could have killed him and did not, so the king and his men left. David must have thought, *The king will restore me. Now the prophecy will come to pass. Surely he sees my heart and will treat me better now. He will be a good and gentle leader.* Oh, how far this was from reality.

He Is Determined to Destroy Me

Only a short time later, men reported to Saul that David was in the hills of Hachilah. Saul went after him again with the same three thousand soldiers. Again Saul sought David's destruction. I'm sure Saul's relentless pursuit devastated David. He realized that it wasn't a misunderstanding, but that Saul was intentionally, without provocation, seeking David's life.

Saul knew his heart but still marched against him. David realized what he had hoped all along was not true: that he was dealing with a wicked leader. How could God place His anointing on such a man?

David, along with Abishai, Joab's little brother, a bloodthirsty young man, secretly slipped into the camp of Saul. God had put them all in a deep sleep. The two men sneaked through the entire army to where Saul was asleep. Abishai pleaded with David, "God has delivered your enemy into your hand this day. Now therefore, please, let me strike him at once with the spear, right to the earth; and I will not have to strike him a second time!" (1 Sam. 26:8).

Abishai had many good reasons why David should order him to strike Saul. First and foremost, Saul murdered eighty-five innocent priests, their wives, and children—in cold blood! The nation was in danger under the leadership of such a mad man. Nowadays many reason in a similar manner, especially with church leaders. Only the leaders haven't done nearly as wicked an act.

Second, God had anointed David the next king of Israel by the word of Samuel. It was time David claimed his inheritance! Did he want to end up a dead man and never fulfill the prophecy? I've heard this reasoning numerous times from disillusioned church staff members.

Third, wasn't Saul out with an army of three thousand to kill David and his men? It was the time to kill or be killed. Surely it was self-defense. Abishai knew any court of law would uphold their actions. Of course, this reasoning wouldn't even be contested in our day. We would embrace it without a second thought.

Fourth, wasn't it God who'd put the army into a sleep so deep that they could walk right up to Saul to carry out His will of ridding the nation of such a wicked leader? They had their chance, and it might never come again. It was the time to seize the fulfillment of the prophecy! How many church boards or staffs have thought this when their leader was down? They think, *God has put him in the place where we can now remove him from leading us.* This reasoning only exposes their insubordinate hearts.

All these reasons sounded good. They made sense, and David was receiving the encouragement of another loyal brother. So if David had the least bit of rebellion within his heart, he would have reasoned to allow his assistant to run the sword through Saul, and he would have felt totally justified. However, listen to David's response: "Do not destroy him; for who can stretch out his hand against the LORD's anointed, and be guiltless?" (1 Sam. 26:9). To put it in today's terms, "Do not touch him with words or actions, for who can attack his leader and remain guiltless?"

David would not kill him, even though Saul had murdered innocent people and wanted to murder him. David would not avenge himself; he left it in the hands of God. It would have been easier to put an end to it right there—easier for David and for the people of Israel. He knew the nation was like sheep without a true shepherd. He knew a wicked person was raping them for his own selfish desires. It was hard not defending himself, but it was possibly harder not delivering the people he loved from a mad king!

David made the decision, even though he knew Saul's only comfort was David's destruction. David had proved his pureness of heart when he spared Saul the first time. Yet he still would not touch him. Saul was the anointed of the Lord. He was God's servant, and David left Saul in God's hand to judge.

David was wise when he chose to let God be Saul's judge. You ask, "Who did God use to judge Saul, His servant?" The answer: the Philistines. The Lord many times will use unsaved men or institutions of the world to bring judgment to His leaders in the church. Saul fell in battle along with his sons. When the news reached David, he did not celebrate. He mourned!

In fact, David executed the man who said he had killed Saul, even though he had not. The man had hoped the news would win David's favor, but the effect was the opposite. David responded, "How was it you were not afraid to put forth your hand to destroy the Lord's anointed?" After the execution, David said to the dead man, "You die self-condemned, for you yourself confessed that you killed the LORD's anointed one" (2 Sam. 1:16 NLT).

David then composed a love song for the people of Judah to sing in honor of Saul and his sons. He charged the people not to proclaim it in the streets of the Philistine cities, lest the enemy rejoice. He proclaimed no rain or crops in the place where Saul was slain. He called for all of Israel to weep over Saul. That was not the heart of a man seeking vengeance, who no longer honored his leader. No, such a man would have said, "He got what he deserved!"

David went even farther. He did not kill the remaining seed of the house of Saul; rather, he showed kindness to them. He gave land and food to them and granted a descendant a seat at the king's table. Does that sound like a man who was happy about his leader falling into judgment? Those who are rebellious in heart rejoice when their spiritual leaders fall. They think, *They got what they deserved.* They usually will help either by slander or by hurtful comments to push them farther into their punishment. They have not the heart that David had. They have not a heart after God.

POSITIONED TO BE BLESSED!

We must keep before us that it is for the ultimate purpose of good that God brings us through unfair treatment at the hands of authorities. He uses it to set us up for a blessing. Peter continued his exhortation: "Do not repay evil with evil or insult with insult, but with blessing, because *to this you were called* so that you may *inherit a blessing*" (1 Peter 3:9 NIV, emphasis added).

The blessing may not consist of natural things, although many times it can; rather, it comes in more important areas, such as Christlike character, advancement of the kingdom, or eternal rewards. When we submit to God's authority, no harm can come to our spiritual well-being. Peter made it clear by asking, "And who is he who will harm you if you become followers of what is good?" (1 Peter 3:13). The context of this statement is to follow Jesus' personal example.

In regard to Christlike character Peter admonished, "For Christ also suffered once for sins, the just for the unjust . . . Therefore, since Christ suffered for us in the flesh, arm yourselves also with the same mind, for he who has suffered in the flesh has ceased from sin" (1 Peter 3:18; 4:1).

Peter instructed us to arm ourselves for the similar sufferings Christ experienced, which in context of his epistle is unfair treatment from authorities. Can you imagine military men going to battle without arms? How ludicrous. Yet many believers are not armed to suffer unreasonable treatment. When assaulted, they go into a state of shock, bewilderment, or amazement. They *react* in the line of reasoning instead of *acting* out of the principle of authority.

Let me give you another example of one who is armed. A crucial part of airline pilot training is the use of flight simulators. In these simulators pilots are confronted by almost every flight emergency they might face. In the safety of this setting they hone their response skills until they can successfully face them. This preparation arms them for emergencies. If something happens on an actual flight, the pilots do not panic—they respond, assisted and guided by extensive training. Even though the passengers may panic and give way to shock and hysteria, the pilots remain calm and in full control. Investigators who review crash black box tape recordings are amazed by the calmness of the pilots. There is usually no panic in their voices even up to the moment of impact. They were armed!

This book could serve as a flight training manual. The Word of God within this message arms or prepares you for the curves that life throws at you in regard to authority. If you respond correctly, you will experience blessing. Peter told us those who follow Christ's example of suffering have ceased from sin. What a statement! In other words, those who correctly handle unfair treatment at the hands of authorities come to a place of spiritual maturity.

There is an even greater promise. Paul asserted,

> This is a true saying:
> If we die with him,
>> we will also live with him.

If we endure hardship,
we will reign with him. (2 Tim. 2:11–12 NLT)

Spiritual authority is promised to those who suffer like Christ. The greater hardship you endure, the greater the authority God entrusts to you. Again, you see that God sets you up for a blessing when you encounter unreasonable authority. But will you respond correctly and receive the blessing, or will you become resentful and bitter? The choice is yours. Choose the way of the overcomer, which is life!

CHAPTER 14

SELF-INFLICTED JUDGMENT

*Those who honor authority walk in great authority,
and respect follows them.*

Not everyone responds to leadership as David did. Too often we delight in seeing defects in our authorities, and then we feel justified to throw off restraint. But our response to the sins of others, especially those who are leaders, is one of the greatest indicators of our spiritual maturity. This being the case, God often uses the faults and mistakes of authorities in our lives to expose the true condition of our hearts. We see how that happened with one of Noah's sons.

RIGHT, BUT WRONG

After the Flood, Noah began to cultivate the ground, and he planted a vineyard. One day after drinking too much, he retired to his tent, and in his drunkenness took off his clothes and passed out naked.

Ham the youngest of his sons, entered the tent where Noah lay, saw his naked form, went outside, and told his two brothers, Shem and Japheth. He told only "family." He might have said, "Guys, Dad is drunk as a skunk and naked as a jaybird!" or maybe even worse, perhaps he invited his brothers to see their spiritual leader naked.

When Shem and Japheth heard the story, they took a garment, held it over their shoulders while walking backward into the tent, with their faces turned away, and covered their father's nakedness. Once Noah woke from his drunken stupor, he knew what Ham had done. Hear what Noah proclaimed:

> Then he cursed the descendants of Canaan, the son of Ham:
> "A curse on the Canaanites!
> May they be the lowest of servants
>   to the descendants of Shem and Japheth."
> Then Noah said,
> "May Shem be blessed by the LORD my God;
>   and may Canaan be his servant.
> May God enlarge the territory of Japheth,
>   and may he share the prosperity of Shem;
>   and let Canaan be his servant." (Gen. 9:25–27 NLT)

Earlier in this book, we discussed the consequences of disobedience to God's authority. Those who willfully rebel come under a curse. Ham learned this truth the hard way. He dishonored and thus showed contempt for God's delegated authority on Noah, which brought a curse on Ham's generations. It is interesting that Ham's transgression brought severe consequence on him, while Noah's drunkenness brought none that was recorded.

The moral failure of Noah became a test to his three sons, revealing the heart of each in turn. One was rebellious and foolish, and two were honorable and merciful. Noah did not set the best example with his drunkenness, yet his behavior was God's to deal with, not those under him. Two sons understood this and continued to honor him. One took matters into his own hands to dishonor and shame his father, and he brought upon his head the very curse he thought destined for his father.

Shem and Japheth would not so much as look at their father's failure. They didn't want to observe or to allow others (wives and children) to see his condition, so they covered him. Because they maintained a reverence for their father's position, they protected his position and their hearts. Ham, however, mocked and discredited his father in a possible attempt to discredit his ability to rule. This provided Ham with an excuse to disobey his father when he so desired. This is true of anyone when insubordination dwells in his heart. By disqualifying authority, he feels released from submission. In his heart he casts off restraint.

In "God's hall of fame" (Heb. 11), God boasts about Noah's faith and obedience, but we don't find Ham listed. Wasn't Ham right? Wasn't Noah drunk and naked? Yes, Ham was 100 percent accurate in what he reported, yet he was wrong in principle. Reasoning would justify his actions; he repeated only what he'd seen; he was only being "truthful." Yet the principles of obedience and reverence say otherwise. Shem and Japheth honored their father and were blessed.

Many, like Ham, are accurate in what they report about leaders, yet they are wrong in God's eyes. They have dishonored another and lost their blessing. They live in the foolishness of their own understanding and reasoning. They lack the hearts of David, Shem, and Japheth. When Saul's downfall was complete, David grieved and proclaimed,

> *Tell it not in Gath,*
> *Proclaim it not in the streets of Ashkelon—*
> Lest the daughters of the Philistines rejoice,
> Lest the daughters of the uncircumcised triumph . . .
> Saul and Jonathan were beloved and pleasant in their lives,
> And in their death they were not divided;
> They were swifter than eagles,
> They were stronger than lions.
> *O daughters of Israel, weep over Saul,*
> Who clothed you in scarlet, with luxury;
> Who put ornaments of gold on your apparel. (2 Sam. 1:20, 23–24,
>   emphasis added)

David suffered severe hardship at the hands of this leader. Natural understanding and carnal reasoning would have encouraged him to rejoice and to proclaim victory. Yet again David proved he lived by principles of authority, and his example communicated this to the men under his authority. As a result, he became a great leader in the kingdom. Those who honor authority walk in great authority, and respect follows them. They have attracted the blessing of God. Those who revile authority, or lightly esteem authority, sow a harvest of disrespect and cause judgment to follow them.

SELF-INFLICTED JUDGMENT

Let's again examine our foundational scripture for delegated authority:

> Let every soul be subject to the governing authorities. For there is no authority except from God, and the authorities that exist are appointed by God. Therefore whoever resists the authority resists the ordinance of God, and those who resist will bring judgment on themselves. (Rom. 13:1–2)

Judgment comes to those who resist authority. Touch authority, and you touch God. I worked for two international ministries before pioneering our own. I saw consistent judgment as a result of resistance to authority. It came in many forms, yet never failed to come. It was especially evident when employees were let go. No matter how unreasonable the leader or the circumstances were, if they criticized or reviled the leader, if they drank of bitterness, they eventually ended up in greater difficulties. For some, it was their finances; for others, jobs; for others, health problems; for others, problems with their children; and some suffered marriage problems. The list is long, but the thread of unusual hardship ran through the life of each person who did not honor his spiritual overseers.

I saw many who were mistreated when they were let go, but they maintained a sweet spirit. They refused to speak against their former employers or listen to others who did; instead, they blessed and honored them whenever the subject arose. They knew God was their Source, and He'd provide for them, care for them, and in turn promote them. I watched them enter positions that were better than they'd had on our staff. I have crossed paths with some of them as much as twelve years later, and they are still blessed in their lives.

How do you keep a sweet spirit? Jesus gave us the secret: "But I say to you, love your enemies, bless those who curse you, do good to those who hate you, and pray for those who spitefully use you and persecute you" (Matt. 5:44). He told us we should pray for those who spitefully use or abuse us. When we do this, our hearts are healed and cannot become critical or jaded.

GIFTEDNESS VERSUS AUTHORITY

I have learned through the Scriptures and seen confirmed through life experiences, those who speak against authority bring certain judgment on themselves. Consider Miriam and Aaron: "While they were at Hazeroth, Miriam and Aaron criticized Moses because he had married a Cushite woman" (Num. 12:1 NLT).

First, let's discuss who Miriam and Aaron were. Miriam was the sister of Moses. Let me also point out, she was his older sister. God called her a prophetess (Ex. 15:20). Aaron was the older brother of Moses as well as the high priest. So we are speaking about two people with significant positions of leadership and notoriety.

They criticized Moses for marrying a Cushite woman. A Cushite is a native or inhabitant of the ancient land of Cush, identified by most scholars as Ethiopia, a country in northeastern Africa. The woman was not a descendant of Abraham; she was outside the covenant of Abraham.

Miriam and Aaron believed Moses had sinned or at best made a bad decision by marrying this daughter of Africa, especially since he was a leader. Were they correct in their opinion? It would appear so if we go by the letter of the law. God had made known His desire for the children of Israel to marry among themselves. He warned that foreign wives would draw away their hearts to foreign gods. This command was given in Deuteronomy. For Moses to marry a foreigner seemed a contradiction. They probably reasoned his influence was too visible and great to behave that way. (Note: Our only command today is that we are not to be unequally yoked with unbelievers. It is no longer a natural bloodline issue, but a spiritual one. See Galatians 3:28. It's perfectly fine for two people of different ethnic origins to marry, according to the New Testament.)

So Miriam and Aaron were right in their assessment, yet wrong as Ham was! Moses was their leader. Criticizing him was out of order. As older brother and sister, they could have discussed it as a family matter with him, but to gossip among themselves or to discuss his behavior within the congregation was absolutely a sin.

What gave them the fuel to speak against their leader? The answer is found in the next verse: "They said, 'Has the LORD spoken only through Moses? Hasn't he spoken through us, too?' But the LORD heard them" (Num. 12:2 NLT).

Had God spoken through them? Absolutely. God referred to Aaron as Moses' spokesperson or prophet. Aaron spoke the messages of God to Pharaoh. Miriam was used to bring forth a prophetic psalm that we still have in the Scriptures. They definitely had spiritual gifts. Yet their error was viewing spiritual gifts or abilities above authority. They reasoned that since Moses had sinned, and they hadn't—and they all had been used by the Lord in a profound way—Moses was no longer qualified as an authority over them. They allowed their spiritual gifting to elevate themselves above the authority that God had placed over them.

As for a New Testament application, Paul said, "There are diversities of gifts, but the same Spirit" (1 Cor. 12:4). This and other scriptures identify the overseer of the gifts as the Holy Spirit. Some of the gifts are the ability to lead, the ability to teach, the grace to give, prophecy, gifts of healings, discerning of spirits, and working of miracles (1 Cor. 12:7–10; Rom. 12:6–8).

Paul continued, "There are differences of ministries, but the same Lord" (1 Cor. 12:4–5). The Greek word for "ministries" is *diakonia*. According to Thayer's Greek dictionary, this word is used to depict "the office of the apostles and its administration, and of prophets, evangelists, elders, etc." Simply put, this word is used to describe the five offices of spiritual authority within the church. From this scripture we see the Lord, or Jesus, is over these offices. Another passage confirms this. When Jesus was raised from the dead, Paul wrote, "He Himself [Jesus] gave some to be apostles, some prophets, some evangelists, and some pastors and teachers, for the equipping of the saints for the work of ministry, for the edifying of the body of Christ" (Eph. 4:11–12).

The authority of the kingdom flows down through the offices, not the gifts, as all authority was given to Jesus by the Father after His resurrection (Matt. 28:18). Jesus in turn gave the fivefold ministries as designated from the passage in Ephesians. Therefore, His authority flows through appointed offices. We must keep before us the fact that a person can be more gifted than his pastor, yet the pastor who stands in the office of authority is over the gifted person.

An assistant pastor on a church staff was very gifted to preach and prophesy. His classes were crowded as the gift of God on his life was evident. He led prayer once a week, and his sessions were heavily attended.

The more popular he became, the more free he felt to criticize the established policies of the church and the senior pastor himself. He said the senior pastor's policies restricted the move of the Holy Spirit, and he shared this insight with those around him. His critical attitude spilled over to another assistant pastor. After a while they jointly led the prayer service on his appointed evening. One night the lead pastor slipped in the back of the building during prayer and watched as the two assistant pastors conducted the service exactly the way he had told them not to do it. Instead of making intercession for the church, the city, and the lost, they were drawing the people into other forms of prayer and rebuking them if they felt they weren't doing it right. The people were confused.

Both men were gifted ministers, yet they weren't submitted to the authority of the church. The seriousness of their offense was covered by the fact the Lord was using them to speak and minister to His people. If this is our standard for approval, we can easily fall into rebellion, just as Miriam and Aaron did. The anointing of God is for the people of God; it is never for the validation of the minister's every comment or lifestyle.

LEARNING SUBMISSION FROM JUDGMENT

Now Moses was more humble than any other person on earth. So immediately the LORD called to Moses, Aaron, and Miriam and said, "Go out to the Tabernacle, all three of you!" And the three of them went out. (Num. 12:3–4 NLT)

Through this scripture, we glimpse one of God's character require-ments for His desired leaders: humility. Moses was the most humble man on earth. But that would not have been Miriam and Aaron's description of him. Their reasoning would have been more along the lines, *He has gotten just a little too big for his britches.*

The Lord called the three of them out to the tabernacle. Other translations use the word *suddenly* instead of *immediately.* Judgment often comes without warning. As the three headed out, it is quite pos-sible Miriam was nodding to Aaron, "Get ready. Moses blew it marry-ing this foreign girl. God is going to make you the leader now because you have been so right in your behavior." This kind of reasoning occurs when we open ourselves to deception through resisting authority.

Of course, what actually happened was very different. God called Aaron and Miriam forward. He reminded them He'd entrusted Moses with His entire house, and He spoke with him face-to-face or directly, not in riddles. Then God posed this question: "Should you not be afraid to criticize him?" (v. 8 NLT). When we criticize authority, we expose a lack of the fear of the Lord. Listen to what happens: "The LORD was furious with them, and He departed. As the cloud moved from above the Tabernacle, Miriam suddenly became white as snow with leprosy" (Num. 12:9–10 NLT).

By resisting authority, we bring judgment on ourselves. This judg-ment can include a lifting of God's presence coupled with some form of calamity. Returning to the two pastors I discussed earlier, it wasn't long before both left the church. One was let go; the other resigned before he was to be released. One started his own church down the road and struggled with a very small congregation that never grew above a hundred. As an associate, he had more than six hundred people under his care. Shortly after his departure, he experienced a personal family tragedy. The other associate left the city and enjoyed a measure of ministry success, but felt isolated and distrustful of most everyone.

Once judgment came, Aaron immediately cried out in repentance for himself and Miriam. God forgave them, but per God's command, Miriam still had to be isolated from the congregation for seven days. There are many questions about why Miriam was struck, but Aaron was not. One reason may be that Miriam was more forceful in her verbal attack than Aaron was. Another common thought is that it was more unseemly for Miriam to speak that way as a woman, and she did not hold quite as pivotal a position. Another reason may be that Aaron, high priest, had to remain in his position with the anointing upon him. Whatever the reason, this incident shows how seriously God views this matter.

Judgment for resistance to spiritual authority is more often than not an opportunity to learn and grow. After such a close call, people who repent often end up among the most faithful in the church. Resistance does not always proceed from an evil heart; it is often committed out of ignorance. Once the realization comes, repentance immediately follows. Sometimes this can take a while because some people have a higher tolerance for the pain that results from kicking against the goads.

It is certain Miriam never forgot her time of humiliation. She did not repeat the behavior, for she was not insubordinate again. However, not all turn as Miriam and Aaron did or learn from their example. Others within the same congregation later rose up against God's established authority. They did not repent, and they received everlasting judgment.

WHY DO YOU EXALT YOURSELVES?

Three men in the congregation—Korah, who was a descendant of Levi, and Dathan and Abiram, both descendants of Reuben—gathered together 250 leaders of the congregation, men of renown, against Moses and Aaron and said, "You take too much upon yourselves, for all the congregation is holy, every one of them, and the LORD is among them. Why then do you exalt yourselves above the assembly of the LORD?" (Num. 16:3).

In simpler words the men, who were in leadership under Moses and Aaron, said, "Hey, guys, why do you exalt yourselves as leaders over us? We are all God's people, and we can obey Him without you ordering us around." You've heard it before! If not these exact words, then definitely the message is frequently portrayed by behavior or subtler words, but it's still the same spirit. You may hear, "We're all equal" or "We're all brothers and sisters" or "We all have the Holy Spirit; why should we have to submit to their leadership?" These people are convinced they can hear the Lord as well as anyone else can.

I understand that a movement within the church called discipleship got out of hand in the 1970s, and submission to leaders teetered out of balance. People were asking pastors about whether they could go on vacations, buy a specific car or other major item, or marry a certain individual. I wasn't involved so I don't know exactly how far overboard it actually went, but some who were involved said that it ended up being unscriptural.

This movement and other abuses of leadership caused a rebound in the opposite direction. Because spiritual authority had been abused, people opted to despise it. This spawned some extreme free agents and spiritual vagabonds ran from church to church, convention to convention, and conducted their own prayer meetings and birthed their own churches often because they couldn't find a pastor perfect enough to submit to. This mentality contributed to the secret power of lawlessness that Paul warned would occur in our day.

The men who rose up against Moses had been under the abusive authority of Pharaoh. Then Moses came, stepped into their lives, and his authority seemed extreme as well, but in a different sense. At times he brought them greater hardship than they had known with Pharaoh. Perhaps they reasoned that they were out of Egypt, Pharaoh was out of the picture, Moses had served his purpose, and every man was on his own. Those guys had had it with authority. It was every man for himself. After all they were God's people, and authorities meant difficulties, so several of them got together and attacked Moses.

I have seen this scenario all too often in my travels. Businessmen, intercessory prayer groups, advisory boards, or other groups within the church gang up on pastors. They have all heard from God, and the pastor is missing it. If they only knew what spirit they were of.

SPIRITUAL AUTHORITY IS APPOINTED

As I've stated, too often Westerners have difficulties with kingdom principles. We live in a democratic society of free enterprise, which varies vastly from a kingdom. A kingdom has a king, by virtue of birthright, and appointed leadership. A democracy elects its rulers. In this free enterprise system leadership is freely available to determined individuals with money, ability, influence, or talent. But that is not the way of God's kingdom, where leaders are appointed.

Jesus appoints the offices of service. No one can place a human being in these positions of authority except the Lord, and He does it by the Spirit of God. When we assume a position of authority without God's appointment, we exalt ourselves. This includes those called, but yet to be appointed. Paul warned, "For I say, through the grace given to me, to everyone who is among you, not to think of himself more highly than he ought to think" (Rom. 12:3).

The writer of Hebrews affirmed the importance of not assuming a position of spiritual leadership: "And no man takes this honor to himself." The preceding verses make it clear he must be appointed. The writer of Hebrews continue, "So also Christ did not glorify Himself to become High Priest" (Heb. 5:4–5). Even Jesus did not assume His position of leadership; the Father appointed Him.

Listen to Paul describe himself: "Paul, a bondservant of Jesus Christ, called to be an apostle, separated to the gospel of God" (Rom. 1:1). He mentioned *called,* then *separated. Separated* is another term for *appointed.* Paul was called as an apostle from the foundation of the world, though he was not placed in the office the moment he was saved. There was a period of testing when he submitted to the church leaders at Antioch. This test lasted years, from his own experience he wrote these instructions for leaders: "But let these also first be tested; then let them serve" (1 Tim. 3:10).

Paul's life established a scriptural pattern for today. Once Paul passed the test of faithfulness in the ministry of helps, he was promoted to the office of teacher (2 Tim. 1:11; Acts 13:1). The Lord's divine order of offices and positions of service are revealed in scripture: "God has appointed these in the church: first apostles, second prophets, third teachers, after that . . . helps" (1 Cor. 12:28).

Paul would be tested not only in the realm of helps but in the office of teacher as well. God's pattern of separation for His servants to a higher office is found again when Paul was promoted from teacher to apostle: "Now in the church that was at Antioch there were certain prophets and teachers: Barnabas, Simeon who was called Niger, Lucius of Cyrene, Manaen who had been brought up with Herod the tetrarch, and Saul" (Acts 13:1). Saul, later named Paul, is listed among the teachers and prophets in the church of Antioch. We know from 1 Timothy 2:11, he was not one of the prophets, but a teacher. Continuing to read, we learn that "As they ministered to the Lord and fasted, the Holy Spirit said, 'Now separate to Me Barnabas and Saul for the work to which I have called them'" (Acts 13:2).

The Holy Spirit spoke, "Now separate to Me." The time had come. It was not a week earlier or later—it was now! And the Lord determined both the timing and the persons to be separated. For years Paul was aware there was an apostolic call on his life. It was revealed three days after his encounter on the road to Damascus (Acts 9:15). Now Jesus had separated the one He had called so many years earlier. Paul had faithfully served without promoting himself.

The Lord used the established leadership of the church in which Paul had faithfully labored. The elders had been appointed in the same manner. Continuing, we read, "Then, having fasted and prayed, and laid hands on them, they sent them away. So, being sent out by the Holy Spirit, they went" (Acts 13:3–4).

Notice that "they sent them." The established leadership sent Paul and Barnabas. Then look at the next verse: "So, being sent out by the Holy Spirit." Jesus appointed and separated Paul and Barnabas by the Holy Spirit through the established leadership. Bottom line, Jesus did it through the proper chain of authority.

Jesus did not use the prophetic intercessory prayer group of Antioch, nor did He send Paul and Barnabas to a prophetic meeting in another city or across town to another church where Paul was not submitted. He did not use an individual in the congregation with spiritual gifts to set the men in leadership.

The Lord used the authority He'd established through the church in Antioch. That was why God warned, "Do not lay hands on anyone hastily" (1 Tim. 5:22). Leaders monitor the faithfulness of those who serve in the church, so when God speaks to their hearts to appoint, they have confidence that it is the Lord's appointment. This is the Lord's method of appointing individuals to positions of leadership in the New Testament church.

PREMATURE IN THE CALL

Moses was called and knew it early in life.

> Now when he was forty years old, it came into his heart to visit his brethren, the children of Israel. And seeing one of them suffer wrong, he defended and avenged him who was oppressed, and struck down the Egyptian. For he supposed that his brethren would have understood that God would deliver them by his hand, but they did not understand. And the next day he appeared to two of them as they were fighting, and tried to reconcile them, saying, "Men, you are brethren; why do you wrong one another?" But he who did his neighbor wrong pushed him away, saying, "Who made you a ruler and a judge over us?" (Acts 7:23–27)

The people he was to lead did not recognize his authority. One said almost the exact words later used by Korah, Dathan, and Abiram, "Who made you a ruler and a judge over us?" Yet he suffered no consequence, for Moses had not yet been appointed. Though the call had entered his heart, the authority of God was not yet upon him.

I believe one of the reasons the people fought Moses so intensely later in the wilderness is, that they did see the authority of God on him, but didn't like it. That would further explain God's words when He said the people were really fighting Him and not Moses. Too often today it is no different. Those who truly have the authority of God are often fought against the most because people really wrestle with divine authority.

SELF-APPOINTMENT—DECEPTIVE AND DANGEROUS

When Korah, Dathan, and Abiram opposed Moses, he had been definitively appointed, and the manifestation of his authority was evident to all. But they were self-appointed, self-righteous, proud men. Their reasoning was a deceptive and dangerous form of rebellion. It was deceptive in the sense they still believed they were serving God through their rebellion. The 250 leaders had convinced themselves they were merely opposing Moses and Aaron; they did not have the slightest inkling that their resistance extended to God, for they wished to serve Him. Somewhere they lost their way, and losing sight of God's authority on Moses gave them the fuel to rise up against him. It was dangerous because it is often accompanied by the greatest judgment. It is after the order of Lucifer's fall.

Upon hearing the words of those men, Moses recognized the spirit behind them and fell on his face. He did not argue with them. Those who are ordained by God have His heart and will not fight to prove their position. Moses knew God intimately and thus knew He would confirm His appointed leadership. Moses said,

> Is it a small thing to you that the God of Israel has separated you from the congregation of Israel, to bring you near to Himself, to do the work of the tabernacle of the LORD, and to stand before the congregation to serve them; and that He has brought you near to Himself, you and all your brethren, the sons of Levi, with you? And are you seeking the priesthood also? Therefore you and all your company are gathered together against the LORD. (Num. 16:9–11)

They grasped for more than what had been delegated to them and found themselves unexpectedly gathered against the Lord. They sought a level of authority God had not given them. Moses repeated to them, "You take too much upon yourselves, you sons of Levi!" (Num. 16:7).

Once it was clear the men would not budge in their stubbornness, the Lord instructed Moses, "Tell all the people to get away from the tents of Korah, Dathan, and Abiram." So Moses got up and rushed over to the tents of Dathan and Abiram, followed closely by the submitted Israelite leaders. "Quick!" he told the people. "Get away from the tents of these wicked men, and don't touch anything that belongs to them. If you do, you will be destroyed for their sins." So all the people stood back from the tents of Korah, Dathan, and Abiram. Then Dathan and Abiram came out and stood at the entrances of their tents with their wives and children and little ones.

And Moses said, "By this you will know that the LORD has sent me to do all these things that I have done—for I have not done them on my own. If these men die a natural death, then the LORD has not sent me. But if the LORD performs a miracle and the ground opens up and swallows them and all their belongings, and they go down alive into the grave, then you will know that these men have despised the LORD."

He had hardly finished speaking the words when the ground suddenly split open beneath them. The earth opened up and swallowed the men, along with their households and the followers who were standing with them, and everything they owned. So they went down alive into the grave, along with their belongings. The earth closed over them, and they all vanished. All of the people of Israel fled as they heard their screams, fearing that the earth would swallow them, too. Then fire blazed forth from the Lord and burned up the 250 men who were offering incense (Num. 16:24–35 NLT).

The severe judgment on those men leaves us two sobering facts. First, they really believed they were still serving God when, in reality, they opposed Him. Second, in the New Testament, Jude warned there would be similar people in the church in the last days, who will "claim authority from their dreams, live immoral lives, defy authority, and scoff at the power of the glorious ones" (v. 8 NLT). Then Jude said, "How terrible it will be for them! For they follow the evil example of . . . Korah, they will perish because of their rebellion" (v. 11 NLT).

Rebellion Is Contagious

This chapter has two separate incidents of rebellion. The first involved Korah, Dathan, and Abiram with the 250 leaders. The second happened the next day when the entire congregation rose up against Moses and Aaron. They railed against them, saying, "You have killed the people of the LORD" (Num. 16:41). They were understandably shaken by what happened the day before, but were mistaken to be upset and to blame Moses. The influence of those men's rebellion was so persuasive that even after witnessing the earth swallowing the upstarts, the congregation didn't get the message of how deadly their rebellion was. This is sobering, and I've seen similar incidents of the grip of this influence in our day.

When the congregation rose up against Moses and Aaron, God became so angry, He wanted to destroy all of them. But Moses and Aaron interceded for the people. As a result, the nation was saved; however, a plague broke out from the Lord, which killed 14,700 people! That's a whole lot more than the day before!

People of God, let me warn you: rebellion is contagious and deadly. The Bible does not say God *dislikes* it. Scripture makes it clear that He *hates* it. His view of it is far more severe than just *dislike*. Lucifer was not asked to leave heaven when he rebelled; he was thrown out as fast as lightning falls from the sky to earth (Luke 10:18). Association with a rebellious person is a death wish. For this reason Paul's final words of exhortation to the Roman church were,

> I urge you, brothers, to watch out for those who cause divisions and put obstacles in your way that are contrary to the teaching you have learned. Keep away from them. For such people are not serving our Lord Christ, but their own appetites. By smooth talk and flattery they deceive the minds of naive people. (Rom. 16:17–18 NIV)

His final words are mine for this chapter as well. I admit, this message may not bring you excitement, but it may save your life. Remember it's a vaccination of truth. It isn't pleasant, but its protection far outweighs the discomfort of its application. I pray you see the love of God in this message. He brings His words of warning for your protection.

CHAPTER 15

ODDS AND ENDS

When we are truly saved and seeking the will of God,
we will recognize legitimate authority in the church.

In previous chapters much of our focus has been on church or civil authorities. Yet as I stated earlier, most of the principles include all categories of authority. In this chapter we'll discuss specific instructions given in God's Word in regard to the different areas of authority, especially the family. Most are pertinent only to their category and, therefore, must be addressed separately. It would be easy to write an entire book on what we will discuss in this chapter. However, if we apply the principles we've already learned, we can extend them to what we discuss in this chapter then the book will be written upon our heart. We will also examine some general instructions, in this chapter, which are not exclusive enough to write an entire book about. For this reason I have titled this chapter Odds and Ends.

THE FAMILY

Before there was church, civil government, or social authority, there was family. Its function is the most crucial because the health of the other three depend on it. You can have defects in other arenas of delegated authority, and the family can remain independently strong. But you cannot have broken family order without its affecting the others. Authority in the family is an essential foundation for the others.

Within the family we find divine order outlined in Scripture:

Children, obey your parents in all things, for this is well pleasing to the Lord. (Col. 3:20)

For the husband is head of the wife, as also Christ is head of the church . . . Therefore, just as the church is subject to Christ, so let the wives be to their own husbands in everything. (Eph. 5:23–24)

These commands, also found elsewhere in the New Testament, set forth God's authority structure in the home. Children are to obey their parents in all things, which includes *every* area of life. This command would not apply only if a parent tells children to do what is contrary to the Word of God, such as encouraging sexual misconduct with the parent, lying, stealing, or choosing between parents, and other such behavior.

A good example of this exception occurred in my family. While at Purdue University studying mechanical engineering, I committed my life to Jesus Christ. Shortly afterward I knew I was called to preach the gospel. I came home one school break and told my parents, who were devout Catholics, I would finish engineering school and then go to Bible college. My news upset them, and they felt my decision was reactionary and impulsive. In fact, my mother said, "Over my dead body will you go to Bible school!"

I responded to my mother with humility and respect, "Mom, I love you and am grateful for all you have done for me, but I must obey God." These words did not comfort or please her in the least. They upset her more.

Jesus said to us, "He who loves father or mother more than Me is not worthy of Me. And he who loves son or daughter more than Me is not worthy of Me" (Matt. 10:37). Strengthened by these words and many similar ones in the Gospels, I knew I had to choose between my mother and father, whom I loved very much, and Jesus' call to serve Him. There was no hesitation in my decision.

Things were very uncomfortable for a few years. I continued to love and respect my parents, in fact, more than I'd ever done before, since I now had God's grace. After time they began to see the fruit of what Jesus had done in my life, and eighteen years later, when my father was seventy-nine, I had the privilege of praying with both parents to receive Jesus as Lord. Now they read our books, watch our videos, and give them to friends. Our relationship is the best it has ever been.

Jesus faced a similar situation. In regard to submission to His parents, we read, "He went down with them and came to Nazareth and was [habitually] obedient to them" (Luke 2:51 AMPLIFIED). However, once His ministry started, the sword began to pierce and expose their hearts and thoughts as Simeon had prophesied when Jesus was just a baby (Luke 2:35). Jesus' strong messages were making many uncomfortable and angry, including His family. Their feelings escalated to the point that His mother opposed Him:

> And when those who belonged to Him (His kinsmen) heard it, they went out to take Him by force, for they kept saying, He is out of His mind (beside Himself, deranged)! . . . Then His mother and His brothers came and, standing outside, they sent word to Him, calling [for] Him. And the crowd was sitting around Him, and they said to Him, Your mother and Your brothers and Your sisters are outside asking for You. And He replied, Who are My mother and My brothers? And looking around on those who sat in a circle about Him, He said, See! Here are My mother and My brothers; for whoever does the things God wills is My brother and sister and mother! (Mark 3:21, 31–35 AMPLIFIED)

He was obedient to His parents in all things until they desired Him to go against His Father's command. The good news is, His own family was found in the upper room receiving the outpouring of the Holy Spirit a few years later. At some point they became followers of the Master.

It Did Not Go Well with Me

To return to the norm and not the exception, the command for children to honor and obey their parents is the first one with a promise: that it may be well for them and that they may live a long life (Eph. 6:2–3; Col. 3:20).

I learned the consequences of disobeying this command the hard way. After graduating from Purdue, I took a job with Rockwell International. I started attending the church I spoke of earlier. After my second service, I went out to eat with several others my own age. I met a leader in the single adult group. He needed a place to live, and I was just moving to the city. After talking awhile, we thought it would be great to share an apartment. I was thrilled because I would save a lot of money, and I was post-college broke at the time.

The next day I called my dad and told him the news. I thought he would share my excitement about saving a couple hundred each month. But he didn't. Instead he said, "Son, I don't like it. Don't do it. You don't know this man." I tried to persuade him by telling him about how involved the leader was in the singles' ministry, but he wouldn't budge from his counsel.

As I hung up the phone, I concluded my father did not understand these things because he wasn't a believer. After all, the fellow had an important position. I ignored my father's words, and the next day we found an apartment together and signed the lease. When we went to get the rental truck, my new roommate asked if I could pay because he'd forgotten his checkbook. When we went to pay the deposit for the apartment, he did the same thing. Similar behavior continued, and I ended up paying for the entire first two month's rent for both of us, as well as the utilities, and his numerous long-distance phone calls.

I lent him my car a few times because he didn't have one. Each time the car was returned early the next morning filled with smoke. He made excuses that he was reaching out to people in need. One morning I found a huge dent in the side of my car. I was very upset, but wouldn't show it. Another evening I came out of my bedroom at 4:00 A.M. and found a total stranger in the living room with a can of beer and cigarettes in his hands. He looked at me as though I was the intruder.

I was tortured in my own home, but as a new believer, I kept thinking, *I've got to walk in love. Don't be angry or judgmental.* So I didn't deal with the issues. These are only a few of my daily struggles with that man.

After several weeks of torment, I learned my roommate was a practicing homosexual. I told him to leave immediately, but he was reluctant. I paid for everything while he lived in sin. About the same time the singles' pastor discovered his lifestyle, and he was removed from leadership. I was one of the last to discover his perverted lifestyle. My disobedience blinded my eyes to discernment.

Because I ignored my dad's advice I lost hundreds of dollars, not to mention my peace. I was devastated, and those were two of the hardest months I'd ever lived through. I cried out to God when it was all over, "Lord, why did this happen? I trusted You for guidance."

The Lord showed me He'd given me guidance, but I refused it. I was baffled, and I questioned, "How did You give me guidance?"

He responded, *Through your father, but you didn't listen.*

"But my dad is not born again," I argued.

The Lord then brought to my remembrance that His Word did not say, "Children, obey your parents *only* if they are born again." He explained, *You are My child; therefore, I place My wisdom and instruction in the hearts of your parents for your guidance and protection.*

I quickly responded, "But I'm on my own now. My dad lives more than a thousand miles away, and he is not paying the bills."

He said, *Just because you pay your own bills, and your parents are a thousand miles away, doesn't mean My command to obey them no longer applies.* His command promises it will go well with us if we adhere, and I can testify it *did not* go well with me!

He showed me at what point a man is released from his father and mother's authority. Right from the beginning God commanded, "Therefore a man shall leave his father and mother and be joined to his wife, and they shall become one flesh" (Gen. 2:24).

The last instruction a parent gives his child is the blessing on a marriage partner. As a side note, after Lisa's father gave me his blessing to marry her, she told me she was surprised. I asked why, and she said, "Because he told me he didn't like you because you're a Christian." This experience served as a confirmation that the heart of the king (those in authority over us) is in the hand of God.

Returning to God's command, his words emphasize that when a man and a woman join in marriage, a new order of authority is set up. The reason God didn't mention a woman leaving her parents is that she does not establish the new family's order; the man heads the authority.

Once children wed, they are no longer commanded to obey their parents, but they are still to honor them. I remember on one occasion asking my parents why they didn't counsel my wife and me when they saw us heading into problems. They simply said, "You never asked us for advice." How godly they behaved! I've seen parents interfere by trying to give instruction the same way they had prior to their children's marriage. Hurt feelings and misunderstandings result because they have not released their children as instructed.

Specific Warnings for Children

After serving as a youth pastor a few years, I saw the dangerous paths many young people tread. I would like to bring out some specific counsel from the Word of God on the importance of honoring parents. I do this in hopes any young person who reads this will avoid the leaven this sin spreads among young people, for it is contagious and deadly. Scripture declares, "'Cursed is the one who treats his father or his mother with contempt.' And all the people shall say, 'Amen!'" (Deut. 27:16).

Across my desk sat a single mother and her teenage son. In the course of conversation this young man spoke to her repeatedly with contempt, as though she was stupid and inferior. I'd corrected him a couple of times already. At the end of the counseling session, to my surprise, I blurted out, "Young man, if you do not repent of your attitude and behavior toward your mother, you'll end up in jail." I was as shocked as they were by my words. The young man was a professing believer and a member of our youth group. How could this happen?

Almost six years later (I was no longer youth pastor, but traveled), the boy's mother saw me one Sunday morning after the service. She said, "Pastor John, do you remember telling my son that if he didn't change, he'd end up in prison? Well, he has been in prison a couple of years now."

I'd almost forgotten it, but it came back to me when she mentioned it. I thought, *How can this mother be excited as she shares this with me.* I learned why. She continued, "He's on fire for God now. He is witnessing to the other inmates and involved in the prisoners' ministry. He is reading your books and receiving greatly from them."

I was in awe of how God's judgment on the young man's life had turned everything around. It would have been better if he had not had to learn from affliction, but had heeded the words spoken years earlier. But what was important—his passion for God—was now in his heart.

We can see the seriousness of children attacking their parents physically or verbally by examining how they were to be handled in the Old Testament: "He who strikes his father or his mother shall surely be put to death" (Ex. 21:15); and "He who curses his father or his mother shall surely be put to death" (Ex. 21:17) And Jesus referenced the Old Testament commands when He said, "For God commanded, saying, 'Honor your father and your mother'; and, 'He who curses father or mother, let him be put to death'" (Matt. 15:4).

Moses gave instruction of how they were to handle a rebellious child:

> If a man has a stubborn and rebellious son who will not obey the voice of his father or the voice of his mother, and who, when they have chastened him, will not heed them, then his father and his mother shall take hold of him and bring him out to the elders of his city, to the gate of his city. And they shall say to the elders of his city, "This son of ours is stubborn and rebellious; he will not obey our voice; he is a glutton and a drunkard." Then all the men of his city shall stone him to death with stones; so you shall put away the evil from among you, and all Israel shall hear and fear. (Deut. 21:18–21)

If these words were applied today, there would be young people within our churches put to death on a regular basis. Even though this order of punishment no longer exists, we still see God's attitude toward rebellious behavior is quite certain and severe. It hasn't changed just because the form of judgment has changed. We must not allow rebellion in our hearts, for it's a killer.

I have warned my children to guard themselves from any form of rebellion. The most deceptive or subtle form is complaining. It despises authority by inadvertently saying, "I don't like the way you are leading me, and if I were you, I would do it differently." This insults leadership. Can you see now why complaining contributed to the children of Israel being kept out of the promised land? Their complaining communicated their contempt toward God, even though it was directed toward Moses. In essence they told God He wasn't doing it right, and they would lead differently.

Honoring our parents brings the wonderful promise of a long and good life. I would rather choose life than judgment. This must be settled in our hearts.

The Marriage

Let's turn our attention to divine order in marriage. Scripture tells us, wives are to submit to their husbands "in everything" (Eph. 5:24). This command applies not just to spiritual things, but to natural areas of life as well. Paul stated, "To their own husbands." Other men do not have authority over the wife, just her husband. A pastor has authority over another's wife in the area of church and spiritual matters, a boss has authority in relation to her job outside the home, and civil authority has authority in civil matters, but when it comes to the home, the husband is her authority.

In the mid-1980s my wife and I fell into an erroneous teaching. We were told the New Testament was written by some chauvinistic men, and we should not adhere to their words when it came to authority between a husband and a wife. We were told Jesus provided equal redemption for all. This is most definitely true, but redemption does not negate authority. For years we had no peace in our home. We were in a constant struggle for leadership.

After years of turmoil, one day I told my wife, "God has made me the head of this home, and I am going to lead, whether you follow me or not." Things started turning around for me, but not for my wife. The Lord had shown me that as a leader, I was never to force those under me to follow. Jesus does not do this with us. If those under our authority don't follow, they suffer.

I entered into a divine rest and peace. However, Lisa continued to carry all the pressures of the home. She was convinced I was an irresponsible leader. I was young and had many flaws, so many of her concerns appeared justifiable by reason of my past mistakes. Sometimes her fears became so extreme, she'd wake me up in the middle of the night to remind me I was not carrying my load, and she was doing much more than her share. I simply suggested giving all the care to God, and I went back to sleep while she lay wide awake beside me, dreading the worst.

The burden increased for Lisa. Worry constantly plagued her. Her mind was never at rest but always scrambling as she mentally ran the spectrum of every imaginable crisis our family could face.

A short while later the tension she carried became almost unbearable. She had to take long showers or baths to try to alleviate the pressure. One night in one of those showers while she was complaining about me, God spoke to her, *Lisa, do you think John is a good leader?*

She quickly responded, "No, I do not! I don't trust him!"

Lisa, you don't have to trust John, He replied. *You have to trust only Me. You don't think John is doing a very good job as the head of this home. You feel that you can do better. The tension and unrest you're experiencing are the weight and pressure of being the head of a household. It is a yoke to you, but a mantle to your husband. Lay it down.*

Lisa immediately saw it. God, not a power-hungry man, was the One who said she was to submit to her husband. The leadership of our home was oppressive to her because it was not her position to fill. God had allowed her to experience the load of responsibility without the anointing or grace to carry it, which He gives the husband. She came out of that shower weeping and asking forgiveness. She entered the peace and rest I had entered a few months earlier, and our home for the first time in years experienced true harmony.

The Holy Spirit's dealing with her that night helped her realize that God didn't say submit only if you agree or like what your husband chooses or decides. She realized if she submitted to God's command, then His protection would be hers. Have I made mistakes since then? Absolutely. Plenty of them. However, God has protected Lisa through my mistakes and given her peace. When she is submitted, His protection is hers, no matter what unwise decisions her husband makes.

UNREASONABLE OR UNSAVED HUSBANDS

This command for wives to submit to their husbands is not just given to those who have believing husbands. Peter said, "Wives, in the same way be submissive to your husbands so that, if any of them do not believe the word, they may be won over without words by the behavior of their wives" (1 Peter 3:1 NIV).

Let's first of all investigate the phrase "Wives, in the same way . . .". Peter had just concluded discussing how to handle unfair treatment from authorities. (We dealt with this in detail in Chapter 13.) But he then immediately offered similar instructions for wives in regard to their husbands. If we were to pull these words together, we would read,

> You who are slaves must accept the authority of your masters. Do whatever they tell you—not only if they are kind and reasonable, but even if they are harsh. For God is pleased with you when, for the sake of your conscience, you patiently endure unfair treatment . . . In the same way, you wives must accept the authority of your husbands, even those who refuse to accept the Good News. (1 Peter 2:18–19; 3:1 NLT)

It is sad but true. I've met some "believing" husbands who are harsher as leaders than unbelievers. However, as a general rule, the most difficult husbands to submit to are those who have not been saved. Again I want to emphasize, if a husband instructs his wife to go a direction contrary to the Word of God, she is not to obey his instruction, but she is to maintain a submitted attitude.

Peter continued by showing how this submitted attitude would be the most powerful witness to the husband, even more than the preached word. I know a woman whose husband was not a believer. For years she preached to him. She left tracts on his workbench, Bibles beside his bed and favorite sitting places, and Christian magazines on the coffee table. When she asked couples over for social gatherings, the men were always strong believers, and she hoped they would witness to her husband.

One day God spoke to her, *How long are you going to hinder your husband's salvation?*

In shock she questioned, "I am hindering my husband's salvation. How?"

The Lord showed her as long as she preached to him and manipulated the circumstances, she was not doing what God had instructed. He showed her the scripture in 1 Peter and instructed, *Get rid of the tracts, magazines, and Bibles, and quit asking strategic couples over for dinner.*

She told me, "John, I just loved him and submitted to him, and within a couple of months my husband gave his life to Jesus." I have stayed in their home, and I know this man loves the Lord very much.

If we would simply believe, trust, and obey what God's Word states, we would see miracles in our homes and enjoy peace that passes understanding. I cannot overemphasize the fact that God, not controlling, manipulating, power-hungry leaders, gave these words. He spoke them for our provision and protection, some of which we'll see in the next chapter. In the midst of hardships we can trust His promise: "For I know the thoughts that I think toward you, says the LORD, thoughts of peace and not of evil, to give you a future and a hope" (Jer. 29:11).

SOCIAL AUTHORITY

In the realms of jobs and schools we are also given specific instructions in the New Testament. Paul instructed,

> [Tell] bond servants to be submissive to their masters, to be pleasing and give satisfaction in every way. [Warn them] not to talk back or contradict, nor to steal by taking things of small value, but to prove themselves truly loyal and entirely reliable and faithful throughout, so

that in everything they may be an ornament and do credit to the teaching [which is] from and about God our Savior. (Titus 2:9–10 AMPLIFIED)

I have rejoiced when I have heard unbelievers who were bosses or owners of companies report to me how they see Jesus in their employees, not because they preach, but because they display His character in difficult situations and in their work ethics. They have said to me, "They never argue, complain, or talk back to me," or "They work harder than the other employees," or "They are the most honest and trustworthy employees I have." These men are open to hear what I say concerning Jesus due to the witness of their employees.

However, I have experienced the opposite. I sat next to a man on an airplane who owned the second largest taxi company in a large city. We were having a pleasant conversation until he found out I was a minister. Then he clammed up and wouldn't speak as freely. Since we'd already established a good rapport, it was easy for me to ask why his demeanor had changed.

He said, "All right, I'll tell you. I had a woman who worked for our company. She was one of those 'born-again Christians.' She preached to everyone in the office, taking away from her and others' productivity. When she left my company, she took things that weren't hers, and left me with an eight-thousand-dollar long-distance phone bill to her son who lived in Germany."

I was heartbroken. Everyone in that office would have a hard time hearing the Word of God after her insubordination and theft. For this reason Paul said, "[Warn them] not to talk back or contradict, nor to steal by taking things of small value, but to prove themselves truly loyal and entirely reliable and faithful throughout." When we submit, work hard, and obey the rules and laws of our employers and schools, we are witnesses of the grace of our Lord Jesus Christ.

Paul said in another place:

Servants, obey in everything those who are your earthly masters, not only when their eyes are on you as pleasers of men, but in simplicity of purpose [with all your heart] because of your reverence for the Lord and as a sincere expression of your devotion to Him. Whatever may be your task work at it heartily (from the soul), as [something done] for the Lord and not for men. (Col. 3:22–23 AMPLIFIED)

Notice the phrase "obey in everything." It doesn't matter how unreasonable your boss or teacher seems. Your obedience to him is actually your obedience to the Lord.

Paul went on to say, "Knowing [with all certainty] that it is from the Lord [and not from men] that you will receive the inheritance which is your [real] reward. [The One Whom] you are actually serving [is] the Lord Christ (the Messiah)" (Col. 3:24 AMPLIFIED). If that woman had known she was really stealing from the Lord, she never would have done it. She lacked understanding and the fear of the Lord as well.

Paul continued in the next verse, "But he who does wrong will be repaid for what he has done, and there is no partiality." I like the way *the Message* brings this out: "The sullen servant who does shoddy work will be held responsible. Being a Christian doesn't cover up bad work."

The woman will most likely not be held responsible by the owner of the taxi service or the civil government; rather, she will be held responsible by the Lord and called to give an account at the judgment seat of Christ: "So we make it our goal to please him, whether we are at home in the body or away from it. For we must all appear before the judgment seat of Christ, that each one may receive what is due him for the things done while in the body, whether good or bad" (2 Cor. 5:9–10 NIV).

GENERAL ISSUES

Many people say they will not listen to leaders who do not live what they preach. Yet does this thinking stem from obedience or natural reasoning? We read, "Then Jesus said to the multitudes and to His disciples, The scribes and Pharisees sit on Moses' seat [of authority]. So observe and practice all they tell you; but do not do what they do, for they preach, but do not practice" (Matt. 23:1–3 AMPLIFIED).

Jesus commanded submission even to corrupt leaders who didn't live what they preached. He pointed the multitudes to the authority upon them, not to their personal lives. Watchman Nee wrote,

> What a risk God has taken in instituting authorities! What a loss God will incur if the delegated authorities He institutes misrepresent Him! Yet, undaunted, God has set up these authorities. It is much easier for us to fearlessly obey authorities than for God to institute them. Can we not then obey them without apprehension since God Himself has not been afraid to entrust authority to men? Even as God has boldly established authorities, so let us courageously obey them. If anything should be amiss, the fault does not lie with us but with the authorities, for the Lord declares: "Let every soul be in subjection to the higher powers" (Rom. 13:1).

> The obedient needs only to obey; the Lord will not hold us responsible for any mistaken obedience, rather will He hold the delegated authority responsible for his erroneous act. Insubordination, however, is rebellion, and for this the one under authority must answer to God. (*Spiritual Authority*, pp. 69–71)

This was written by a man who was unjustly treated by authorities. In the 1930s and 1940s he helped establish local churches in China completely independent of foreign missionary organizations, and he was instrumental in bringing many into the kingdom of God. His activities infuriated the authorities, and he was arrested in 1952 and found guilty of a large number of false charges. He was imprisoned until his death in 1972. Yet his reverential fear of the Lord was a witness to many in prison, and many were saved through his testimony. His writings still speak to multitudes many years later.

RECOGNIZING AUTHORITY

I have pointed out throughout this message how to recognize appointed authorities, but as I conclude this chapter, it would be expedient to reinforce what's been said. In civil and social areas, recognizing legitimate authority is not difficult. We read, "Be submissive to every human institution and authority for the sake of the Lord" (1 Peter 2:13 AMPLIFIED). We recognize public officials as those sworn into office or hired as government workers. Then there are leaders of companies or hired teachers or directors of educational institutions, and we know their authority is authentic.

Authority in the home is easily recognizable. When a woman marries a man, she comes under his authority, protection, and provision. When a child is born into a family, the parents are his authority. If a child is adopted, he should honor his parents as if they were his biological parents. A child in an orphanage or foster care should respect the leaders as his authority.

Discerning legitimate authority is a little more complex in the church. Scripture warns of false apostles, prophets, and leaders found within the church; we are not to submit to them. As Paul said, "To whom we did not yield submission even for an hour" (Gal. 2:5). False leaders can manifest in two ways. First, they teach doctrine that does not line up with Scripture. In the context of what Paul just said, he wrote, "But even if we, or an angel from heaven, preach any other gospel to you than what we have preached to you, let him be accursed" (Gal. 1:8). For that reason Paul would not honor those leaders with submission.

Second, false leaders arise within the church through self-appointment. God's appointment is initiated by the Holy Spirit and confirmed by the existing ruling elders who have observed the candidate's life. In the Old Testament this process is illustrated in Joshua's ordination. God said to Moses,

> Take Joshua son of Nun, who has the Spirit in him, and lay your hands on him. Present him to Eleazar the priest before the whole community, and publicly commission him with the responsibility of leading the people. Transfer your authority to him so the whole community of Israel will obey him. (Num. 27:18–20 NLT)

God chose Joshua, but confirmed His choice through the existing appointed authorities, Moses and Eleazar. Those men had observed

Joshua's life for years. This pattern appears in the New Testament as well (Acts 13:1–4).

Paul asserted, "For not he who commends himself is approved, but whom the Lord commends" (2 Cor. 10:18). Submitting to self-appointed authorities is a dangerous move. God will always confirm His appointments before the church where the candidates have served faithfully. Jesus rebuked the believers of Thyatira for submitting to the teaching and counterfeit authority of the self-appointed prophetess named Jezebel (Rev. 2:20–25). I wrote an entire book on how to recognize self-appointed ministers. titled *Thus Saith the Lord?* it is a good reference for this message; it deals with the abuse of spiritual authority as well as the counterfeit.

When we are truly saved and seeking the will of God, we will recognize legitimate authority in the church. Jesus said, "If anyone wills to do His will, he shall know concerning the doctrine, whether it is from God or whether I speak on My own authority" (John 7:17). The key is found in the words, "If anyone wills to do His will." When we have a heart after God, He gives us discernment by the Holy Spirit. As John confirmed, "You have an anointing from the Holy One, and you know all things" (1 John 2:20).

Watchman Nee wrote, "If we would indeed learn how to obey God, we would then have no trouble recognizing on whom God's authority rests" (*Spiritual Authority*, p. 62). To know God is to know authority, for He and His authority are inseparable.

God rewards those who diligently seek and obey Him. In the next chapter we will move on to see some of the many and great benefits for submitting to authority.

CHAPTER 16

GREAT FAITH

The greater our level of submission, the greater our faith.

In this final chapter we'll focus on the benefits of taking the "vaccination shot," in other words, the tremendous rewards and blessings to all who come under cover. A volume of books could be written expounding the benefits alone. Though we will cover only a few, you are destined to discover more through your own personal study and experiences in Christ.

LORD, INCREASE OUR FAITH

A few years ago I went into my office at 5:30 A.M. to pray as I'd done so many mornings before. Yet before I could begin, I heard the Holy Spirit's directive: *Go to Luke chapter 17 and start reading from verse 5.*

Excitedly I turned to the reference and noticed it was a portion of scripture I was very familiar with. I'd even preached messages out of it before, but this didn't deter my enthusiasm. I knew from past experiences, if He told me to read specific verses, I'd learn something I'd missed before. Let's look at it.

The apostles asked the Lord, "Increase our faith" (Luke 17:5). Before we go on to discuss what He showed me that morning, let me point out the reason those men cried out to have their faith increased.

Had Jesus just raised a dead person? Had He just fed the five thousand with a few loaves and fish? Or had He just calmed the raging sea by speaking to it? The answers are no, no, no! Jesus had just told those men, "Take heed to yourselves. If your brother sins against you, rebuke him; and if he repents, forgive him. And if he sins against you seven times in a day, and seven times in a day returns to you, saying, 'I repent,' you shall forgive him" (vv. 3–4).

Notable power miracles had not inspired their cry for greater faith. It was the simple command to forgive those who had wronged them. Those men lived under the law and were accustomed to responding to an offense with the mind-set of an eye for an eye and a tooth for a tooth. Jesus was directing them to walk in a way that seemed totally unreasonable. The command to walk in the character of God jarred them. How could they obey such a tall order? The answer, "Increase our faith!" Those men knew obedience and faith were directly connected, something I was about to see in a whole new light.

Upon hearing their cry for greater faith, Jesus told this parable: "If you have faith as a mustard seed, you can say to this mulberry tree, 'Be pulled up by the roots and be planted in the sea,' and it would obey you" (v. 6). I felt I understood this point. I'd taught along these lines and was familiar with Jesus' teaching to have the faith of God, and if we say to the mountain to be removed and cast into the sea and would not doubt in our hearts, we would have what we say (Mark 11:22–24). This was no different. He was only using a mulberry tree instead of a mountain.

Also illustrated in these words is that faith is given to each and every believer, as a mustard seed. It is the kingdom principle of seed time and harvest: "The kingdom of God is as if a man should scatter seed on the ground" (Mark 4:26). When we were saved, we were allotted a measure of faith (Rom. 12:3). This faith is in seed form, and it is our responsibility to cultivate and grow it. How does it grow? The answer is forthcoming.

A SERVANT'S PROPER TIME TO EAT?

I read on carefully because the next four verses always stumped me. I was about to discover Jesus wasn't giving His disciples mere formulas on how to increase their faith. He was about to direct them in a way of life that deals directly with the area of obedience to authority. Listen to His parable:

> Which of you, having a servant plowing or tending sheep, will say to him when he has come in from the field, "Come at once and sit down to eat"? But will he not rather say to him, "Prepare something for my supper, and gird yourself and serve me till I have eaten and drunk, and afterward you will eat and drink"? Does he thank that servant because he did the things that were commanded him? I think not. (Luke 17:7–9)

I had always questioned why the Lord apparently changed subjects. He went from speaking about the faith that plucks up trees to protocol for a servant. It just didn't make sense to me, but that morning I would understand.

Reading these verses again slowly, I listened to my heart for His inspiration. Suddenly I heard, *What is the ultimate purpose of a servant who works your field? What is the ultimate purpose of a servant who tends flocks? What is the end result?*

I thought a moment. Then it came to me: to put food on the table. I realized what Jesus was communicating. If the end result of the servant's labor is food on his employer's table, why would the servant eat before his master was served? Wouldn't he complete his job first? Of course he would! An unfinished job can be just as bad as one not started. Why plow your fields and not eat? Why tend your flocks and not partake of the wool, meat, or milk?

Once I saw this, I read Jesus' next statement: "So likewise you, when you have *done all* those things which you are *commanded*, say, 'We are unprofitable servants. We have done what was our duty to do'" (Luke 17:10, emphasis added).

He turned the example back to us. As I read, the words *done all* and *commanded* jumped off the page. Jesus connected this servant's obedience to his master with our obedience to God. In doing so He made three significant points related to increased faith:

1. There is a direct connection between faith and obedience to authority.

2. Faith increases only when we complete what we're commanded to do.

3. An attitude of true humility is of utmost importance.

Let's discuss each point from the scripture.

THE CONNECTION BETWEEN FAITH AND OBEDIENCE TO AUTHORITY

The first point, the direct connection between faith and obedience, is seen in an officer's encounter with Jesus in the Gospels. Jesus entered Capernaum, and a Roman soldier holding the rank of centurion sought Him out. He pleaded with Jesus to heal his servant who was paralyzed and tormented. Jesus responded, "I will come and heal him" (Matt. 8:7).

The centurion interjected, "Lord, I am not worthy that You should come under my roof. But only speak a word, and my servant will be healed" (Matt. 8:8).

Jesus was willing and ready to go to the man's home, but the soldier felt unworthy and begged Him not to. He asked Jesus to give the command from where He stood, and his servant would be healed. The centurion explained his reasoning: "For I also am a man under authority, having soldiers under me. And I say to this one, 'Go,' and he goes; and to another, 'Come,' and he comes; and to my servant, 'Do this,' and he does it" (Matt. 8:9).

Let's discuss his position. There were six thousand soldiers in a Roman legion. Within the legion there were sixty centurions who reported to the legion commander. Each centurion had one hundred soldiers under his command.

The Roman officer communicated to Jesus that he had the respect and submission of his soldiers because he was submitted to his commander. Therefore, he had the backing of the authority of his commander, who in turn had the backing of the authority of Rome. In simpler terms he said, "I am under authority; therefore, I have authority. So all I have to do is speak a word, and those under me respond immediately to my orders."

He said, "For I *also* . . ." He recognized Jesus was a Servant of God under His kingdom's authority; therefore, the soldier knew Jesus had authority in the heavenly realms of the spiritual world, just as the soldier had authority in the military world. He understood all that was necessary was the command, and infirmity would have to obey, just as those under his authority jumped when he gave command.

How did Jesus' respond? "When Jesus heard it, He marveled, and said to those who followed, 'Assuredly, I say to you, I have not found such great faith, not even in Israel!'" (Matt. 8:10)

The greatest faith Jesus encountered in more than thirty-three years on earth was not John the Baptist's or His mother Mary's. It was not from any of the children of Israel who received healings or miracles. It was not from any of the Twelve. It belonged to a Roman citizen, a soldier, one of Israel's conquerors. What made his faith so great? *Because he understood and walked in submission to authority.*

That was what Jesus was communicating in His parable of how to have great faith. The authority in which we walk is directly proportional to our submission to authority. The greater our level of submission, the greater our faith. Now tie this in with what Jesus said to His disciples who desired increased faith: "If you have faith as a mustard seed, you can say to this mulberry tree, 'Be pulled up by the roots and be planted in the sea,' and it would obey you" (Luke 17:6). Jesus said all you have to do is speak a word, and the tree will obey you! Who does this mulberry tree obey? The one who "did the things that were commanded him" (Luke 17:9).

Obedience to Completion

The second major point Jesus communicated is that faith increases as we complete what we're commanded to do. His exact words were, "So likewise you, when you have *done all* those things which you are *com-*

manded." A servant is responsible to carry out to completion the will of his master, not just a portion or a sampling of it. Too often we begin assignments we never finish because we lose interest, or the labor and suffering become too intense. The true and faithful servant completes the project, no matter the hardship or obstacles. He works the fields, brings in the fruit of his labor for his master, and prepares the meal. His actions represent true obedience.

Abraham is called the father of our faith (Rom. 4:11–12). Abraham was childless. God appeared to him at the age of seventy-five and promised that he would have a son through whom he would become the father of many nations. After years of waiting and obedience, Abraham had the promised son at one hundred years of age.

God allowed Abraham to grow very close to Isaac. Once their love was strong, God tested him by commanding him to take Isaac to the land of Moriah and put him to death as an offering. Scripture records, "So Abraham rose early in the morning" (Gen. 22:3). Notice his instant obedience. Some people mull around for days, weeks, months, and sometimes even years contemplating whether to obey God. They lack holy fear, which is the reason they don't have great faith. Once we know God has spoken, we should respond immediately. If it is a major life change, however, we are wise to seek confirmation with the authorities who are over us.

It took Abraham three days to get to Moriah. The three-day journey gave him time to think things through. If he was going to turn back, he would have done it then. But he didn't. Abraham continued all the way to the top of the mountain and bound his only son on the altar they built together. He raised the knife to slay Isaac when the angel of the Lord stopped him, "Do not lay your hand on the lad, or do anything to him; for now I know that you fear God" (Gen. 22:12).

Abraham obeyed to completion! He did not stop short, even by letting go of the most important thing in his life, his Isaac, his heir, his hope, his promise from God. Isaac's death would represent letting go of his own life. Abraham proved his passion for obedience outweighed his desire for the promises. We must have this resolve in our

hearts as well. *O Lord, raise up a generation of these men and women today!*
As a result, God spoke,

> By Myself I have sworn, says the LORD, because you have done this
> thing, and have not withheld your son, your only son—blessing I will
> bless you, and in multiplying I will multiply your descendants as the
> stars of the heaven and as the sand which is on the seashore; and your
> descendants shall possess the gate of their enemies. In your seed all
> the nations of the earth shall be blessed, because you have obeyed My
> voice. (Gen. 22:16–18)

Look at what was promised Abraham, as well as his descendants,
because of his obedience to completion! "Your descendants shall pos-
sess the gate of their enemies." Why do you think Jesus said, "The gates
of hell shall not prevail against the church"? The obedience of father
Abraham opened the door for Jesus to provide this for the church. His
faith or obedience still speaks.

Now read carefully what the writer of the book of Hebrews declared
about Abraham's obedience:

> We desire that each one of you show the same diligence to the full
> assurance of hope *until the end* [completion], that you do not become
> sluggish, *but imitate those who through faith and patience inherit the promises.*
> For when God made a promise to Abraham, because He could swear
> by no one greater, He swore by Himself, saying, "Surely blessing I
> will bless you, and multiplying I will multiply you." And so, after he
> had patiently endured, he obtained the promise. (Heb. 6:11–15,
> emphasis added)

Abraham was diligent unto the end. He obeyed all the way to completion—he patiently endured. Compare his acts of obedience with the
behavior of King Saul, discussed in an earlier chapter. He was diligent to
go to war and completed more than 99 percent of what he was commanded. He spared only a fraction of the best, and that he reasoned was
for the Lord. The bottom line: he didn't finish what God had com-

manded him. Outwardly he came close to completion, yet his disobedience cost him greatly. He got right up to the point of putting food on the "Master's table," but his heart motives were revealed in what he withheld. He turned the command into something beneficial for himself rather than honoring the One he served.

How many people, like Saul, start out on fire with enthusiasm, then when things get uncomfortable, difficult, or results aren't as fast as expected, they disobey? Or with others they see an opportunity to benefit themselves while only slightly detouring from the directives of authority. All the while they justify it with religious purposes or reasonings, as Saul did when he spared the best sheep for sacrifices to God, sheep that were to be destroyed according to the word of the Lord. If obedience is not complete, faith will not increase, but dwindle!

Abraham received the promises through true faith and endurance, which translates to obedience to completion. His faith and obedience were inseparable, as James so clearly pointed out (in this scripture I am going to substitute the words *obedient actions* for the word *works*):

> But do you want to know, O foolish man, that faith without *obedient actions* is dead? Was not Abraham our father justified by *obedient actions* when he offered Isaac his son on the altar? Do you see that faith was working together with his *obedient actions*, and by *obedient actions* faith was made perfect? And the Scripture was fulfilled which says, "Abraham believed God, and it was accounted to him for righteousness." And he was called the friend of God. You see then that a man is justified by *obedient actions*, and not by faith only . . . For as the body without the spirit is dead, so faith without *obedient actions* is dead also. (2:20–24, 26)

In the final verse, faith and obedient actions are compared to the body and spirit of a man. In his example, you'll discover faith is compared to the physical body, and obedient actions are likened to the spirit of a man. The two must have each other to express themselves in this world. If the spirit departs the body, the body dies. Once the spirit departs, the body cannot be raised unless the spirit returns, as in the case of Lazarus. Thus, James showed from his example how faith completely depends on obedient actions. That was why James said, "Show me your faith without your *obedient actions*, and I will show you my faith by my *obedient actions*" (James 2:18).

Faith is not true faith apart from obedience. Make no mistake about it. Scripture makes it clear that "by *obedient actions* faith is made complete!"

The apostles cried out, "Lord, increase our faith." Jesus then talked about obedient actions all the way to completion! Oh, my dear fellow believer, do you now see why in the beginning of this book I wrote of the urgency and importance of this message? We all need to heed these words in this hour of increased lawlessness.

You may say, "I thought faith comes by hearing and believing." Yes, this is true, but the evidence of belief is actions that accompany the confession. For this reason we're told if we hear the word and do not obey, we are deceived. Then our faith is not real, but counterfeit.

GREAT BOLDNESS IN THE FAITH

This truth is seen again as the apostle Paul described those who serve in the church: "Before they are appointed as deacons, they should be given other responsibilities in the church as a test of their character and ability. If they do well, then they may serve as deacons" (1 Tim. 3:10 NLT). A deacon is not a leader, but one who executes another's command. W. E. Vine says that the Greek word for "deacon" "primarily denotes a 'servant'." He further states it identifies one under another's authority. Paul told us once deacons serve faithfully, their obedience positions them for the following: "For those who have served well as deacons obtain for themselves a good standing and great boldness in the faith which is in Christ Jesus" (1 Tim. 3:13).

Two things are promised the servants Jesus described in our opening parable: (1) good standing, which includes spiritual promotions (Ps. 75:7); (2) great faith for those who fully obey. Faith and obedient actions are seen as inseparable and dependent on each other in the Scriptures. Examples abound throughout the Bible:

- Abel's faith was revealed by his obedience, and his testimony still speaks thousands of years later (Heb. 11:4).

- Enoch's faith, manifested by obedience, caused him to walk with God and then to be taken and escape death.

- Noah's faith was evidenced by his obedience and salvation was provided for his family while condemning a world completely saturated with sin.

- Abraham's faith, which was evidenced by his obedience, made him the father of many nations.

- Joseph's faith, manifested by his obedience, brought his family deliverance.

- Joshua's and Caleb's faith, through their obedience, granted them an inheritance of the promised land. Joshua was faithful to serve Moses and became his successor. He led the younger generation into the promised land of milk and honey.

- Rahab the prostitute was "considered righteous for what she did when she gave lodging to the spies and sent them off in a different direction" (James 2:25 NIV). Her obedience saved her whole household. It was the evidence that she had true faith.

- Hannah's obedience and submissive attitude to the priest who insulted her opened a womb that would provide revival for the nation.

- David's obedience not to attack his leader made him a great king with a heart after God, not after the order of Saul.

- Daniel, Shadrach, Meshach, and Abed-Nego's obedience brought them great favor with God and the king.

And what more shall I say? For the time would fail me to tell of Gideon and Barak and Samson and Jephthah, also of . . . Samuel and the prophets: who through faith subdued kingdoms, worked right-eousness, obtained promises, stopped the mouths of lions, quenched the violence of fire, escaped the edge of the sword, out of weakness were made strong, became valiant in battle, turned to flight the armies of the aliens. Women received their dead raised to life again. And others were tortured, not accepting deliverance, that they might obtain a better resurrection. Still others had trial of mockings and scourgings, yes, and of chains and imprisonment. They were stoned, they were sawn in two, were tempted, were slain with the sword. They wandered about in sheepskins and goatskins, being destitute, afflicted, tormented—of whom the world was not worthy. They wandered in deserts and mountains, in dens and caves of the earth. And all these, having obtained a good testimony through faith. (Heb. 11:32–39)

The writer of Hebrews intermingled faith with obedient actions. They're inseparable. If faith was given just to receive miracles, then why would he include those who wandered in the deserts and mountains, afflicted and tormented? Those men and women finished well. They obeyed to completion. This is true faith.

If you desire great faith, then obey God's authority, whether direct or delegated, all the way to completion. Your faith is directly proportional to your obedience!

THE SAFEGUARD OF HUMILITY

The final point Jesus impressed upon His disciples was to keep an attitude of humility. He said, "So likewise you, when you have done all those things which you are commanded, say, *'We are unprofitable servants. We have done what was our duty to do.'*" When we maintain this attitude, we position ourselves for the reward that comes from the Master. Those who exalt themselves will be humbled. However, those who are base in their own eyes, the Master exalts. James urged, "Humble yourselves in the sight of the Lord, and He will lift you up" (4:10).

To remain lowly in heart is to remain positioned for the rewards of obedience. To pride yourself in your own obedience is to position yourself for a fall, even though you've obeyed. This can spoil everything you adhered to. You could follow the counsel or Word of God in this book, yet by pride lose all you gained through obedience.

Lucifer was anointed. He was the seal of perfection, full of wisdom and perfect in beauty. He was established by God, and he resided on His holy mountain. He was perfect in his ways until pride was found in him. Then he was thrown out of heaven as fast as lightning comes down from the sky. Paul instructed those appointed to a position of authority never to be "a novice, lest being puffed up with pride he fall into the same condemnation as the devil" (1 Tim. 3:6).

Paul accomplished many things by his obedience to the call of God. But the longer he lived, the more he grew in humility. In the year A.D. 56 he wrote to a church he started in the virgin territory at Corinth during his third major missionary journey of the four he completed. He was ten to eleven years away from death and a seasoned veteran in the service of Jesus. Yet hear his words: "For I am the least of the apostles, who am not worthy to be called an apostle" (1 Cor. 15:9).

Do you hear the humility in his words? He did not even consider himself worthy of the title "apostle." I want to point out: this is not false humility. Counterfeit humility knows how to use politically correct words in order to *appear* humble, yet there is no lowliness of heart or mind. It is deceptive and untrue. But when writing scripture under the inspiration of the Holy Spirit, a man cannot lie! So when Paul said he was the bottom of the barrel of the apostles, he wasn't using politically correct jargon. He was expressing true humility.

Now look at Paul's very next statement: "I labored more abundantly than they all, yet not I, but the grace of God which was with me" (1 Cor. 15:10). "I labored more abundantly than all the other apostles!" Wait, was Paul bragging? That comment sounds arrogant, yet it is not. It precedes another declaration of Paul's dependence. He followed his assessment of himself as the least of the apostles with an acknowledgment that all he had done had been done only by God's grace. He was fully aware that all he had spiritually achieved flowed from the ability that God had given him.

Paul's self-description as "the least of the apostles" is hard to swallow. In his day and throughout church history, he has been esteemed as one of the greatest apostles. Now consider what Paul said to the Ephesians in A.D. 62, four to five years prior to his departure. In those years since he wrote 1 Corinthians, he accomplished more than at any time period in his life. He described himself, "To me, who am less than the least of all the saints, this grace was given, that I should preach among the Gentiles the unsearchable riches of Christ" (Eph. 3:8).

Years earlier he called himself the least apostle, and here he described himself as lower than the least of all the saints! What? If anyone could boast in his Christianity and leadership, it surely was Paul. Yet the longer he served the Lord, the smaller he viewed himself. His humility progressively grew. Could this be why the grace of God on his life increased proportionately to the older he became? Could this be why God revealed His ways so intimately to Paul that it even baffled the apostle Peter (2 Peter 3:15–16)? The psalmist declared, "The humble He teaches His way" (Ps. 25:9). In the light of this, could it be why Moses knew the ways of God so well, the very man God describes as "very humble, more than all men who were on the face of the earth" (Num. 12:3)? Perhaps both knew a secret to obtaining great faith with God that few others had learned.

At the close of Paul's life, circa A.D. 64 to 66, he sent two letters to Timothy and therein described himself, "This is a faithful saying and worthy of all acceptance, that Christ Jesus came into the world to save sinners, of whom I am chief" (1 Tim. 1:15). He called himself the "chief of sinners"! Notice he didn't say, "I was chief."

No, after years of great accomplishments, His confession was not, "I have done it all, and my great ministry should be esteemed." Nor did he boast, "I have done a great work and deserve the respect of a true apostle." He didn't even write, "I am the least of the apostles," as he had several years previously. Nor did he write, "I am the least of the saints." He declared, "Of all sinners, I am chief." Though he understood that in Christ he was the righteousness of God (2 Cor. 5:21), he never lost sight of God's grace and mercy. In fact, the longer he lived, the more dependent he became on God's grace. His attitude continually portrayed, "I am an unprofitable servant; I have done only the things commanded me."

This explains Paul's other statement toward the end of his life: "Brethren, I do not count myself to have apprehended; but one thing

I do, forgetting those things which are behind and reaching forward to those things which are ahead, I press toward the goal for the prize of the upward call of God in Christ Jesus" (Phil. 3:13–14). Can you hear the humility in his words? "I haven't arrived, and what I have achieved, I leave behind in my thought life." He declared his accomplishments as "nothing" compared to his quest to fully know Christ Jesus. Remember God reveals Himself to the humble! Paul said, "I press toward the goal." To press meant he experienced resistance and opposition. One of the greatest opponents to the upward call is *pride*.

As we study the life of Jesus, we find He did not accept praise but redirected it toward His Father. He even told the ones He healed not to report what happened to the general public, but give God the glory.

A rich young ruler said to Jesus, "Good Teacher." Yet Jesus quickly responded there was no one good but God. Was He not God's Son? Was He not good? Absolutely! Yet He would not accept the praise of man; He wanted only the glory of His Father. However, the virtue He did boast in was humility. He said, "Take my yoke upon you and learn from me, for I am gentle and *humble in heart*, and you will find rest for your souls" (Matt. 11:29 NIV, emphasis added).

The love of God breeds true humility. We read that love "is not boastful or vainglorious, does not display itself haughtily [or proud]" (1 Cor. 13:4 AMPLIFIED). Pride seeks its own; love seeks not its own. Pride despises any obedience that does not benefit its own agenda; love seeks the glory of the One it serves. We obey because we love; we desire success because we want Him honored. We long to see Him glorified. Perhaps that was why Paul said, "Though I have all faith, so that I could remove mountains, but have not love, I am nothing" (1 Cor. 13:2).

FULFILL YOUR DESTINY

We are called to produce fruit and be champions for our God. Only when we walk in His ways can we truly bring honor to His wondrous name. I pray you will see this message as both for your good and for His glory. Adherence to His Word may seem foolish to the reasoning process, but didn't He say, "God was pleased through the foolishness of what was preached to save those who believe" (1 Cor. 1:21 NIV)? On the other hand, we are told, "For the foolishness of God is wiser than man's wisdom" (1 Cor. 1:25 NIV). Remind yourself, we are to "refute arguments and theories and *reasonings* and every proud and lofty thing that sets itself up against the [true] knowledge of God; and we lead every thought and purpose away captive into the *obedience* of Christ" (2 Cor. 10:5 AMPLIFIED, emphasis added).

Reasoning that contradicts obedience is proud. It resists the counsel of God. It does not acknowledge God's Word as final authority. As we've seen throughout this book, it is dangerous. God will have a people in these days who will walk in great faith, authority, and boldness. They will be the ones Paul said will "punish every act of disobedience, once [their] obedience is complete" (2 Cor. 10:6 NIV).

The time is short, so we must be effective. Obedience keeps us effective. When I was first born again, I was quite active, but short on obedience. I was ineffective, not to mention at times detrimental. The more I grew, the more I realized even though my diligence in obedience didn't always appear to get me anywhere at the time, it proved in the end to be effective.

Your destiny in God is before you. When you choose obedience, you choose to fulfill destiny. Nothing and no one can stop you. For years it looked gloomy for David, as with Joseph, as with Moses, as with Joshua, as with Hannah, as with Noah, as with Esther, as with the rest of the patriarchs. But remember, there is a hall of fame for those who fulfilled their destiny, and these listed here made it. God is looking for men and women in these last days to add to the list of patriarchs to be honored at the judgment seat of Christ. I pray we can be among those who fulfill the commission to bring glory to our wonderful Lord.

CHAPTER 17

CONCLUSION

The fruit we eat as we abide under His cover ushers us into His banquet. It is there we partake of His abundance.

We began this book with the tragic decision of the first married couple. This husband and wife stepped out from under the cover of the Almighty, and found a source of right and wrong outside of the umbrella of God. They spurned His authority, but we have and can continue to learn from their failure, as well as those who followed after them.

Let's conclude with the flip side—the reward for those who remain under the shadow of the Almighty.

> I sat down under his *shadow* with great delight, and *his fruit was sweet* to my taste. He brought me to the banqueting house, and his banner over me was love. (Song 2:3–4 KJV)

Under His shadow is the tree of life. This fruit has enduring sweetness. The fruit Adam and Eve ate looked good through the eye of reason, but in the end, brought death. This is true of all fruit eaten from the tree of reason. The fruit we eat as we abide under His cover ushers us into His banquet. It is there we partake of His abundance.

While reading this book it is quite possible you felt the pain of conviction. Pain is not always bad, in this case it indicates two things, first your conscience is tender, and sensitive to the Holy Spirit. Second, there is a way of escape—it's called repentance. There is a fundamental difference between conviction and condemnation. Both are accompanied by pain, but one has a way out, while the other does not. Repentance is as simple as a change of heart that produces a change of mind and actions. In essence you say, "Lord, I've done it my way, and seen my futility, now I chose to submit to Your ways." It is a choice to leave the way of reason birthed from the tree of the knowledge of good and evil, and return to the way of obedience.

Through prayer and meditation open your heart and allow the Holy Spirit to pinpoint the areas of disobedience in your life. If needed review various chapters which uniquely apply to your situation. Allow the word of God to survey your life. The light of His Word exposes areas of disobedience. These areas may deal with either God's inherent or delegated authority. List them on a separate piece of paper. Once you've done this let's pray together to receive forgiveness and restoration.

Heavenly Father in Jesus name forgive me for disobedience and insubordination. I've lived by my own reasoning and consequently rebelled in the following areas.

I have: (from your list, confess each area of sin to His authority.
Include both direct as well as delegated.)

I repent of each of these areas of thought and behavior. I ask you to forgive me and cleanse me with the blood of my Lord Jesus.

I purpose to submit to Your authority, and in doing so will submit to the family, civil, church, and social authorities which You have placed over my life. Give me Your grace to not only desire, but to do of Your good pleasure. I ask for a heart that delights in submission and obedience. I commit my life to my Lord Jesus Christ and forsake all manner of rebellion. In whatever way You've called me to glorify Your name I eagerly submit. Amen.

If appropriate go in person, or write a letter to those in the positions of authority you listed, and ask their forgiveness. This is not a time to place blame or to argue your cause, but an opportunity for you to take responsibility for your part in any difficult manner. This will position you to see the hand of God move on your behalf.

Thank you for choosing a path so opposite of the course of this world. By our obedience we hasten the purposes of our marvelous King. The reward for your obedience will be great.

Now to Him who is able to keep you from stumbling, and to
present you faultless before the presence of His glory with exceeding joy,
To God our Savior, who alone is wise, be glory and majesty, dominion and
power, both now and forever. Amen.
Jude 24–25

Remember:
Stay UNDER COVER!

ABOUT THE AUTHOR

JOHN BEVERE is the bestselling author of several books, including *A Heart Ablaze, The Bait of Satan, The Fear of the Lord,* and *Thus Saith the Lord?* John and his wife, Lisa, a bestselling author as well, founded John Bevere Ministries in 1990. Since that time the ministry has grown into a multifaceted international outreach that includes a weekly European television broadcast, *The Messenger.* John ministers in conferences and churches both nationally and internationally. He and Lisa reside in Colorado with their four sons.

OTHER BOOKS BY JOHN BEVERE

A HEART ABLAZE

THE BAIT OF SATAN

THE BAIT OF SATAN STUDY GUIDE

BREAKING INTIMIDATION

THE DEVIL'S DOOR

THE FEAR OF THE LORD

THUS SAITH THE LORD?

VICTORY IN THE WILDERNESS

THE VOICE OF ONE CRYING

BOOKS BY LISA BEVERE

BE ANGRY BUT DON'T BLOW IT!

OUT OF CONTROL AND LOVING IT!

THE TRUE MEASURE OF A WOMAN

YOU ARE NOT WHAT YOU WEIGH

CO-AUTHORED BOOKS

PATHWAY TO HIS PRESENCE DEVOTIONAL

THE SPIRIT OF CHRISTMAS

To receive JBM's free newsletter, *The Messenger,* and to receive a free color catalog of ministry resources, please contact:

John Bevere Ministries

UNITED STATES
PO Box 888
Palmer Lake, CO 80133-0888
800-648-1477 (US & Canada)
Tel: 719-487-3000
Fax: 719-487-3300
E-mail: jbm@johnbevere.org
Web site: www.johnbevere.org

EUROPE & AFRICA
PO Box 2794
Walsall
WS2 7YQ
UNITED KINGDOM
Tel: 44 (0) 870-745-5790
Fax: 44 (0) 970-745-5791
E-mail: jbmeurope@johnbevere.org
Web site: www.johnbevere.org.uk

AUSTRALIA
PO Box 6200
Dural CD NSW 2158
AUSTRALIA

The Messenger television program airs on the God Digital Network in Europe and the Australian Christian Channel. Please check your local listings for day and time.

VIDEO MESSAGES

BY JOHN BEVERE

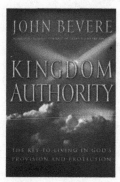 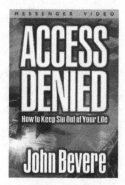

KINGDOM AUTHORITY & ACCESS DENIED
COMPANION VIDEOS TO *UNDER COVER*

OTHER VIDEOS:

THE BAIT OF SATAN
DECEIVED BY GRACE
BREAKING INTIMIDATION
DOES GOD KNOW YOU?
HOLINESS
HUMILITY
FREEDOM FROM SIN
THE FEAR OF THE LORD
PASSION FOR HIS PRESENCE
CULTIVATING A PURE HEART
DEVELOPING A STRONG SPIRIT
CHANGED FROM GLORY TO GLORY

BY LISA BEVERE

YOUR PAST IS NOT YOUR FUTURE
ESCAPING ANGER